Legacy and *Testament*

Legacy and Testament

THE STORY OF COLUMBIA RIVER GILLNETTERS

IRENE MARTIN

Washington State University Press
Pullman, Washington

Washington State University Press, Pullman, Washington 99164-5910

Library of Congress Cataloging-in-Publication Data
Martin, Irene, 1946-
    Legacy and testament : the story of Columbia River gillnetters / Irene Martin.
       p. cm.
    Includes bibliographical references (p.   ) and index.
    ISBN 0-87422-109-9 (pbk.)
    1. Gillnetting—Columbia River—History.   2. Fishers—Columbia River—History.   I. Title.
SH221.5.C64M37   1994
639.2'1'09797—dc20   94-14431
                                              CIP

Cover photogravure, "Salmon Fishing on the Columbia," from a painting by A. Hencke, after a sketch by Victor Perard.

To my husband

I don't mind the wet and cold,
Just don't like the growing old.

—Gordon Bok

Contents

Acknowledgments

The work on this book has been lived during the past nineteen years, while gillnetting with my husband on the Columbia River, Willapa Bay, and on Bristol Bay, Alaska. I originally envisaged it as an ethnography, then a history with anthropological overtones, but none of these disciplines really spoke to what I wanted to capture. How does one make a book on an obscure technology intelligible to the lay person, authoritative enough to satisfy the professional historian, authentic enough to satisfy the anthropologist and folklorist, and detailed enough to satisfy the fisherman? Marine anthropology probably comes closest in its theoretical framework to providing the model I sought, but it is my belief that theory is only validated by the truth of people's lives. I have used every resource at my disposal to ensure the accuracy and comprehensiveness of the facts delineated here. I have added substance to these facts by using the words of the fishermen themselves. Am I objective? No, I am not. I have a unique and subjective view of the Columbia River gillnet fishery which comes from having lived it for so many years. I view this opportunity to participate in fishing as having been a marvelous chance to gain a unique perspective on a living tradition.

If there is one thing I have most wanted to do, it is to make this book rich and full enough so that fishermen reading it will be able to say, "Yes, that's the way it is." Many fishermen already have a sense of being part of a living history of Oregon and Washington. Capturing this consciousness and expressing it to others has been my ultimate goal. There is a wonderful creativity and vitality in the Columbia River gillnet fishery which has ensured its survival for over a century. If there are gaps in this book, and I am sure there are, please remember that the Columbia River fishery is still being lived. My perception of the story, while unique, has the limits of time and space and my own personality. In some cases events, thoughts, and feelings have been described because I believe they are important, but I am yet too close to analyze them.

The issue of the use of the terms "fishermen" and "fisher" has come up on a number of occasions. Virtually all of the gillnet licence holders in the Columbia River fishery are male, so I have used the term fishermen throughout when referring specifically to them. Some women do act as crew for fishermen on the Columbia, usually for their husbands, and I have noted such instances where appropriate. The term "boatpuller" is the general rubric covering both male and female crew members. When referring to fishing methods and fleets outside the Columbia, I have usually used the term fishers, as there is a higher ratio of females to males in such fisheries. The question of gender-related terminology is sensitive, as many fishermen view the term "fisher" as pejorative. As one man I know put it, "A fisher is a little brown animal. I'm a fisherman." There is also the connotation that a fisher is not the owner or licence holder, but simply a person who fishes, usually for someone else, with little in the way of decision-making power. There is some blurring of authority, too, as the woman's role is often that of bookkeeper and manager of the operation, a key function with a great deal of decision-making involved. The terminology usage in this book may not satisfy everyone, but I think it reflects both the composition of the fleet and the roles various parties play.

I have had a great deal of help from a long list of individuals and institutions during my years of research and study. Among the institutions, I would like to mention the fine collections and service of the Oregon Historical Society, the Multnomah County Library, the Washington State Library, the Washington State Historical Society, the British Columbia Archives and Records Service, the Longview Public Library, the Cowlitz County Historical Society, the Astoria Public Library, the Prince Rupert Public Library, the University of British Columbia libraries, the Vancouver City Library, the *Samson* V Maritime Museum in New Westminster, B. C., the University of Washington Suzzallo Library, the Washington State University Library, the Pell Sea Grant Library in Rhode Island, the

Wahkiakum County Museum, the Pacific County Historical Society, Noreen Robinson and the Ilwaco Heritage Museum, the Abernathy Salmon Culture Facility, the Skamokawa Community Library, Noreen Holten of the Cathlamet City Library, the Columbia River Estuary Study Taskforce, Audrey Conroy of the Canadian Department of Fisheries and Oceans, and especially the Columbia River Maritime Museum and its director, Jerry Ostermiller.

Among individuals, I would like to thank Jack Marincovich, executive secretary of the Columbia River Fishermen's Protective Union (C.R.F.P.U.), and Arlene Graham, secretary, who have always welcomed me on my many trips to dig out information. Many of the individual members of the C.R.F.P.U. answered questions and encouraged my writing through so many years, and their names appear throughout. Likewise, Bob Eaton, Jody Hoag, and Thane Tienson of Salmon for All were most supportive. Ralph Ennis, Bill Finucane, Eldon Korpela, Jim and Yvonne Hogan, Bruce Cruikshanks, Manny Mustola, Bob and Darliss Hyke, Dean Badger, Dan Silverman, Alan and Linda Takalo, the Doumit family, and Beverly Badger are all part of that larger fishing community that has had such an influence on my life. Our drift-mates are Johnny Anderson, Craig Nettles, Gary Huber, Mark Laukkanen, and David Nelson. Jim Bergeron, Marine Extension Agent with Oregon State University, had the vision and determination to tape record the oral history interviews with old-time gillnetters that have proven so important. Bob and Thea Pyle, Ruth Kirk, Judith Irwin, Thomas and Elizabeth Vaughan, Carlton Appelo, Bruce and Diantha Weilepp, Larry Gilmore, Larry Johnson, Hobe Kytr, Anne Witty, Kit Helsley, David Freece, Jack and Elaine Edwards, Rick and Kathy Minor, Bent Thygesen, Larry Weathers, Esther Snowden, Janet Gilmore, and Merle Reinikka are all writers or students of history who have helped with advice and support. Wendell Ankeny of the Ocean Park Methodist Camp booked me to teach several Elderhostel classes, providing a very useful way to try portions of the book out on a live audience, which provided both support and advice.

The staff of a number of fisheries agencies have proved helpful, supplying statistical data and other information when requested. I would like to mention Dick Laramie, Joe Salte, Ed Manary, Kirk

Beiningen, Don McIsaacs, Steve King, Jack Donaldson, Guy Norman, Ron Roller, Dennis Austin, Jim Martin, and Wolf Dammers in particular.

There is much that could be said about the many friends who have been a blessing in my life, and about the community in which I live. Let me mention in particular the Friends of Skamokawa Foundation, who encouraged my historical endeavors, St. James Episcopal Church, whose members uplift me in prayer daily, Iris Hamm, Pauline and Don Barra, Norman and Ruth Martin, Sunrise and Jessica Fletcher, Carol Carver and George Exum, Virginia Grundstad, Larry and Linda Orenstein, Gay Abbate, Cindy Mead, Dale and Chris Mead, Arnold Andersen, Eric Andersen, Maija Blaubergs, J'Anne Hook, Steve and Debbie McClain, Sarah and Chuck Slape, Mary Goble, Sue Cotter, who provided enthusiasm and meticulous research, Gerry Brennan, who nursed my failing computer along, and Keith Petersen, the most patient of editors. Finally, my most heartfelt thanks go to my family: my parents, who always encouraged me to write, my brother Robert and sister-in-law Cinta, my husband's parents and so many relatives, whose stories helped tie both personal and community life together, my two daughters, Varsha and Menoka, and my husband, Kent, for whom gillnetting is art, science, and passion.

The Martins and friends launch their new gillnet boat, the *Floozie,* in 1977. *Photo by Terry Norberg.*

Prologue
Vision of the Wet World

Part One

Well, here it is, early May again. Same old familiar routine. The airline tickets are purchased, after numerous calls to various travel agencies to haggle over prices. As usual, it costs proportionately more to fly out of Anchorage to King Salmon than it does to fly from Portland or Seattle to Anchorage. All the equipment, supplies, nets, and other gear went out weeks ago by barge. There was the usual last minute flurry of activity to get everything inventoried and packed into heavy wooden crates. The finality of the trip to Seattle with the pickup groaning under its load of stuff bound north always comes as a shock. The long summer absence of the Columbia River fishermen is at hand.

preparation for the season.

It helps to know that other families, dozens of them, are going through the same experience. A chance encounter with a friend produces the same ritual of questions: "When does your husband leave? Has he shipped his stuff north yet? Got all his gear hung? Are you going up this year? What about your boy?" This scene repeats over a period of weeks in all the small towns along the Columbia from Portland down to Astoria: Grays River, Deep River, Pillar Rock, Skamokawa, Cathlamet, Clatskanie, Mayger, Knappa, Westport, Kalama, Longview. Departure times vary, depending on which town in Alaska a fisherman is going to: Cordova, Naknek, Dillingham, Ugashik, Egigik. Run predictions are rehashed, improvements planned for boats are discussed for hours, and last minute paperwork is completed.

It takes organization to make a long summer absence possible. The last few weeks before departure are a round of visits to banks to arrange any transactions requiring a husband's signature, to a lawyer to have a power of attorney drawn up, to marine stores to order forgotten items. "Are you sure you know how to pump out the boat while I'm gone?" "Don't forget to check on the Corps of Engineers dredging schedule." What my husband refers to as "Honey-dew stuff," that is, "Honey, do this," and "Honey, do that," occupies the last few days. Tasks may include plumbing in an irrigation system for the garden, cutting and stacking the winter's firewood, fixing the lawn mower. It is an axiom of our lives that during the first week of my husband's absence, at least one major appliance will break down.

Excursions with the children are also part of the routine, as soon there will be no Dad at home. All along the Columbia these patterns repeat in family after family. Some men start to complain of the heat when the first warm days of spring begin. Others grow irritable and tense as departure day approaches. I have heard some say that the sound of geese honking in the sky as they fly north sets up an answering restlessness within. Last minute checks on their Columbia River boats reassure some that there is life after the Alaska season. Potential homecoming dates are circled on the calendar. Times are set for the weekly phone call home.

The summer routine for a fishing wife is one of child care, responsibility for all business problems and decisions, letter writing, and handling any crisis which may arise. Wives call each other to share letters and phone calls from up north. Any newspaper articles regarding missing boats are read with a terrible anxiety. News is sketchy at times, but women console themselves with the thought that perhaps it's heavy fishing and there isn't time to write or call. The phone calls can be as frustrating as the silence. There are often long lines of men waiting to use the single telephone, which means that calls are neither private nor as long as one could wish. One of our calls ended abruptly when a bear dug up the phone line somewhere in the tundra, severing connections for several days. Women who have actually been north are more aware of the primitive conditions in the fish camps and seem better able to cope.

And what is it like up in Bristol Bay? It's gray weather where the clouds form strange sculptural shapes. It's spinning at the top of the globe, where a look across the Bay can show several different weather patterns sweeping over the water. The geography seems proportionately more water and sky than land. The water and land are both madly fecund, in a race to see whether the mosquitoes will outnumber the salmon or vice versa. A bizarre progression: juvenile salmon eat mosquito larvae, grow to be adult salmon which fishermen prey on, and fishermen are in turn preyed on by mosquitoes. Perhaps not the divine plan, but certainly a function of it. And what crazy god dreamed of walking on tundra, which is like walking on mattresses a foot thick, so springy it is, and covered with flowers and berries.

The bunkhouse of our Alaska camp was built of tongue-and-groove lumber sometime during the World War I era. Old stoves in the hallways blast out heat through the rows of clothes hanging to dry. Here and there a rickety card table stands, waiting for all-night poker games during closed periods. Nude pinups and faded calendars decorate the walls of the bare rooms, but are not enough to keep the wind from whistling through the cracks during a gale. There are still a few of the original woolen army surplus blankets around, but many fishermen have replaced them with electric blankets.

The food is wonderful, with three substantial meals and three mug-ups or coffee breaks per day. Mug-ups would qualify as full meals anywhere else in the world. Amazingly, some fishermen go to all six meals a day. In the years when I went to Bristol Bay, I had to forego much of this banquet, however. My weakness is seasickness. At the time, a kind fisherman reassured me that "No-one ever died of it. . . . You only wish you could." I remember Sverre, the elderly gillnetter, a halibut fisherman until age seventy, who often regaled me with tales from the past, bragging about his winter job as night watchman for a shipping yard. "A warm job," he assured me, the criterion of a man who had often been cold.

We are, of course, fishing for salmon, particularly red (sockeye) salmon, here in Bristol Bay. The Bay is a series of gutters and sand bars. There are names for various places—Johnston Hill, Graveyard Point, the Banana Trees, Dead Man's Sands. Our boat is old, heavy, round-bottomed, originally a cannery boat. It rolls in heavy or light seas. It has two bunks and its previous owners put up shelves and benches and lockers for food storage. The radio is probably the most important item of equipment, as fishermen work in groups to explore for fish and cooperate in order to maximize catches. These groups are often family-based or may be formed, at least in part, of the men one fishes with on the drift on the Columbia.

The radio chatter also provides an outlet for the men. When the weather turns bad, old jokes come crackling through the static. "Weather's so bad I had to keep my mouth open to keep my face dry." The radio is always there if someone needs help. Up until 1952, the Bristol Bay fishery was conducted from sailboats, a management technique called conservation by inefficiency. Conservation by killing fishermen was the underlying function. The old Columbia River saying, "A salmon head is worth a dollar, but a man's head is worth nothing," was most true in Alaska.

During closed periods the men are bored and often lonely in the bunkhouses. They wander through town, go to the bars and drink, or go to the local movie, usually one several years old. They are resented by the Alaska residents as "outsiders" but are driven north by necessity, because dams, first on the Columbia and later on the Snake River, decimated the summer salmon runs on which they once depended. As the Alaska summer wears on, with the long days of fishing, the thought of home becomes more and more tempting. The sockeye runs taper off, while chums and silvers appear more frequently, indicating that the end is in sight. The first fisherman arranges to leave, and then there is a stampede for flight reservations. Homesickness is powerful.

Back home, the women are waiting for the phone call that says "Meet me at the airport." There will be presents from Alaska, salt salmon for pickling later, and the welcome paycheck. There is also that tentative period of husbands and wives getting to know each other again. And then the focus shifts to preparing for the August and fall fisheries on the Columbia.

Part Two

I am seated in our boat the *Floozie* as I write this. It is the opening night of yet another Columbia River August gillnet season, and my husband and I are here fishing at the mouth of the river near Astoria, Oregon. Not much fish around. We have four salmon, a sturgeon, and a couple of flounders for take-home fish in the fish locker. Very poor for opening night of the season. However, it's been raining for days, and the fish are undoubtedly on their way upriver and in the creeks by now. Somehow, though, tonight, I do not seem to mind the lack of fish. Does that mark me as no true fisherman? My priority should be to catch fish, but the fish are secondary to the experience of the river at night. A little while ago we were running up Blind Channel in the darkness. Look down and the foam is rushing by, lighted by the gleam from the cabin windows. There is a sensation of movement quite unconnected with the boat. Looking at the lights on the horizon, there is a sense of movement again, but slower this time, as if the boat were merely gliding. And now, look up. Our red running light is moving slowly, slowly, among a crowd of stars in a black sky. The Fishermen's Union pennant flaps suddenly against the darkness, like the twist of a fish's tail.

With the engines on, all other sound is masked so that we can believe we are the only people who exist out here. Other boats glide by, dark shadows on the water, with only their red running lights on. No visible human beings steer them. But when we shut off our engine, the hum of the boats resembles traffic on a freeway. The heartbeat of the fishery is heard again, and the ghostly movements of the boats become once more the embodiment of individual desires and human decisions.

All of the senses are utilized in fishing; sight and sound are simply the obvious ones. Judging position from landmarks, looking for the little firefly light on our buoy at the end of the net far off in the darkness, peering through the fog to find a mark—were our eyes meant to cope with such strain? The sound of the engine is a constant, but any slight change in volume or rhythm can mean trouble.

Each kind of fish has its own smell. Flounder smell of seaweed; salmon have a clean, fresh odor, like soap or watermelon; sturgeon smell musky; dog sharks smell of ammonia. The smell of the engine in the cabin mixes with the other smells, especially of damp clothes drying. We have been drifting for several hours and it is time to pick up the net. We each climb into our rain gear and peel our gloves off the engine manifolds where they have been drying; a few seconds of luxurious warmth before wet begins to seep through again.

Dampness and cold are conditions of life aboard a Columbia River boat, even in August. The scratchiness of woolen underwear is counter-balanced by the knowledge that wool stays warm even if it gets wet. It has sometimes seemed to me that fishermen do not feel the cold as other people do. I have heard that Scandinavian fishermen have nerve endings further under the skin than other people, a possible physiological reason why they do not feel cold so acutely. In addition, it is possible to cultivate an attitude of indifference to physical discomfort. Dress for the conditions, avoid them where possible, and then forget them. The body will survive. Wet and cold are transitory.

On go the picking-up lights. I grab the buoy and the reel begins to turn and wind in the net. Sometimes strange objects come up from the river bottom. I recall an anchor we found once, left over from sailing-boat days. Generally, chunks of wood and sometimes whole trees become entangled and must be released again. There is always the fear of getting a load of jellyfish or hake. Once I got a piece of jellyfish in the eye, and I realized how one could be driven mad with pain. The first salmon comes over the roller and I remove the fish locker boards as my husband shares the common superstition that it is bad luck to open the fish locker before there is a fish in the boat. We get three more salmon on this drift. Not very fishy out there.

This afternoon we ran down the river from Skamokawa to Astoria and tied up at North Shore, a former fish-buying station. Now only pilings mark its former existence, and the remnant of one building, formerly the stationmaster's house, with a rusty iron bedstead in it. As usual, there were a few boats tied up there, including two of our drift-mates, Johnny and Craig. There was also one beautifully kept-up old bowpicker there. The owner must have been asleep, as we never saw him, just his lovely boat, white trimmed with red. The bowpicker reached its peak of perfection with boats like this and then became obsolete.

The boats were tied in a line and we all gathered on Johnny's, the *Viking Queen*, drinking coffee. Very peaceful. Just the sound of water slapping against the boat, quiet conversation, and the occasional cry of a seagull. Craig spotted two bald eagles, both males with white heads. Occasionally a car went by on the highway, but traffic wasn't heavy and was far enough away to make only a muted rushing sound.

Although it is calm now, I have seen days when the weather was wet and stormy in August. I have also seen openings in September when the weather was tropically hot.

As the night wanes, the brain grows fuzzy with lack of sleep and intense concentration. If one can conquer the urge for sleep for a certain period, however, a numbness sets in, and fishing becomes mechanical. After the last drift of the night is done, though, and the fish are delivered to the receiving scow, four hours' sleep becomes the greatest luxury imaginable. Dawn is now bright on the river.

Later in the day we go into town for a meal, as the tides are not right for fishing. A quick look in the mirror first, to make sure there are no fish scales adhering to the face, and then a careful walk along a dock. We are so used to motion that the solid surface causes us to lurch. The restaurant is decorated in a nautical theme, but the romantic "toilers of the sea" imagery is artificial when contrasted with my grubbiness and my husband's day's growth of beard.

Back at the boat we resume the work of gear-mending and tidying up in the cabin. We also try for a few more hours of sleep, but it is hot in the cabin, even with the windows open, and there is a persistent fly buzzing around. I move my sleeping bag and pillow out onto the deck to try to find a cooler spot, but am in danger of being rolled off the deck by the wake of the other boats going by. Just one more night of fishing and we can go home.

But things do not go well this night. As we begin to haul in the net for the first time, we hit a snag and can't pick off it. A net further upriver drifts down on top of us, and we realize to our horror that it is full of short sturgeon. Although the men in the other boat are picking as fast as possible, the two nets clinch, the sturgeon thrashing around become entangled in our net as well, and the two nets knit themselves together. After disentangling as much as possible, the men in the other boat cut off part of their net, a drastic action. We pull off the snag, pull the remainder of the net in, and disentangle the sturgeon, returning them to the water. So much time and gear lost. And there are fish around.

On the next drift the end of the net bunches so that several layers of web become tangled together, making it too heavy to haul in. Unable to tow it to shore, as it is too close to the propeller, we put out a radio call to our drift-mates for help. It takes four men to haul it in, and despite all precautions it tangles in the prop. A friend tows us to a safe anchorage and we go to sleep.

At dawn my husband goes over the side, groaning about the cold water, and dives repeatedly until he is finally able to cut the net free. There are fish all over the boat, some even in the cabin, still entangled in the net. We head across the river to Astoria and set to work on the dock to untangle the mess, estimating it will take at least six hours. But other fishermen join us until there are eight people working on the net, and in an hour we are back on the river.

At the change of the tide the wind shifts to the east, making the water very rough. Although the sun is shining in a cloudless sky, we both wear rain gear drenched with spray. All this for one salmon. We decide to call it quits, ship our catch to the buyer, and head upriver for home. The river grows calmer with each mile, and by the time we reach Brookfield it is hot, a different world from the one we have just left.

Why do we do it? In our time we use the term "lifestyle" to imply a fashion of living generally related to choice of career, friends, and the latest consumer goods. Fishing is not a lifestyle. It is a traditional way of life, handed down from one generation to the next. It chooses you. It is a life based on wind, weather, and tides, in a world where these elements seldom affect anyone anymore. The brutal action of the wet world on human flesh brings a freedom of personality from convention and restraints. All activities become superfluous except those directly focused on fishing, until the boat, net, and person become one.

And now there is the exhilaration of the trip home, the winding down after two days of intense labor, gladness at the sight of our own green slough, and home.

Part Three

For us, Labor Day is a day to rest from labor, and a time to prepare mentally for more labor. It comes about halfway between the return from Alaska and the beginning of the fall season. There's snagging and gear work going on, and school about to begin, and our friends' schedules to coordinate, but somehow the annual Martin excursion always manages to take place on Labor Day. After days of phone calls and planning it all comes together around noon when we gather at the dock and start loading stuff. And what a lot of "stuff" there is in the late twentieth century. Chairs, coolers, children, diaper bags, picnic baskets, buckets, towels, dogs, windsurfing boards, even a kayak, sun screen, blankets, an axe. The only thing missing is a brass band.

When we reach Price's Island, Kent drives the boat onto the beach. The teens jump into the water to help unload everyone and everything. There's usually at least one craven dog who has to be bodily lifted ashore. When all are off-loaded Kent takes the *Floozie* out and anchors. Then he jumps in the water and swims ashore, in what has come to be called his annual cardiac test: if he jumps into the water and survives, he's good for another year. Meanwhile, those already on the beach have been inspecting the campsite. There are logs to sit on and an old piece of plywood to prop up for a table. There's the "sofa," an old car seat that we throw into the brush each year beyond the high water mark, and retrieve each year for gala seating. The children are everywhere—beachcombing, swimming, helping find wood for the fire. This year there are twenty people and three dogs. The proportions vary each year. The afternoon is spent talking, eating, beachcombing, swimming, and settling squabbles between children and dogs.

Across the channel on Welch's Island there is another family of gillnetters and their entourage from Svensen. They are the only other people in view. Our view is downriver on a golden afternoon full of laughter and the intimacy of dear friends. News of a pregnancy, a job promotion, is interrupted by children who have lost their marshmallows in the fire and must be comforted. Some are sunworshippers and some use a number 15 sunscreen. The vegetarians in the group miss out on the hot dogs, but viewing the charred remains of the children's efforts, perhaps they are better off. At least one dog will attempt to steal a piece of pie. The occasional ship goes by, and the children run down to the water's edge to wave. An occasional salmon rolls. Kent takes the *Floozie* back to the dock once or twice to pick up latecomers and take in those who have to leave early.

As the sun begins to descend over Three Tree Point it's time to load everything again, in haste now, as thoughts of school and work become uppermost. Load after load is ferried out in a skiff to the *Floozie* at anchor. The teens are diving off the boat in a last crazy laughing frenzy. I fling the last bucket of water on the fire and get into the skiff for the short ride. The engine starts and the *Floozie* heads for home, just as the sun slips behind the hill. "Look at the after-glow," cries someone. We all turn to look upriver at the deep blue hills with pink glowing above them.

As we float up Steamboat Slough, the golden western sky is reflected in the windows of Skamokawa Landing and Silverman's Emporium. We dock and there is a last minute sorting of shoes and towels. Children are either crying or asleep. There is a low growl from a dog too tired to move that is being urged out of the boat. I take one last backward glance at the *Floozie*, transformed for a day from a fish boat to a ferry, a pleasure boat. A friend catches my backward glance and says quietly, "The children will remember this forever."

Part Four

It's the last day of fall fishing, and we are drifting together in the Channel Drift. Cold November. A typical blustery, squally day, with occasional periods of brilliant sunshine. We have come out together for winter fish, always our custom on the last day of the season. Winter fish are those that we can and freeze and salt for our own use during the winter months. Actually, we have already taken care of most of our own needs, but we'll probably give away part of the catch to neighbors and friends and smoke some in the smokehouse.

In all our years of marriage we have only missed fishing the last day of the season together once, and that was due to my illness. Time was when I came out fishing much more often, but the arrival of children changed that pattern. Usually there's not much fish around in mid-November. We don't do it for the volume but for custom and companionship. The pressure to produce is over.

We are drifting with our diver net in the Channel Drift, one of two drifts we own. The Gut, our other drift, is too dirty to fish right now—full of sticks and leaves and chunks of logs, due to recent high tides that have floated a lot of debris off the beaches. The Channel tends to stay cleaner, though as the name implies, part of it is in the ship channel and has its own dangers.

I've been sitting in the cabin on the bunk, reading. Kent is outside in a squall, watching the net. He comes inside and we open the lunch bucket. It's hard to be creative with lunches for a long period, especially when trying to keep up with a food intake of 3,500 to 4,000 calories a day, my estimate of what it takes to keep him going. Roast beef sandwiches, fruit, chips, and Oreos—a concession to my craving for chocolate.

After half an hour Kent pulls on his rain gear again and goes out to pick up the net. I watch from the cabin door, though normally I'd be out there too. The levelwind grinds and lurches its way along its track, feeding the net onto the reel; build up the net on the sides of the reel for easier handling. There's a trick to everything. When we fished the bowpicker together, the net had to be piled properly so that it would lay out again smoothly, with no twists or turns. Three silvers on this drift, one with the rich belly portion ripped out by a seal we never saw. We decide to move, since we know the seal won't leave us alone on the drift now that it knows we are fishing.

We head downriver to Three Tree Point, planning to make an "ebber" or two, drifts on the ebb tide, but with a floater net instead of a diver. The sun comes out suddenly, illuminating the yellow leaves still left, which glow against the dark green of the hemlock and fir. It takes more than a hundred inches of rain a year to support this luxuriant growth. As I look ahead to the dark winter months of fog, rain, and mud, I remember the remark of a friend: "We pay a high price for so much beauty."

Pilings in the water mark the site of the Bayview Cannery, the first cannery built by R. D. Hume, brother of the man who brought the salmon-canning industry to the Columbia River. It was here that his first wife and two children died, the latter of childhood illness, the former of grief. He left the Columbia for the Rogue River, as the price was too high for him here. Next comes Turner's Canyon, with its big cherry tree that still blooms every spring. Then Rockland, then Glenella, where a bald eagle is perched on a piling, his white head dazzling against the dark shadows. At Three Tree Point a silver salmon is leaping in Duncan's Cove, former home of a long-dead bachelor gillnetter. Fragments of the clay pipes he used to smoke still litter the beach. As we swing close to the rocks, the arched ferns clinging to their crevices tremble in the drip from the seepage above. There is eighty feet of water below us and the current is swift. The net quickly rounds the point and floats by a shallow bay. The pilings in the bay are remnants of an early George

Myers cannery named Fisherton, already a memory by the turn of
the century. It was named, appropriately enough, for a gillnetter
named John Fisher. He died in 1891, possessing only a sailboat,
spars, oars, oarlocks, a net, a grindstone, and one dollar cash.

We pick up the net. Three silvers and a small salmon, unusual
for so late in the season. We decide to lay out again. A gust of wind
turns the air suddenly colder. We turn to each other with the same
question: "Do you remember when we fished here when the snowflakes were the size of silver dollars, drifting down in the hush and
disappearing into the black water?" "Do you remember when we
saw the fawn drinking from the river in Duncan's Cove?" "Do you
remember when we found the stoneware beer bottle dating from
the 1860s or '70s, lying there on the beach, in perfect condition?"
We have it yet, along with other fishing memorabilia: the sailmaker's
kit, the two Swede stoves, the rusty sturgeon hooks, the needles
and mesh boards made by Great Grandpa Erick Martin.

"Erick Martin was the only man I ever knew who could cook
salt salmon so the boys would eat it three times a day." Such was
the opinion of John Harrington, owner of Pillar Rock Packing Company. Great Grandpa Erick was renowned for his ability to sail one
of the little gillnet boats of the 1870s. On the other side of the family, there's Great Grandpa John Strom, who jumped ship at Westport,
Oregon, to escape the grindingly long conscription period of the
Swedish merchant seaman. Both men homesteaded in Skamokawa,
our home, farming, fishing, and logging in order to survive.

We pick up the net again. One silver, one dog salmon—a female, still alive. Dog salmon, once common on the Columbia, are
now scarce, though showing signs of reviving. We turn her loose,
to spawn and assist in the slow recovery of her race. It is colder yet
now. On the Swing Drift one boat is still out but is picking up. There's
a boat on Hungry Harbor, and one of the Clifton boys is out somewhere across the cattails. We hear him say on the radio, "Fishing
season 1990 is over."

We arrive at the dock, tie up, and load the fish in the truck. As
we drive up the darkening valley the lights are winking on. We stop
at neighbors' and friends' houses on the way to drop off fish. Ahead
is our own home, where our daughters have the lights on and are
waiting for us. Salmon for supper, and much laughter. "What's more
fishy than gillnetting?" asks Varsha, our older daughter, in one of

the silly jokes of childhood. Menoka remembers when she released balloons during a long day's fishing, laughing as they escaped in the breeze. "Do you remember when we launched the *Floozie?*" I checked in *Emily Post* for the proper etiquette for conducting a boat launching. Emily, for once, was silent. So a friend of mine advised me to put the wine bottle in an old sock and wrap it in foil so that the glass wouldn't fly around when the bottle broke over the bow.

Later that night, just before bed-time, the wind grows stronger. And I wonder, "Who was the first to name empty expanses of water, to recognize them as a territory?" "Who conceived of the idea of nets so complex that after seventeen years of work I still have only a rudimentary grasp of how to fish them?" Erick Martin and John Strom are dead. We can go to the cemetery and look at their graves and the graves of other fishermen, some with gillnet boats engraved on the headstones. But they are silent and tell us nothing of the intervening seasons. We look in the treasured photo albums and the faces we see are our own. There's the Strom mouth, going back to Great- Great- Great-Grandmother's portrait. There's the Martin chin. And there are the unidentified ones, known only by the photographer's name, "John Dryselius, Kalmar," Sweden. There is the faded poem in Swedish, written on Oct. 19, 1873, by Mathilda Nelsson for her friend, Christin Berg, on the occasion of her wedding to John Strom. Her wedding day was also the day she left Sweden, never to return. "Farval! Farval! Christin." One friend left behind, a woman who came to the Columbia and died in 1899 in childbirth.

I too am an immigrant, trying to cope with a life I was never prepared for. Like grasping a salmon it is to try to understand this fishing life. So solid and substantial, and you just think you have it firmly in your hand and it slips away and skates across the deck. And still I chase it, foolish but determined.

Who was it that created this rhythm of seasons, of customs, of boats, of gear? Look in the old scrapbooks, the faded clippings. The occasional sentence in a book, sometimes even a whole paragraph, provide clues. The photos in the attic, the will found in a courthouse, all yield their small bits of information. Listen to the memories of the old-timers, and the younger ones who remember the memories of those now dead. Piece it all together and you have a story, our story. I sink down deeper into bed and drift off to sleep.

Chapter One
"It's the Net that Catches the Fish"

"It's the net that catches the fish," commented my husband some years ago. This statement provided a point of entry into the history of the drift gillnet and of the technology that developed around it, as well as the social organization which grew up at the same time. However, the research proved to be curiously unsatisfactory, as there was always something missing from the various descriptions of the early gillnets of the Columbia River. That something proved to be the names of the people who used the nets. The observers of the past century, whether travelers through the area or scientists, provided dimensions and materials of the nets they saw. They occasionally noted variations, but seldom addressed the question of why certain variations appeared in specific locations. They were trying to provide a general view to their readers by focusing on the object, almost excluding the people who created it. For me, the opposite focus, on the creator of the object, is primary. The questions that always interest me are the people questions.

My first assumption, in writing this book, is the title of this chapter, that it is indeed the net that catches the fish, and that the net will be, must be, the first priority in a fisherman's thinking. In planning a strategy for catching fish, a fisherman will design a net to suit the grounds he is fishing, the type of fish he is after, the technological constraints under which he operates, and his own unique flair for fishing. The net is thus an extension of a mental process, a series of parameters and choices. It is also an extension of the individual personality, as well as the focal point of social organization. The development of the drift gillnet has been the driving force behind the development of the social fabric of the Columbia River gillnet fishery for over a century.

Influences upon the drift gillnet reflect technological changes in North American society. Originally fishermen used sailboats, which were also powered with oars when needed. These imposed their own limitations upon the gear. Considerations of wind and tide and the weight of the gear, which had to be pulled in by hand without the help of any mechanical device, provided powerful restraints. Introduction of the gasoline engine in the late 1890s and early 1900s released fishermen from these restraints, although not without some reluctance. Oliver Dunsmoor, a fisherman who witnessed the transition from sail to power, described a double-end boat used by an older fisherman he worked for: "He had a double cylinder 7 horsepower Palmer, and that was about as much power as anybody had at that time. He carried a sail along for the mast . . . for a couple years after I started with him. . . . They didn't have too much confidence in that old gas engine at that time."[1] Later generations, which put their faith in the power of technology to resolve problems, may have difficulty relating to this statement! A similar tongue-in-cheek account relates that a fisherman named "Doc" Monroe named his boat the *Perhaps* because "Boats at anchor, or being rowed while the owner toiled over the engine, were more common than boats running."[2] A favorite joke concerned the complaint that an engine wasn't running because of "gasoline in the water."[3]

The transition from sail to power took place over a period of years because canneries with fleets of boats—which they leased to fishermen—proved reluctant to face the major expense of refitting the vessels. Independent fishermen who owned their own boats were free to experiment with fishing difficult areas relatively inaccessible to sailboats. This competition undoubtedly applied pressure to the cannery owners to capitulate and modernize. The fisherman with the gas-powered boat could make more "drifts" than the fisherman with the sailboat, as he could return more rapidly to the area where he wanted to lay out his net. The gasoline engine led to the redesign of the sailboat into what became known as the Columbia River bowpicker, which by 1931 had a power roller in the bow. These allowed the fisherman to eliminate hiring a crew, thus creating a more profitable one-man operation and providing "a faster means of handling nets in the strong currents of the Columbia."[4]

Competition among gear types, as well as among gillnet fishermen, led to experimentation with gear in order to increase productivity. Aboriginal Columbia River fishermen used set gillnets, with the net anchored in the water. They also used traps, seines, and weirs. Early immigrant fishermen brought the drift gillnet to the Columbia, although they, too, used seine and trap technologies. Newspaper accounts of huge hauls by these latter methods appeared frequently in the latter part of the nineteenth century. High productivity was also a feature of a well-placed fishwheel. Competition existed, not so much between the fishermen using the different types of gear, but between the gillnetters and the packers, who often controlled the seines, traps, and wheels.[5] Gillnetting was a relatively low-cost technology, needing only an owner/operator and possibly one or two crew members. Seines, traps, and wheels were capital intensive, requiring large investments and big crews. Although there were individual trap and seine owners, the major canneries gradually either purchased or leased the most productive grounds.

Each gear type had its strong points and its weaknesses. Traps, seines, and wheels were stationary, set in a location where fish regularly appeared. If the fish did not show, more mobile gear—the gillnet—emerged as the winner. Freshet conditions could paralyze traps, seine, and wheel operations, while the gillnet was more flexible, able to fish in high-water conditions. As the numbers of fishermen in each type of fishery grew, competitive pressure in order to stay profitable increased. Clashes occurred among the different user groups, and gillnetters continually refined their gear to make it increasingly competitive. One of the results of this intense competition was the need to control overfishing. Both the Oregon and Washington departments of fish and wildlife had their genesis in the nineteenth century, spawned by a need to do something to regulate the intensive exploitation causing runs to decline. The 1894 *Report of the Commissioner of Fish and Fisheries on Investigations in the Columbia River Basin* stated the need for season limits and closed seasons in order to permit salmon to pass into the headwaters. In 1918 Congress ratified the Columbia River Compact, mandating that both Oregon and Washington manage the Columbia by mutual consent in order to avoid conflicting regulations. Management agencies also regulated mesh sizes, length of nets, and areas where gear could be placed in order to control catch and allow sufficient salmon to spawn.[6]

Obviously, gillnetting did not and does not operate in a vacuum. Many of the pressures present in the early history on the Columbia remain. Competition and technical innovation are still realities that must be faced when trying to design a gillnet. Tracing the history of the design and continual redesign of the Columbia River drift gillnet also poses the problem of trying to determine which of many technical innovations came first or in what order they appeared. The accounts are scattered and fragmentary, and original sources can be difficult to locate. Nevertheless, the history of the evolution of the gillnet used on the Columbia River is the foundation of the story of the fishermen themselves.

**

In 1844, for the purpose of trading in salt salmon, Captain John Couch established a trading post at a location known as Bayview about a mile below Skamokawa.[7] In 1846 James Birnie retired from the Hudson's Bay Company and established a trading post at Cathlamet. Couch's enterprise lasted only a short time, and after several transactions, Birnie finally bought the property in 1854, along with another fishery-related property on Tenasillihe Island. His accounts, however, indicate that he was buying and salting fish at least a year previously. He purchased fish from Indian fishermen and also employed non-Indian fishermen, supplying nets to them. His journal entries do not make clear whether the nets were drift or set gillnets or seines.[8]

Early sources tell us that two men, Hodgkins and Sanders, were using a drift gillnet by 1853 in the vicinity of what is now Oak Point, Washington.[9] Hodgkins was born in 1826 in Woolwich, Maine, which is located on the Kennebec River, a well-known salmon stream. He fished during his earlier years and then moved west, arriving in Portland, Oregon, in the spring of 1853. He took up a donation land claim near the present-day town of Clatskanie, Oregon.[10] He may have brought the net he used with him from Bath, Maine, or he may have made it locally.[11] He returned to Maine in 1857 and again took up fishing on the Kennebec. He fished there another ten years and then returned to Oregon, ultimately developing the H & B Seining Ground.[12]

Meanwhile, the Hume family of Augusta, Maine, was also involved in a westward migration. William Hume had gone to the Sacramento River in California in 1852, joining his Uncle David, who had arrived there some years previously.[13] The Humes had fished the Kennebec River for salmon since the 1790s and had fished salmon in Scotland before then.[14] David Hume engaged in fishing for salmon in the Sacramento in order to supply California gold miners. In 1856 William Hume returned to Maine and brought his brothers John and George out west with him.[15]

Another of the Humes who made the westward journey during this period was Robert Hume, a half-brother of William, John, and George. He described the situation he left on the Kennebec in 1853:

> At this time . . . the catching of a salmon . . . on the Kennebec River was of rare occurrence, usually the catch for a season being three or four, and a half dozen being a large take for the year. At this time the principal supply of salmon for the markets of the United States was procured from the Penobscot river in Maine and the waters of the British provinces [now Canada], namely Mirimichi river and the rivers putting into the Bay of Chaleur. . . . Up to the age of eighteen, the time the writer left home for the Pacific Coast, although some of his family were engaged in the fishing business, it had never been his fortune to taste salmon but once, and it is doubtful if but few in that State of his age had ever seen one.[16]

Hume blamed "civilization" for the decline of the Atlantic salmon on the Kennebec and other New England rivers. Under this rubric he lumped such factors as dams, traps, hydraulic mines, pollution, and the logging of watersheds. Studies by other parties corroborate his views regarding the salmon rivers along the east coast.[17] The influence of the east coast fisheries, however, provided a prime background for the development of the Columbia River. Not only did the Hume family and Hodgkins fish the Kennebec, but a number of early lower-Columbia pioneers also named the Naselle River the Kennebec when they first settled in the area.[18] Only some years later did it revert to its aboriginal name. Obituaries of early Columbia River gillnetters occasionally mention east coast fisheries in which the deceased took part.

On the Sacramento, miners in the gold fields purchased salmon for a dollar a pound, a huge price in those days.[19] As Emma Adams mentioned, this trade proved to be lucrative for William Hume, who shipped fresh salmon in express wagons to the gold mines as "The miners were a class of men who would not be denied any article of food they desired, however extravagant the price."[20] San Francisco also provided a market for fresh salmon, as did the salt fish trade. Besides the Humes, other immigrants in the San Francisco area experimented with gillnets. Three men from New Haven, Connecticut, tried a number of different types of twine, finally settling on shoe thread, which was strong enough to hold a twenty- to thirty-pound salmon.[21] Gillnetting on the Sacramento expanded somewhat during the 1850s, with Greek, Italian, and other Mediterranean fishermen joining the New Englanders. There are also references to Chinese fishermen in the area in the 1850s, but whether they driftnetted for salmon is not clear.[22]

In 1861 H. N. Nice (Rice in some accounts) and Jotham Reed began salting salmon at Oak Point on the Columbia, using a net fifty fathoms long and three fathoms deep, with an eight-inch mesh. Nice had constructed the net from flax purchased locally which he spun himself on a spinning wheel.[23] Although Hodgkins and Sanders had salted fish on the Columbia in the 1850s, early pioneer Peter Crawford kept a journal in which he noted that the salt salmon trade became much more extensive in the 1860s.[24] The Indian population on the lower Columbia had supplied most of the salmon used in the salt salmon trade during the first half of the nineteenth century. By the mid-1850s diseases had decimated their populations. Obtaining a supply of salmon necessitated the use of non-Indian fishermen who employed gillnets, seines, and traps to catch the fish, all methods they had seen used back in New England.

William Hume had brought his own gillnet with him to the Sacramento while H. N. Nice made his locally. Regardless of whether the early gillnets were imported from the east coast or constructed locally, it appears certain they were modelled after those used on the various New England rivers such as the Penobscot and the Kennebec. These were "simple, straight nets, buoyed at the top and leaded at the bottom."[25]

In 1863 George Hume went back to Maine and persuaded Andrew Hapgood, a former schoolmate, to return with him to the Sacramento to help set up a cannery for salmon. Hapgood had had some experience canning fish in both the eastern U. S. and eastern Canada. In 1864 the first pack of canned salmon was put up on the Sacramento.[26] In 1865 the salmon runs on the Sacramento were poor, due to increasing pollution from growing urban areas and destruction of spawning grounds by hydraulic mining. It must have been *deja vu* for the Humes, and in 1866 they moved to the Columbia, accompanied by their tinsmith, Hapgood.[27] In their first year of production they canned 6,000 cases of salmon. During this year the only drift gillnets being used were owned by Jotham Reed at Oak Point and by their own company, Hapgood Hume and Co., at Eagle Cliff, Washington Territory. Their nets were 125 fathoms in length and 32 meshes deep, "the gillnet of Mr. Reed being of much less size. . . . All the gill nets put together would not make one of the dimensions used in 1907."[28] The fishery expanded rapidly. An 1868 article in the Portland *Oregonian* described the fisheries in the vicinity as follows:

> Seven different fisheries are now carried on in the vicinity, on both sides of the river. Last year, over 3,000 barrels of two hundred pounds each were taken in these fisheries and salted down. Messrs. Hagood [sic] and Co. and Mr. Hume are engaged in putting up Salmon in one pound cans for exportation, and this year they expect to put up not less than 300,000 cans. The Salmon put up this way, are cooked in the cans, and will keep fresh for years. They are pronounced by salmon-eaters as the best way of cooking, and preparing salmon for the table. Nearly all their Salmon are sent to the Australian market. Taking it altogether, the Oak Point fishery on the Columbia River, and the salmon put up there, have attained a reputation for being put up in good order, and full weight, which is likely to be kept up, as all the parties engaged in the business are responsible men, who understand the business and will make it a point to keep up the reputation of Oak Point Salmon. The fisheries of course use a large number of tight barrels, which have nearly all been heretofore made at other places; but preparations are now being made to manufacture the greater portion, if not all of them, in one neighborhood.[29]

With the entire length of the Columbia River to choose from, why did the Humes and others choose the Oak Point vicinity as their fishing grounds? Here one must enter the realm of conjecture. It is known that both the Humes and Hodgkins went back to the east coast at various times, and that they had fished the Kennebec. It seems quite possible that news of Hodgkins's early fishing near his donation land claim might have reached the Humes on one of their trips, and that when the Sacramento proved disappointing, they relocated near the site where another Kennebec fisherman had enjoyed some success. In addition, lumber was available from the nearby mill owned by George and Alexander Abernethy, who had also salted salmon until deciding that lumbering was a more lucrative business. Since much of early San Francisco was built of lumber from the Abernethy mill,[30] it is tempting to speculate about connections the principals may have had in California.

The Humes canned their first pack on a scow located at Eagle Cliff. Although canning was a secret process at that time, it did not remain so for long. Numerous other canneries followed during the decades of the 1870s and 1880s. Gillnets, seines, and traps supplied these canneries with the necessary raw product. Robert Hume used nets 125 fathoms long and 32 meshes deep in 1871, but by 1876 the length had increased to 150 fathoms. He noted that "While canneries increased in numbers rapidly, the development of gear proceeded more slowly in proportion while salmon remained plentiful."[31] There was as yet no competition for a limited supply of fish. Rather, getting a share of what was available depended upon the number of fishermen and boats a cannery had and the skill of the fishermen. R. D. Hume also devised a way to get ahead of his competition by purchasing a launch to tow the sailboats out to the drifting grounds in the evening and back to the cannery in the morning, thus saving time and energy for the fishermen.[32]

An article in the *Tri-Weekly Astorian* in 1873 described the gillnetting of the early 1870s in some detail:

> The nets are about two fathoms wide [deep] with sinkers on one edge and small buoys on the other which cause them to float perpendicularly when stretched in the stream. They vary in length from 100 to 300 fathoms. Two men with a boat attend each net. The net is extended across the channel and allowed to float down with the tide while the boat passes back and forth along the line of buoys, watching for fish and keeping the line aright. [When a fish was gilled it disturbed the buoys, so the men lifted that part of the net, took the fish out, killed it by a blow to the head, and dropped the net again, a process known as under-running.] Thus they will work till the boat is full of fish or they have drifted the proper distance when they take the net into the boat and go back to the fishery. 'Drifting' is generally done at night so the fish cannot see the nets, but many were caught last season during the day in cloudy weather.[33]

At this time there were eight canneries in operation on the Columbia, with six more being erected.

The *Report of the Commissioner of Fish and Fisheries for 1875-76* described the typical Columbia River gillnet as being 1,200 feet long and 20 feet deep, drifted over three or four miles.[34] In 1878 Nellie Megler, wife of pioneer cannery owner Joe Megler, wrote an article for the *New York Grocer* in which she described gillnets as being 250 fathoms long, 20 feet deep, with an 8 3/8 inch mesh.[35] Since nets were made of linen, a heavy twine visible in clear water in daylight, they were fished mostly at night, except in periods of freshet in June, when daylight fishing was possible due to murky waters. The cannery would send out a launch each morning to tow the fishing boats home. Each cannery had a net-tender who examined the nets and mended any holes to prepare them for fishing again that night. The canneries owned nearly all nets and boats during this period. It is clear from the way the length of the nets expanded that increased production was needed as canneries proliferated and the size of their individual packs grew. The depth of the nets appeared to vary from twelve to twenty feet, about the maximum depth that could be handled by the technique of under-running which was standard at this time. The shallowness of the nets also reflected the attempt to balance fish production against snag damage.

During these early days of the fishery there were no regulations regarding fishing gear. Gillnets were effectively controlled by the canneries who leased them to the fishermen. The fishermen, particularly those in the Astoria area, were mainly transients with no stake in the fishery. The fleet is described in this 1882 observation:

> In the actual work of fishing about 2,500 white men were engaged from April 1 to August 1–four months. Half of these are masters of boats and the other half assistants or pullers. Independent fishermen who own their boats and nets and sell their catch to the canneries receive 60 or 62½ cents per fish. As a rule, however, the canneries own the outfits, for the use of which the fisherman gives one third of his catch, receiving only 40 cents per fish from the cannery. Each fisherman employs and makes terms with his own boat puller [the person who rowed the boat], the usual rate for this service being a share in the catch, about the equivalent of $70 per month. One hundred dollars per month, after charges for boat and net and pay of boat puller are deducted, is considered only a fair return to the

fisherman, and the average is rather above than below this estimate. Only white men engage in fishing, the greater proportion, however, being Italians, Fins [sic] and other foreigners, men without families, who come to the river from San Francisco only during the fishing season.[36]

Fishermen in the areas upriver from Astoria homesteaded the many valleys along the Columbia, becoming permanent residents earlier than those who fished the mouth.

Another detailed description of the fishery just two years later was contained in a report of the Secretary of War:

As an average the gill-nets are 1800 feet long and from 20 to 30 feet deep, with meshes of $4^1/_2$ inches [9 inches in today's terminology]. To hold down the lower edge lead sinkers are placed at intervals of 12 inches. Of course it is in the interest of this class of fishermen to leave as little free water-way as possible below their nets for the fish to pass through, and hence they almost drag the bottom and close the whole waterway for a portion of time while floating. The whole number of gill-nets operating about the mouth of the river is about 1,600.[37]

Cannery ownership of nets was a problem for the canners because they were expensive. They had to pay a net-tender, and losses occurred when nets were badly damaged or lost entirely. As fishermen did not own the nets, they had little incentive to care for them, let alone experiment with their design to increase productivity. The May and June freshet posed a problem for the fisherman who wanted to fish for the premium spring and summer chinook then entering the river on their upstream migration. Warm weather thawing the snowpack in the mountains created high and swift water in the Columbia, along with a great deal of debris. Muddy water conditions were advantageous for the fisherman, permitting him to fish in the daytime as well as at night. However, crest heights of the river might be twenty or more feet above normal, and in exceptional years, such as the flood year of 1894, the river crest at Portland was thirty-three feet above normal.[38]

R. D. Hume was the victim of a freshet, as he described in his autobiography:

Being inexperienced, I took the advice of people who had lived in the neighborhood, [and] drove the piles for a wharf on a point of land where the water cut the bank away. I was building this dock with the expectation of getting some money out of the business of the firm of Hume and Cook, and before [I] got any returns from that business a freshet came and washed away my wharf. I stood on the porch of my house and saw it swept away without any power to save it. Had been waiting a long time to get a cannery started, and it made me feel very much discouraged; while pacing up and down, looking at the work of destruction going on, my wife came to me and placed her arm around my neck and said, "Rob, the darkest hour is just before day." I patched up what remained of the wharf.[39]

High water posed a problem for the migrating salmon, too. In order to conserve energy in their upstream passage, salmon tend to "sound" or move to the bottom of the river where the current is not so strong, especially during the ebb tide and during periods of freshet. This habit made them inaccessible to fishermen whose nets were only twenty feet deep. The *St. Helens Mist* of April 1897 described the frustration felt by fishermen trying to work during periods of high water. The fishermen "are a badly demoralized lot of fellows. When the season first opened fishing prospects were good, but they continued so only a brief period, for the high water came and now it is almost impossible to catch a fish." The same article reported driftwood playing havoc with fish traps at Chinook.[40]

The presence of sunken debris that would snag and tear nets hampered fishermen in their efforts to catch the fish which they knew to be near the bottom of the river. In addition, the extra depth of a net designed to fish in deeper water was prohibitive in a day when boats were powered by sail and oar and the fisherman had only his back and arms for hauling in gear. Such a net would also have had a prohibitive price. As the number of canneries continued to increase during the 1880s, however, the fish runs began to dwindle due to the fishing pressure. At this point competition between canneries to maintain and increase their pack size became fierce. Competition among fishermen also increased, as each sought to maximize his individual catch of a shrinking resource. Cannery operators began to encourage fishermen to own their own nets in order to reduce cannery operating costs. As the saying was, "A man rarely catches a steamboat with his own net."[41] Increasing competition among fishermen, plus the ownership of nets, encouraged experimentation with gear, leading up to the development of the "diver" net.

The New England style of net is what is now called a "floater" net on the Columbia. Floats buoy its upper edge while lead weights along the bottom edge ensure that it will hang properly in the water from the surface down. Salmon swimming upstream, unaware of its presence, get caught in it by their gills or occasionally by their teeth or back fins. The diver net, by contrast, is heavily leaded so that it sinks to the bottom of the river and hangs suspended in the water buoyed by corks along its upper edge. It fishes from the bottom of the river up. Both floater and diver nets are drift gillnets, drifting downstream with the river current or upstream on the incoming tide. The floater was and is fished predominantly on the flood tide, while the diver was and is fished on the ebb, or in parts of the river where there is only a downstream current and no tidal effect.

The origins of the diver net are uncertain and its exact date of development unknown. Certainly there were precedents in the nineteenth century among other fisheries, both in Europe and North America, for sunken gear. Descriptions in newspaper accounts of the late nineteenth and early twentieth centuries help establish parameters for the period in which this gear appeared. The *Cathlamet Gazette* of December 18, 1891, reported that

> Two enterprising sturgeon fishermen are preparing a net to catch sturgeon instead of using hooks and lines as at present. The meshes will be from twelve to fifteen inches in size and will be sunk to the bottom of the river and well buoyed. This plan works successfully on the [Great] Lakes and there is no reason why it should not succeed here.[42]

Whether it did succeed or not was never reported. However, the net described is obviously a diver net to be used for sturgeon.[43] The New York market created a demand for sturgeon, which was shipped east in refrigerated railroad cars during this period. Sturgeon are found close to the bottom of the river and were at this time fished by Chinese "gang lines," rows of hooks attached to a line placed along the bottom.[44] In developing a net to catch sturgeon, the unknown but "enterprising" fishermen were utilizing what was already common knowledge about the location of sturgeon and adapting it to a net technology. Entering the realm of conjecture again, it is entirely likely that some salmon were caught along with the sturgeon in this experiment, and it was but a short step to transferring the knowledge gained to the intentional capture of salmon. A short item mentioning a "sinker net" appeared in the *Skamokawa Eagle* of February 6, 1896, and an article in the July 23, 1903 *Eagle* mentioned gillnetters fishing with "small mesh diver nets."[45] A June 11, 1908 article in the same newspaper mentioned that "Sixteen years ago . . . the . . . diver net was not in use."[46] These quotations place the development of the diver net in the decades of the 1890s and 1900s.

Oral tradition places the location of the first divers variously in the Willamette River, Mayger, Puget Island, Skamokawa, and Brookfield. There is no written evidence to either certify or deny any of these claims. It does appear to have an upriver origin, where fishing always took place on the ebb, there being no tidal influence in May, June, or July. Mrs. Katherine Ytredal, daughter of an early Columbia River fisherman, made the following comments:

> My father always claimed to have taught the fishermen around Brookfield how to use diver nets, and to have organized and kept going the first diver drift in the area, Jim Crow, as well as another one later on which was the Grassy Island drift. . . . My memory was that diver fishing didn't work on the lower river [i.e. at the mouth near Astoria] . . . anyway, my father's early fishing was on the Willamette, and that is probably where he learned to fish with divers.[47]

An examination of the inventories of the Columbia River Packers Association canneries in 1913 indicated that diver floats were stored in company facilities from Cottardi to Rooster Rock, but not in the Astoria establishments,[48] thus indicating a probable upriver origin for the net. Its use caught on rapidly, whatever its origin, so that by February 1920 an article in *Pacific Fisherman* noted:

> Fishermen on the lower Columbia River are predicting that the "diver" net will practically supersede gillnets [floaters] in that stream within the next few years, particularly if the cost of gillnet webbing keeps up to its present level. Many nets of the "diver" type were operated last season in the upper part of the river and are said to have been quite successful. As the diver net is made of cotton webbing, it is very much cheaper than a gillnet of equal capacity.[49]

H. N. Nice had spun his own twine for his gillnet. During his first winter on the Columbia, R. D. Hume reminisced that "We spent the winter making cans and making nets having brought the material with us. It is a very lonely place there, the nearest neighbor being three miles off. . . . It rained forty days and forty nights without interruption."[50] W. H. Barker also remembered the very early years of net making. "The fishermen spun their own twine from small balls of shoemaker's thread and wound it up into skeins ready for knitting. Nets were only 125 to 150 fathoms long and 30 to 35 meshes deep, and were hung on manila lines."[51]

The supply of flax or linen affected gear construction materially. Flax had been grown in Oregon since 1844 in varying amounts[52] and remained as part of the fiber industry of the west coast for decades.[53] After its introduction in the 1890s cotton substituted for linen when the latter's cost became prohibitive. Such was the case during World War I. Linen twine which had cost $1.25 per pound in 1914 rose to $2.55 per pound by 1917.[54] Much of the world's supply of fiber flax had come from Russia, but the disruption of the war cut off supplies. As a result, on the Columbia there was a shift from gillnetting to other kinds of fishing. The June 1919 issue of *Pacific Fisherman* stated it bluntly: "Owing to the increase in the cost of gear, many former gillnetters have turned to trolling."[55] This option was available mainly to those gillnetters who lived near the mouth of the river. Those who lived further upstream turned more and more to diver nets which required less web and were cheaper than floaters.

Linen became more plentiful by the middle of the 1920s, due at least in part to the development of the flax-growing industry in Oregon. Although the fishermen by then owned their nets, the canneries would order twine in bulk for the fishermen who shipped their fish to them, thus achieving a cost savings. The nets were knitted at home from the linen twine, although machine-made web was available. Machine-made web was generally considered to be of inferior quality, especially during the first years of its manufacture:

> The [net-making] machine leaves the knot too loose in the large nets, so lots of us make them by hand. There are a great number of women who make their living this way. . . . This one will be 1500 feet long and 20 feet wide. We make them of pure linen yarn-192 pounds in one like this. If one is good at the knitting he can make a pound an hour. . . . Those who knit nets are paid 50 cents a pound for the work. In the early spring we use the eight inches meshes. Later we use the nets with 9½ inches.[56]

By 1931 *Oregon Magazine* could boast that an Oregon spinning mill "is supplying a major portion of the net twine for our great salmon fishing industry."[57]

By the 1930s the nets were becoming very much more complex. Compare the following description of a trammel diver with the early descriptions of the simple floater net:

> 150 fathoms hung, has 386 aluminum floats with a small size. The lines are practically new and is what is commonly called four-web net, in other words it has one cork line and two lead lines. One web is of 40: 10 ply, 10 inch mesh and 8 meshes deep. The second web is 40: 7 ply, 7 inch mesh and 17 meshes deep. The third web is 40: 8 ply 11¹/₂ inch mesh and 6 meshes deep. The fourth web is 40: 7 ply, 6³/₄ inch mesh and 18 meshes deep . . . it takes all four of these webs to complete the net of 150 fathoms hung.[58]

A trammel net had a curtain of large mesh webbing hung on one or both sides of smaller mesh webbing. When the salmon hit the smaller mesh webbing, the impact would cause the web to form a pocket in which entangled the fish. Trammels could be used on both divers and floaters. Mesh sizes for gillnets started changing in 1893, when canneries started packing and paying for smaller fish in addition to the large chinook salmon that had been their mainstay.[59] It was only a matter of time before fishermen began to develop gear that would take more than one size of fish. The *Astoria Budget* reported on this development in 1922, describing in great detail a trammel net used during the previous year:

> Two of the nets are of cotton twine with meshes from 32 to 35 inches square. Between these two the third net is strung. It is made of linen twine and has from 8 to 8¹/₂ inch meshes. The main object of the new type of gear is to provide a net which will catch both large and small salmon, that is, those of commercial size, and thus obviate the necessity of an individual fisherman being equipped with two nets, one of 7¹/₂ and another of 9¹/₂ inch mesh, in order to catch the different sizes of fish which enter the river.
>
> The idea is and it has proven to be correct, that the smaller mesh net will hold the salmon weighing from 17 to 22 lb. each. When a larger fish strikes this small net it will not be gilled but will force a section of the net through a big mesh of one of the outside nets and thus form a sack or pocket from which it cannot escape.

It is also asserted that should the anticipated runs of sock-eyes in the Columbia River materialize, this combination floater can be rigged to catch them also by simply reducing the size of the mesh in the linen net to about 5 inches.

The principal drawbacks in operating these new floaters are their weight, which makes them harder to handle than is the ordinary net, and the fact that they float so much faster than a gillnet that they often overtake and become entangled with other floating gear in the river.[60]

A certain upriver-downriver rivalry regarding gear development appeared in the *Skamokawa Eagle*'s response to the article just quoted:

> The Astoria Budget had an article in its Monday issue describing a "new type of net" to appear in the 1922 fishing. By the description we recognize the tripple [sic] net in use around Skamokawa since 1916. Some of the upriver fishermen not only have the tripple rig but have an apron or two in the bargain, which proves a labyrinth to Mr. Chinook once he sticks his nose into it.[61]

There is some confusion in the literature regarding Columbia River gillnets, as occasionally an author will talk about trammel nets being a third type of net, in addition to divers and floaters. Fishermen, however, view all nets as either divers or floaters.[62] They may, however, be trammel divers or trammel floaters, but trammels are a part of the net itself, not a different kind of net. In addition to the technique of catching a fish by its gills, they provide the added option of entangling a fish.

The apron referred to in the previous quotation was an additional curtain of webbing weighted so that it would float at an angle to the straight wall of webbing. In this way a fish which might try to escape being gilled in the backwall, or straight wall of webbing, by swimming upwards and over the net, would be caught in the apron. Some aprons even had a "slacker," an additional shallow piece of web hanging down to catch any fish which managed to escape the backwall and apron. As Elmer Hurula explained:

> Well, they first started in with straight nets and then they started stringing them and then they had trammels, some had small trammels and some had trammels up to fifty inches even or more. . . . And then some of them had aprons. An apron was to catch those foxy salmon that wouldn't hit the back wall. They'd

come crawling up and they would hear the lead line grinding on the sand or something and they'd back up and hit the apron. When they got close to the lead line they could hear it and they'd turn back and up and they'd hit the apron.[63]

Experimentation with gear was not without its consequences in the larger world. In 1915 the State of Oregon enacted the first regulations on the Columbia River regarding mesh size, establishing a minimum mesh size of five inches.[64] In 1935 the maximum length for gillnets was established at 250 fathoms, a regulation rescinded in 1937 and re-established in 1957. Since the 1930s gillnet changes have occurred largely in the realm of newer and different materials, including aluminum, plastic, and foam corks, nylon web, and polypropylene lines. Newer methods of pulling a net into a boat, beginning with the roller found on the early bowpicker, continuing with the hydraulic roller developed in the early 1950s, and culminating in the single and double reels or drums used today, have allowed the development of heavier, deeper gear. Today's new wrinkle is the deep floater, designed to fish from top to bottom of the river. Such a net would have been an impossibility a century ago, as human power alone could not pull in so heavy a net.

The basic principles of gillnetting have not changed, despite changes in materials, net lengths and depths, and mesh sizes. Fish behavior is still the same, and thinking through the creation of a net is still the pursuit of each individual fisherman.

**

A number of the preceding accounts of the development of the drift gillnet lack the flavor of personal experience. The writers were observers of the fishery, but not necessarily participants. Most were unaware that nets are individual creations, constructed upon basic principles and with specific fishing grounds and types of fish in mind, products of the competitive pressures of fishing and of an individual's skill in the techniques needed to construct a successful net.

The constant push for more production, more fish, drove the development of the drift gillnet on the Columbia. While Robert Hume could put up a pack based on one man's production in the days when there weren't a half a dozen canneries on the river, the expanding markets demanded expanding production. Increasing production was not a problem at first. Nets simply became longer, and perhaps a little deeper, and canneries hired more fishermen. However, once peak production was achieved, the runs began to decline, due to overfishing. In an effort to address this issue, salmon propagation by means of hatcheries drew the interest of the packers, in particular R. D. Hume, who conducted experiments in this area. The pressure to produce ever-larger catches of salmon to fill markets caused fishermen to look at ways to maximize harvest on portions of runs previously unfishable due to freshet conditions, and led to the development of the diver net. Once the spring and summer runs had declined to the point where they could no longer fill market demand, other market niches for such runs as steelhead and fall chinook salmon developed. In turn, fishermen created combination nets which would take several sizes of fish. During the period of expansion of the fisheries during the second half of the nineteenth century, it should be noted that fishing was almost completely unregulated by government, leading to the uncontrolled expansion of the fishery and subsequent overfishing.

The question of who developed the Columbia River gillnet in each of its stages is unanswerable if one searches for the names of the individuals. It is possible, however, to find out more about the different groups of fishermen who came to the Columbia by examining the great waves of immigration which transformed the Pacific Northwest and the Columbia River region in the second half of the nineteenth century.

Chapter Two

"They Were All Gillnetters"

Who invented the diver net? Who first thought of pulling snags? Who developed drift rights? I have not been able to answer any of these questions with a specific name or date. Instead, I have recast the questions themselves, based on the concept of the drift right. Drift rights were a community's way of organizing access to fishing grounds. The ethnic basis of the various communities is the link, then, to understanding the origins of the gear, boats, and customs of the fishermen. Further, it is necessary to replicate the thought processes of the immigrant fishermen faced with making a living by fishing in a new territory in conjunction with immigrant neighbors who were not all from the same country. New questions need asking, including: Where did the fishermen come from? Why did they leave their homes to come to the U. S.? How did they learn about the Columbia River fishery? What customs did they bring with them? What types of gear technology were they familiar with?

Hudson's Bay Company and east coast American traders who sent ships to the Columbia River and purchased fish from the local Indian fishermen developed the post-contact trade.[1] They packed salted salmon in barrels and sold them wherever they could find a market—in London, China, Chile, and Hawaii. Quality control was a recurrent problem. The shortage of coopers skilled in barrel-making, labor skilled in preparing the fish, and long journeys to markets all contributed to the deterioration of salt fish.

Despite these problems, the salt salmon trade increased. A number of the early salmon canners got their start in this fashion. P. J. McGowan came to Chinook from Ireland in 1852[2] and set up a saltery, purchasing fish from Chinook Indians who operated a seine.

John West[3] began salting salmon in about 1857 in Westport, Oregon. The early packers came mainly from the east coast or Great Britain, and they used their connections with communities back home to encourage migration to the Columbia. Hall Kelley and other enthusiasts publicized the Oregon Country, attracting more settlers. The California gold rush received wide publicity, bringing still more immigrants to the west coast.

Canning of salmon began on the Columbia in 1867. It expanded rapidly, and on April 1, 1869 William Hume advertised in the Portland *Oregonian* of the need for "Twenty young men and boys to work at canning fish at Hume & Co.'s packing establishment." In 1870 a similar ad requested twenty-five people. Chronic labor shortages were the norm for the first few years of the canning industry, which competed with a still-vital salt fish trade.[4] In the early 1870s R. D. Hume returned to Maine to visit his family and recruit labor for his Bayview Cannery. He brought back his nephews, Abraham Webber and Johnnie Hume, a sailor named Jack Driscoll, and "several other good men."[5] Booth Fisheries, headquartered in Chicago, established a cannery in Astoria in 1874.[6] The firm had fishing and wholesale interests on the east coast and Great Lakes, both sources of labor and technology.[7] The fishermen on the Great Lakes were primarily American, Indian, and Norwegian immigrants who had arrived during the 1850s and 1860s.[8]

A number of early immigrants' manuals and similar documents circulated among U. S. fishermen during the 1870s, promoting the development of the Columbia River. J. L. McDonald's book, *Hidden Treasures or Fisheries around the Northwest Coast*, published in Gloucester, Massachusetts, in 1871, targeted a fishing audience:

> The Chincook [sic] salmon found in the Lower Columbia are very large, solid and fat. Several establishments are located along the banks of this river devoted to the catching and pickling of this fine fish. We noticed two or three fishing stations on the Washington side of the river in which salmon were prepared and put up in tin cans, hermetically sealed. The salmon fishery on the Columbia is profitably developed.[9]

McDonald's book pointed out the need for laborers, particularly coopers, in the west. *The Fishermen's Own Book*,[10] published in 1882, devoted several pages to the Columbia River, encouraging fishermen to consider emigration to the fishery. Other publications, intended for a general audience, also extolled the value and potential of the Columbia River fisheries. A promotional booklet, *Columbia River Salmon Statistics: The Product of Six Years. Where and How to Sell to Best Advantage*,[11] attempted to position Astoria as a viable trans-shipment port, should a railhead develop there. Its statistical tables indicated that the salmon pack was being marketed in the eastern United States, Great Britain, New Zealand, and Australia. *Oregon, Facts Regarding its Climate, Soil, Mineral and Agricultural Resources, Means of Communication, Commerce and Industry, Laws, Etc., Etc.*, included salmon statistics as part of the "etc." These early publications attempted to attract labor and capital to the Columbia River area. By the early 1880s, however, the attraction of tourists to the region provided additional impetus to publishers. L. Samuel published *Columbia River Illustrated*,[12] a tourist guidebook containing pictures of the salmon industry. By this time, Cleveland Rockwell was also publishing his illustrated articles in *Harper's Magazine*,[13] so that knowledge of the Columbia River salmon fisheries was widely disseminated in North America.

Immigrants' manuals also appeared in Europe. A monthly publication in Czech[14] printed in Hamburg, Germany, during the 1880s kept prospective immigrants up to date on immigration centers in North America. In 1899, *Suomalaiset Amerikassa*[15] described in detail the good life available to Finnish fishermen on the Columbia, showing pictures of the comfortable homes of those who had already emigrated, of multitudes of salmon spawning, and of settlements such as Astoria and Deep River, with their large Finnish populations.

The reports of the U. S. Commissioner for Fisheries which began in the 1870s were a potent force in disseminating information and strengthening communications. Translations of key fisheries research undertaken in Europe, especially in the Scandinavian countries, appeared in the reports on an annual basis. Results of experimental gear research and fish stock assessments conducted in the U. S. also were reviewed. In addition, a number of international fisheries expositions occurred from 1876 to 1883 in which the U.S. participated, yielding many valuable contacts for the U.S. delegations.[16] These expositions also served to disseminate information to European fishermen regarding the potential of U. S. fisheries, and the Columbia River usually had a prominent display. Newspaper articles appeared in host countries, which included France, Germany, Sweden, Denmark, Norway, and Great Britain, thus giving additional international exposure to the developing U. S. fisheries.

All of the preceding methods—importation of fishermen by packers; publications; expositions—served to attract fishermen and labor to the burgeoning fishing industry. The fishermen themselves in turn attracted other fishermen, friends and relatives from their communities of origin. In addition, turbulent economic, social, and political conditions in Europe compelled fishermen and others to leave. The stories of the lives of individual fishermen who emigrated during that time illustrate the difficulties facing many of those who lived in nineteenth century Europe.

An example is Erick Martin.[17] Born in Stavanger, Norway, on January 25, 1851, his real name was Erick Martinius Tollefson, and his father was Tollef Tollefson. Somewhere around the age of thirteen or fourteen he began to go to sea, and at some point took part in the cod fisheries of Norway. Although family records are not complete, it appears that after the death of both of his parents in an epidemic, Tollefson left Norway and in 1870 arrived in Portland, Oregon, where he jumped ship (and changed his name). In 1871 he came to Skamokawa and fished during the summer salmon seasons for the following thirty years, mainly for Pillar Rock Packing Company. In 1878 he married Anna Oline Marie Johansdatter in Astoria, Oregon. In April 1898 he became an American citizen, and he died in 1923. He resided on a farm in East Valley, Skamokawa, from 1879 until he died. Among the relics left in the family possession there is a model of a Norwegian cod fishing schooner, made by him in the 1880s for his son, Emil, a mesh board inlaid with a salmon carved in either ivory or bone, several other needles and mesh boards, and a sailmaker's needle.

John Strom also landed in Portland in 1870. The following account, printed in 1908, tells the story of his life:

> A pleasant Christmas dinner was that enjoyed by the families of Messrs. John A. Strom and N. P. Anderson. In 1866 Messrs. Strom and Anderson, both young men, left Sweden to follow the sea in a Swedish bark. Their wanderings took them to England where they left their home vessel and shipped in a "limejuicer." They spent two years in the English vessel and

left her at Bremen to ship in a German ship. They went to China in this vessel and in 1870 she came to Portland. This was the opportunity they were looking for and they left the German in Portland and came down to Westport, Or. They soon found work gillnet fishing, Mr. Strom pulling boat for the late John Polwarth . . . and Mr. Anderson acting in like capacity for the late Jacob Wilson. They made their home in Westport and vicinity until 1873 when they came to Skamokawa and Mr. Anderson bought a farm. . . . Mr. Strom then bought 42 acres of Mr. Anderson and also homesteaded 160. The two old friends now had their farms and they needed wives, so Mr. Strom went back to Sweden in 1873 and married Mrs. Strom and her sister returned with him and Mr. Anderson was married to Mr. Strom's sister-in-law at Westport. All these years they have lived near to each other and every Christmas finds them celebrating the day together. Only once in 41 years have these two old friends missed eating their Christmas dinner together.[18]

John Strom was born in Kalmar, Sweden, on June 11, 1847. The newspaper article euphemistically states that he and Nels Anderson "left" their ship. Life in the Swedish merchant navy was arduous, and a tour of duty lasted many years. In actuality, they jumped ship and hid out some months at the Polwarth establishment. John Strom's younger brother, Charles Strom, also emigrated to the U. S. Family legend has it that communications were so poor in those days that the two brothers had completely lost contact until they met by accident in the streets of Astoria. Charles Strom worked for the Hanthorn Company, fishing, canning, and boat-building. The Stroms left Sweden due to economic crises and crop failures in the 1860s, known as the Great Famine.[19] Christin Berg, who married John Strom, waited for him for seven years. When they left Sweden, a friend of Christin's, Mathilda Nelsson, wrote a poem bidding her farewell, knowing that in all likelihood they would never meet again. The journey in those days took the long route around Cape Horn in a sailing vessel. A few family relics include the battered copper tea pot which came on that journey, and the poem written by Mathilda Nelsson. The final verse is translated below:

Farewell! You two young people, May God bless you even on a path far away in a distant country, and give you his peace. I pray for this. Then you will be safe, Yes, all the way to the beach of heaven.

In both Sweden and Norway, a willingness to be flexible was essential in order to make a living. As families increased in size and divided up family farms, the amount of acreage per farm grew proportionately less, making it more difficult to support a family.[20] Those who had a pluralistic adaptation of farming and fishing, or farming and logging, were better able to adjust to the economic pressures, but conditions began to deteriorate in the fishery as well. The major Norwegian cod fishery occurred annually in the Lofoten Islands, and its decline began in about 1866. Declines either in numbers of fish in some years, or in prices in other years due to competition from fisheries in places such as Newfoundland,[21] continued for some twenty years, bringing great hardship to the Lofoten fishery:

> Who has not heard of the Maelstrom? It may not be so generally known, however, that the fishermen of these parts well acquainted with its peculiarities enter it in light open boats, and, driven by the current, cast out their nets and only avoid it when at times it rises threateningly. . . .
>   Twenty thousand fishermen come to these inexhaustible seas every year; traders come in their yachts and everything is life and bustle. But what a life of labor and danger! In the darkness of the long night the fishermen enter their boats, for the brief day-time often shortened by gloomy skies would be by far too short for the work which has to be accomplished.[22]

Fishermen came to the Lofotens from all over Norway. Interviews done as part of the Oregon Sea Grant Columbia River Project indicated that the Norwegian ancestors of a number of the interviewees participated in this fishery.[23] The maternal grandfather of the author's husband got his start fishing there as a boy of thirteen. He spent part of his teenage years on schooners transporting salt cod to England, France, and "Riga Russia" (present-day Latvia). In addition to the downswing in the cod fisheries, the European herring fisheries failed in 1876,[24] with losses felt particularly by the Scots, Dutch, French, and Norwegians.

The Scandinavian countries exhibited a number of the problems that served to drive fishermen out of their communities. Population pressures, particularly on limited agricultural land, widespread economic problems, famine, downturns in fisheries which had been mainstays, all provided the impetus for fishermen to look elsewhere in order to make a living. Upon their arrival in the U. S. they tended to settle in areas where there were other immigrants from the old country. As recently as 1955, in an article about Puget Island, a reporter could write that:

> The real model for this water-borne society in the middle of the Columbia was an obscure fishing village somewhere in the fjords of Norway. . . . Like so many other American immigrant groups, these children of the midnight sun drifted into a place which most closely resembled their former environment. They had grown up in verdant country where the air was moist from the nearby sea. Handy with a net and a milk pail, they took up the accustomed ways of making a living: Fishing and dairying.[25]

The Scandinavian countries were not the only nations with fishing communities that were in trouble. The fisheries of the Mediterranean and the Adriatic were also in a state of flux during the period from 1860 to the 1890s. The Austro-Hungarian Empire, which ruled parts of Europe, including Yugoslavia, Poland, Hungary, Austria, and parts of Romania, Czechoslovakia, and Italy, was undergoing difficulties similar to those in Norway and Sweden by the late 1870s:

> The years of poor harvest with their food shortages, overdue unpaid loans of the population, and in the maritime provinces the decline of sailing ships, fishing and wine-making industries in addition to the economical and political negligence of that region triggered mass emigration.[26]

The preceding quotation referred to the provinces composing what became Yugoslavia. However, it could equally well apply to other areas controlled by the Hapsburgs. Each province had fishing laws on the books which dated back hundreds of years. Attempts were made to resolve some of the inconsistencies, but the changes could also be disastrous for local fisheries. For example, in 1864 the province of Galicia [Poland] tried to organize its chaotic laws by bringing them before the imperial ministries:

> The reports of former Galician officials and of the Galician agricultural societies faithfully depict the chaotic state of the fishing-laws, which in many parts of the province had almost entirely exhausted this source of national wealth, and had seriously injured the salmon and sturgeon fisheries in the Galician rivers, which had formerly been very extensive. In some districts, the fisheries are carried on by the land-owners; in others, they are managed by the village-communities as the

common property thereof, and the revenues derived from them are used for meeting the common expenditure; while in other parts, they are the independent property of private individuals.[27]

Another province of the Empire, Bukowina, received the following description:

With the exception of the ponds and a few mountain streams, nearly all waters in Bukowina are almost entirely deprived of their former wealth of fish by reason of the utter want of system in all matters pertaining to the fisheries; and it will take a long time for a fishing-law to gain ground.[28]

In addition to the internal administrative problems brought about by an expanding empire, international problems also occurred. The writer who described the situation in Austro-Hungary also pointed out that:

In large connected fishing territories, divided between several countries, each one is dependent on the others for its fisheries. Every country by itself can do much to destroy the fisheries of the whole territory; but, without the co-operation of the other countries, it is not able to keep them up, even with the best and strictest fishing laws.[29]

The Elbe and Rhine river salmon runs served as particular examples of this kind of problem. Attempts to negotiate an international fisheries treaty on the Rhine date from 1869. However, a convention was not signed until 1886. It included the German Empire, the Netherlands, and Switzerland.[30]

Census and newspaper accounts of the latter part of the nineteenth century shared the confusion in nomenclature of the emigrants from the Austro-Hungarian Empire. Slavs, Yugoslavs, Hungarians, Slovaks, Croats, Slovenians, Austrians, Italians, and other rubrics all served to define a population on the move from the Empire to what they hoped were better conditions. Political purges and poverty were the chief pressures behind their emigration.[31] "It is commonly said that America is a nation of immigrants. However, speaking of the Yugoslavs, one can say that they are the nation of emigrants."[32] Saxony, which borders the Elbe River, was the home province of Joe Megler, who established the Brookfield

Cannery in 1873 and brought in fishermen from the Dalmatian Coast to fish for him.[33]

The stark poverty which drove the Austro-Hungarian fishermen from their homes followed them to America, where they struggled to make a living. The estate of Nicholas Marincovich, one of Joe Megler's Brookfield fishermen who died in 1887, listed as his only assets a boat worth $75, "one old net" valued at $50, a gun valued at $12, and two blankets worth $2. The effects were sold and the proceeds sent to his Austrian relatives, as he had no near kin in the U. S.[34] An account by John Vlastelicia described early immigrant life in America:

> Vis is the town they come from, the island too is Vis. From an island in the Adriatic Sea. About 25 miles off shore, I guess it was. . . . They had vineyards over there. . . . They also fished but in those days you know, they talked about the United States where money was flowing all over and they all came over here to make big money and he [his father] came over here and he worked for a dollar a day. Can you imagine that? For a dollar a day they worked. They barely got by.[35]

The marine fisheries of Austro-Hungary were located in the Adriatic Sea. Approximately 10 percent of the fishermen were Italian subjects, whose catch per man was about double that of the Austrians. The latter, however, appeared to have utilized a pluralistic adaptation, being "fishermen only during the best part of the season and . . . engaged in farm work or some other employment at other portions of the year."[36]

The evidence regarding the Italian fishermen is somewhat more fragmentary than that for other nationalities. It was an Italian, Captain Giovanni Dominis, who began the salt salmon trade from the Columbia River in 1827.[37] Italian fishermen were apparently in the Portland area during the 1860s, supplying the local demand for fresh salmon and some salt fish for winter use.[38] Italians had emigrated to the Sacramento River fisheries beginning in the 1850s,[39] but the largest waves of immigrants arrived in the following three decades, as the continued struggles for Italian unification kept the country in a state of chaos. A contemporary account noted that the fisheries were declining in the Bay of Naples by the 1870s,[40] an additional impetus for leaving.

Since the Sacramento salmon runs dovetailed with the Columbia River summer season, Italian fishermen fished on the Columbia during the summers and then returned to fish the Sacramento.[41] This migratory pattern continued with Italian fishermen eventually substituting Alaska for the Columbia River when the fishery changed. The Italian and Greek fishermen of the Sacramento were the subject of Jack London's book, *Tales of the Fish Patrol*,[42] which, while somewhat ethnically biased, does convey the hardships of the immigrant fishermen in the early days of gillnetting out of a sailboat.[43]

Finns also made up part of the transient population which migrated to the Columbia for the fishery. During the 1870s and 1880s Berkeley, California, served as the winter base for the majority of the Columbia River Finnish fishermen.[44] As families were established, more permanent settlements and neighborhoods grew up in the Columbia River area. Communities such as Deep River, Washington, had significant numbers of resident Finnish settlers by the late 1870s.[45] The biography of B. A. Seaborg is a classic immigrant story.[46] He left Finland in 1867, driven from his farm by total crop failure. After a period of time in New York, he migrated westward in 1873 and lived in Portland until 1875, when he went to Astoria and began salmon fishing. In 1879 he moved to Ilwaco and opened the Aberdeen Packing Company, the first of several salmon canneries he eventually owned. Akseli Jarnefelt featured him in *Suomalaiset Amerikassa* as a major Finnish success story, a "local boy makes good."[47]

Rural living in Finland declined during the 1880s due to crop failures and famine. Landless rural workers migrated to urban industrial centers either in Finland or America. A second wave of Finnish emigrants in the late 1890s and early 1900s, encouraged by the stories of those who had gone earlier, sought to avoid conscription and political persecution by the Russian government.[48] Jarnefelt's rhapsodies about Finnish life on the Columbia River suggest the push and pull, the divided loyalties which must have faced so many immigrants:

> An Astoria Finn does not get tired of bragging about Oregon climate and about the mighty Columbia River. I have often thought, while listening to those devoted praises: If any country will succeed in capturing his love of his fatherland from a

Finn, it must indeed be Oregon. A Finn who has lived in Oregon wants urgently to return there again–at times even more eagerly than to his land of birth, Finland. And a westerner wonders: Who wouldn't long for the gentle stroking of the Zephyr, the delightfully even temperature with a cool breeze after one has experienced it there. Oregon, Oregon, that name next to the name of Finland, echoes even more precious to many.[49]

The Thompson family of England is another example of a Columbia River family with a fisheries background. In 1922 John Thompson wrote an account of his life:

> I was born in the town or parish of Chepstow, in the county of Monmouth, England, a small town situated on the river Wye about four miles from its mouth which empties into the Bristol Channel. . . . My Father . . . was a seafaring man. Ever since I can remember he was master or captain of a small coasting vessel. Most all my relations followed the sea for a livelihood.
>
> My Grandpa on my father's side also followed the sea. . . . My mother's . . . father was brought up on a farm somewhere near Frampton in Gloucestershire. He followed the sea, and later in life moved his family to Chepstow and followed salmon fishing. [John Thompson married, and he and his wife had two children while in England. However, his brother had emigrated to the U. S.] Keeping up correspondence with my brother Tom in America and knowing conditions in England, I began to feel that I would rather see my rising family have a chance to better their conditions, as I was well aware that in the crowded condition of England it was a struggle for existence. So my brother Tom offered assistance to bring us to the U. S. I accepted his offer.

Thompson's brother Thomas Thompson was an English seaman who jumped ship in 1871 at either Portland or Westport, Oregon. During ensuing years he worked as a boat puller and eventually settled on a farm in Skamokawa. His son, Thomas Thompson Jr., farmed, but principally fished for a living.[50]

It should be evident from the previous discussion that fisheries resources both on the east coast of the U. S. and in Europe generally were in a period of eclipse, due to overfishing and environmental problems which contributed to low fish populations. Low fish prices were also an issue in particular fisheries. Political and social unrest contributed to the difficulty of making a living, as national boundaries affecting fishing territories and the fish runs themselves were subject to change. The pluralist adaptations developed over many years were no longer successful, due in part to population pressures and to agricultural failures. All of this combined to send waves of migrant fishermen to the Columbia River.

There were a number of impediments to the development of a fishing community on the Columbia. Immigrants brought with them different customs from their home communities, different gear types, and different ways of organizing access to fishing grounds. They spoke a variety of languages, and for the first years many made up a transient population which did not settle on the Columbia. Communications systems such as the telephone were unknown. Many communities were water-based, with no roads, especially on the Washington side of the river. On the Oregon side, the Spokane, Portland and Seattle Railroad served to connect communities from the 1880s on. Until then, riverboats linked the small scattered villages and towns on both sides of the Columbia. The connecting road to the sea was not completed on the Washington shore until the 1930s. The European fishermen utilized a number of different gear technologies in their homelands, with both set and drift gillnets common. Educational backgrounds of the immigrants varied widely, with a fairly high level of literacy in the U. S., from Finland, and the Scandinavian countries, and a much lower level of literacy on the part of the Mediterranean immigrants.[51]

The Clatsop County, Oregon, census for 1860 listed only three fishermen, one from Germany, one from New Jersey, and one from North Carolina. The census for Clatsop County for 1880 revealed that of 1,293 fishermen, over 90 percent were single, and six out of every seven lived in boarding houses. These figures indicated a large transient population, 84 percent of foreign birth, residing in the Astoria area.[52] However, an examination of the census records of other riverine counties indicated a somewhat different pattern, that of a more pluralistic adaptation. Occupations were frequently lumped together. Erick Martin, for example, appeared as a farmer-fisherman in the 1880 census. Definitions were fluid, so that a fisherman might be listed as a carpenter or a logger, an occupation he followed for a portion of the year during the off-season. A fisherman who owned a small farm might be listed as a farmer, although the principal source of income was fishing.

Fishermen tended to settle in ethnic enclaves along the Columbia. Brookfield was predominantly Slavic, Clifton was part Slavic, part Greek, part Italian. The Mayger-Clatskanie and Deep River areas were predominantly Finnish and Puget Island was 100 percent Norwegian. Astoria had a number of different ethnic communities, as well as a large migrant population of laborers who arrived from California to work at seasonal jobs such as canning.[53] Family connections helped increase the size of small communities, as successful immigrants earned money to send home for relatives and brides.

The various communities differed in their adaptations to their surrounding geography. A community such as Clifton depended almost entirely upon the fishery for its economic mainstay, while villages such as Skamokawa, with its fertile valleys, tended to have a more mixed fishing-farming-logging adaptation. By 1900 most of the communities of the lower Columbia had achieved a certain cultural stability, with no new waves of immigration coming in.[54]

One of the major catalysts in overcoming the various potentially divisive elements among the immigrant fishermen was the Columbia River Fishermen's Protective Union. The forerunner of the Union, the Columbia River Fishermen's Beneficial Aid Society, organized August 16, 1875 and included members from Astoria to Cathlamet, among them John Strom. Its principal purposes were to provide insurance so that the widows of fishermen who died while fishing received a sum of money, and to regulate access to the lower-river fishing grounds. A news item in the *Daily Astorian* of May 4, 1876 described the organization:

> At a special meeting of the Columbia River Fishermen's Beneficial Aid Society, the following regulations for the government of all concerned were adopted. That the following drifts and Tow Heads be established for the fishing season of 1876:
> First Drift from Woody Island to Brownspoint.
> Second Drift from Brownspoint inside of Snag Island to the 12th red buoy.
> Third Drift from the 15th Buoy to Tongue Point.
> Fourth Drift from Tongue Point to a point a little west of Booth's Cannery at a place to be designated by a spile or some permanent mark.
> Fifth Drift from the termination of the fourth drift to Smith's Point.

Sixth Drift from Smith's Point to the Pacific Ocean.

Seventh Drift from the red buoy in the Prairie Channel to Tongue Point up or down.

Eighth Drift the big snag in Chinook Shoot will be considered a Tow Head.

The Fishermen in Astoria in council have mutually agreed to bind themselves to be governed by the foregoing drifts and it is expected from boats outside of the Society that they will also conform to same. Any fisherman who is not fortunate enough to be a member of this Society has still another opportunity to join this Society by applying before the 10th of May, 1876, in accordance with the notice published elsewhere in the Astorian. After which time the initiation fees will be raised to twenty-five dollars.

By order of the Society,

Thomas Dealey, Secretary.[55]

A reading of the names of the fifty-three signatories of the organizational documents of the Society[56] indicated that its charter membership was composed almost entirely of fishermen of Scandinavian, British, or U. S. ancestry.

Due to the burgeoning numbers of fishermen in the late 1870s, some form of organization on the fishing grounds was necessary in order to maintain order and reduce the safety hazards of too many boats competing for the same area. This form of organization became known as a drift or drifting ground. Not only did a drift encompass a certain fishing territory, it also entailed rules to govern access to the area:

> The nets and fishermen are so numerous in some parts of the river that there is not room for all to work at the same time, without being so near as to destroy all chance for the higher nets to catch anything; but by common consent, certain rules have been adopted regulating the times when each boat shall have its turn.[57]

The Columbia River Fishermen's Protective Union formed in 1879[58] and went through a number of reorganizations during the next two decades, affiliating with the American Federation of Labor in 1886. Its early officers were Robert Marriott, president, N. Gilmore, vice president, W. J. Weber, secretary, J. G. Robeson, treasurer, and John McCann, financial secretary,[59] their names an indication of the ethnic composition of the fishing fleet. The numbers of Columbia River fishermen continued to grow, until the C.R.F.P.U.

estimated that there were 1,400 boats and 2,800 fishermen employed in 1888.[60] The Union's membership consisted of a large majority of these men.

The Union recognized both the ethnic and economic nature of its membership. The difference in adaptation between the Astoria fishermen and those further upriver was also well understood, as noted in an 1890 Union publication:

> The Columbia River Fishermen's Protective Union is composed exclusively of gill-net fishermen, and has about 2,500 members, of whom about 900 are permanent residents of the city of Astoria, at which place the union's head office is located. The rest of the members are living along the river–on both banks of the same–and when not fishing a great many of them are engaged in clearing up their land and making other improvements, as a majority of them are real, live home builders in the fullest sense of the word. Again, in the city of Astoria, a large number of our fishermen who reside there are property owners, and their interests and the interests of the city and county are identical.[61]

The Union had representatives at all the canneries along the river. Their job was to sign up members and represent their local membership at Union meetings. In this fashion, news could be effectively disseminated to the rank-and-file and their views made known at Union headquarters in Astoria. The Union operated a reading room at its headquarters, subscribing to newspapers which fishermen could read while they were in Astoria. A number of these were ethnic publications. The Union thus played several roles: a bargaining agent with the canneries, a body which organized access to fishing grounds at the mouth of the river, and a social center. By the 1890s membership included large numbers of Finnish, Scandinavian, and Slavic fishermen. Despite the obvious language and cultural differences, the Union's power was never greater than during this period.

The organization's real strength lay in the fact that it was a union of gillnetters only. There were other types of gear on the river, notably seines, traps, and fishwheels. The trapmen had their own organization, the Washington Fishermen's Association, formed in 1894.[62] However, the clustering around a gear type and a specific geographical area—the Columbia River—rather than developing an organization of all the different gear types, or a coastal or state organization of gillnetters only, proved to be the tool necessary for survival.[63]

The following definition of ethnicity illuminates this situation. An ethnic group is one "which shares common cultural norms, values and identities and patterns of behavior and whose members recognize themselves and are recognized by others as an ethnic group."[64] A description of the Oregon fishing community of Clifton by one of its former residents reinforces this concept: "Yes, the Italians were at the lower end, the Yugoslavs were in the center, and the Greeks were in the upper town. The three nationalities, they all got along pretty well together. They're all gillnetters, that's all they ever done."[65] While there were a number of ethnic identities among the communities along the river, there was another "ethnic" identity, that of Columbia River gillnetter, which the Union fostered. An 1890 booklet published by the C.R.F.P.U. described the fishermen of the Columbia in these terms:

> And now, a word about the nationality of these men. . . . Of our 2,500 fishermen, about 40% or 1,000 were born in other lands, but of these 1,000 nearly 90% have foresworn all allegiance to the land of their birth and have become, or are about to become, full-fledged American citizens. Out of a total membership of 2,500 men about 45% are married and have families, or 1,120 are heads of families.
>
> The men of Scandinavian birth form the largest part of our foreign born members. These hardy sons of the Vikings and Norsemen of old take naturally to the sea for a livelihood, and are a credit and honor to any community wherein they dwell. As a rule they are moral, sober and industrious, and soon enter into the spirit of our free institutions.
>
> Next come the men who first saw the light of day in far off Finland, and too much cannot be said of the steady thrift and perseverance of these people. Idleness is to them unknown. They are wide awake, sober and intelligent. In the westernizing part of the city of Astoria a number of the natives of Finland reside, and have erected very substantial dwellings and buildings, and in other ways materially aid in the general advancement of the city.
>
> There are, next, about 300 men from Austria. They are as a rule a happy and generous race, and it can be said to their everlasting credit that it is very rarely that any of them are ever known to commit a criminal act. Coming, as many of them do, from the Dalmatian coast, where they early in life learned the

art and profession of the fisherman, they become first-class salmon fishermen.

The Latin race is also well represented, and, of course, the omnipresent natives of Germany, Great Britain, Canada and other countries, are to be found here.[66]

The pamphlet continued by extolling the salutary effect the Union had on life in Astoria, which at one time was called "the wickedest town for its size on earth" by the *Oregonian*. The pamphlet claimed that drunkenness among fishermen was a thing of the past, that transient fishermen were no longer in evidence, and that marriages and stable families were on the upswing. In brief, "a mighty moral uplifting has taken place . . . we have a higher and nobler type of manhood than ever before in the annals of this industry."[67] While the prose was purple and slanted to persuade members of the public and the government to a certain point of view on issues affecting gillnetters, the ethnic background of the fishermen was clear. Clearer yet was the forging of an identity as fishermen, a kind of supra ethnic identity.

It is significant to note what did not happen. As alluded to earlier, gillnetters did not organize on a coast-wide basis. Instead, the C.R.F.P.U. had a bi-state membership focussed on the Columbia River. Fishermen did not organize on an ethnic basis. There was no "Swedish Fishermen's Brotherhood," as it were, although there were numerous other organizations such as churches and fraternal societies which were organized around nationality. The *raison d'être* for the C.R.F.P.U. was the Columbia River gillnetter.

These ethnic beginnings are still in evidence today among Columbia River fishermen. References to "squareheads" (Norwegians) and the "Slav Navy" are common, as is the ability to swear in several languages. At the same time, being a Columbia River gillnetter, as opposed to being a gillnetter from any other location, or a fisherman of a different gear type, confers status, rather like being on a winning basketball team. "Columbia River gillnetters are the best in the world" is a quotation which occurs frequently and reinforces the identity developed over a hundred years ago.

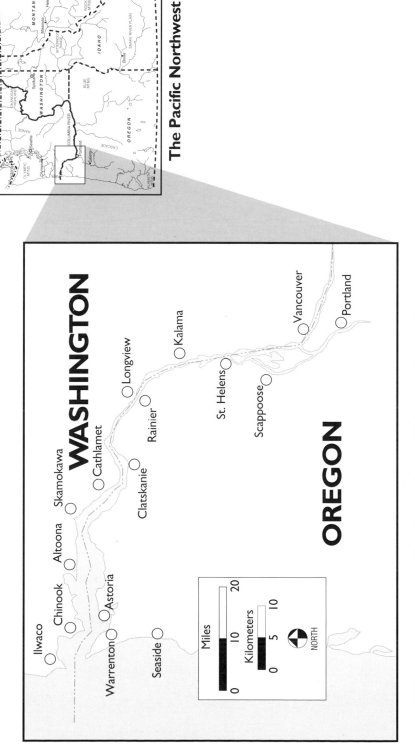

The Pacific Northwest

The Lower Columbia River Region

Courtesy Skamokawa Community Library.

Courtesy Skamokawa Community Library.

In the early years of gillnetting on the lower Columbia, fishermen worked primarily for canneries. Upper left: launch *Harrington* at the Pillar Rock Packing Company. Lower left: interior of the Pillar Rock Packing Company. Above: the Pillar Rock cannery at North Shore. Below: fisherman and cannery workers' housing at a cannery in Eureka, Washington.

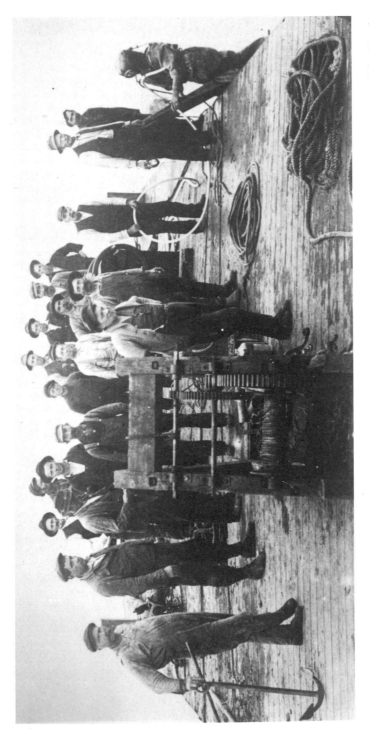

Sands Dritt Snagging Crew, Puget Island, Washington, c. 1915. *Courtesy David and Cheryl Nelson. Left-hand group, l to r:* John Breck, Conrad Steresen, Herman Hansen, Jacob Gjerp, Jorgen Gilbertsen, Ronvald Nelsen, Lars Pedersen. *Center group:* Torlaft Flato (standing by wench); *front row, l to r:* Gus Brubach, Gens Gjerp, William Dixon, John Vik; *back row, l to r:* John Berg, Albert Gjerp, Marcus Gilbertson, Bernhart Gjerp. *Right-hand group, l to r:* Juan Vidal, Joe Crandall (owner), Olaf Carlsen, Bert Cory (diver).

Colorful canning labels depicted the life of fishermen and pride in the lower Columbia region. *Author's collection.*

Courtesy Skamokawa Community Library.

Fishwheels, fish traps, and seines were highly effective ways of catching salmon, so effective they threatened to exterminate the runs and were outlawed in favor of more selective gillnetting. Above: fishwheel on the Columbia. Upper right: Andrew Peterson's seining outfit, with sailing gillnet boats, at Skamokawa. Lower right: after a successful day's seining on Sand Island, off of Ilwaco, 1903.

Courtesy Gene McClain.

Author's collection.

Because of its selective nature and efficiency, gillnetting came to dominate the lower Columbia commercial fishery. Above: towing boats to the drifting grounds. Below: boats in harbor at Svenson, Oregon.

Above: Eddie Rasmussen's boat and float house. Below: gillnetter Eddie Rasmussen pulling in his net, c. 1920. *Courtesy Washington State Archives.*

Motorized gillnet boats at Astoria. *Courtesy Columbia River Maritime Museum, neg. #79.27.*

Frank Nelson laying out his net in 1945. *Courtesy Columbia River Maritime Museum, #85.55.1394/1634.*

Until recent times, men have predominated in the lower Columbia gillnet fishery. But women have always played key roles in the success of the family operations, from providing bookkeeping services to assisting in maintaining equipment. Above: Edwin Carlson, Billy Peterson, Norman Olson, and Victor Peterson relax in a gillnet boat. Below: Agnes Hendrickson works on the engine of her brother Harry's boat.

Photo by Terry Norberg, author's collection.

Photo by Stan Chen, author's collection.

Author's husband and fishing partner Kent Martin removes fish from his gillnet at two different times in his career on the lower Columbia, in the top photo in 1964, and in the lower photo in the 1980s.

Net racks in Ilwaco. *Author's collection.*

Bluestone tanks in Ilwaco. Nets are soaked in a saturate of anhydrous copper sulphate and water in such tanks. *Author's collection.*

New England net rack and gillnet boats in Ilwaco, 1977. *Photo by David Myers, courtesy Washington State Archives.*

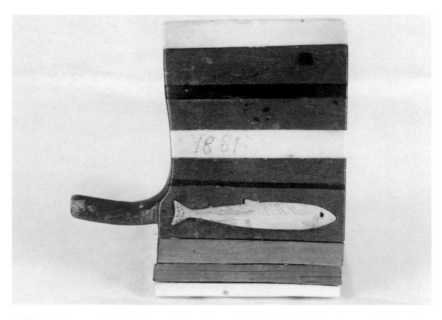

A highly decorative inlaid meshboard made by Erick Martin. A mesh is the diamond-shaped portion of the web of a gillnet, and meshboards are measuring devices used to ensure that meshes are of an even size when sewn into the net. *Photo by Mr. C's Photography, Longview, Washington, author's collection.*

Courtesy Thelma Whitten.

Courtesy Columbia River Fishermen's Protective Union.

"Underwater loggers"—divers—keep drifting grounds cleared of snags which can destroy gillnets. Above: diver Billy Whitten. Below: Columbia River Fishermen's Protective Union snag scow in 1968. Ross Lindstrom is the diver.

COLUMBIA RIVER STURGEON
AND ROYAL CHINOOK SALMON.

750 LBS

65 LBS

Salmon have always dominated the commercial fishing market on the lower Columbia and its tributaries, but secondary fish have been and continue to be caught for commercial markets. Above: Columbia River Smelt Company boats on the Cowlitz River, c. 1900. Below: two good-sized fish from the Columbia taken in 1909—a salmon and a sturgeon.

Chapter Three
"He May Have Been a Drunk But He Was a Damn Good Net Man"

The chapter title expresses the universal respect fishermen feel for a person who is "good at the twine." The story goes that a local fisherman had to serve some time in jail for an offense related to alcohol. Unable to leave fishing behind, to while away the hours he asked for and got permission to work on his net in his cell. In the intervening years, the story has been retold many times as a fishing fable, with the moral being "He may have been a drunk but he was a damn good net man." Different fishermen describe putting up a net as both art and science. It involves numerous separate tasks, decisions, tools, and skills, some dating back to the Stone Age. To understand the background behind the decisions involved in creating a gillnet, some basic knowledge of Columbia River fish runs is necessary.

Columbia River chinook enter the river from February through May. There is a great variation in the size of the fish, due to age (i. e., whether the salmon is a three, four, or five-year-old) and home watershed. Those destined for upriver areas are larger, as they need more stored fat to enable them to make the journey to their spawning grounds. The earliest fishing of the year now takes place in February and March. At one time, steelhead were an important component of this fishery, but today only the capture of chinook is permitted. These Columbia River spring chinook are of very high quality and command premium prices in the marketplace. After a closed period in April there was traditionally a fishery on the May component of the spring chinook run. Following another closure, fishing began on summer chinook. Neither the May nor the summer chinook fisheries have been opened for many years, as the populations of these two runs plunged after construction of mainstem and Snake River hydroelectric dams. Limited gillnet fisheries for shad and blueback—the well-known sockeye run of the Columbia—occur during the summer. In August runs of both chinook and coho enter the river, and fishable runs of both species continue to arrive in September, October, and November: the fall season. Incidental harvests of sturgeon also occur during fishing seasons. In addition, some fishermen fish for smelt, first using a gillnet in the mainstem Columbia and then shifting to a dipnet as the smelt migrate into the Cowlitz River, or occasionally into other tributaries. Smelt appear during the winter, from late December through March. Chum salmon, once in great abundance on the Columbia, are now caught incidentally during the fall fisheries. As the options for fishable runs of salmon have diminished, fishermen have had to make their gear more effective in order to maximize returns.

The art or science of putting up a Columbia River gillnet is both sophisticated and subtle. Factors such as the grounds to be fished, deep or shallow water, the type of fish being sought, the type of boat being used, and the individual's own preference as to the type of net to be used all influence the final outcome. Some prefer diver nets, others like to fish floaters:

> Floater fishing is much more a science of position. There are floaters and floaters. Some fish better than others. But really it's a science of position, of estimating where the tide will stop and where you want to be when it stops. It's like playing pool. You're fishing a much larger section of the water column. With diver fishing, the tide stopping is not so critical. You're only fishing the bottom twelve feet or so of the water column. There's certain stages of the tide where you want to have your net in the water. Just because your gear is in the water doesn't mean you'll catch 'em. You have to regulate your net, have it tailored to maximum efficiency so that net is fishing its best when fish are available. The crux–it can all be boiled down to one word, buoyancy–the degree of negative buoyancy that you have. That's why some of the real artists, like George Emery, John Passmore, and Anton D. Marincovich would add lead or take it off depending on the stage of the tide.[1]

Fishermen are aware of conditions such as a sandy, muddy, or rocky river bottom, and the existence of any deep holes. The slope of the river bottom is also important, with a climbing bottom being preferred for a diver net ebbing downstream. Knowing the grounds is critical. Water temperature, which affects the buoyancy of the floats, must be factored in when regulating diver nets by adding or removing lead as water temperature changes during a fishing season. Each drift area has its own formula for how many leads balance a certain number of floats.

The earliest nets were knitted by hand from linen[2] during the winter months. Knitting net could be a social affair. The Finns even had a word for a net-knitting or work party, calling it a "talkoot."[3] Frequently women knitted the nets, as they had a reputation for being more careful. Jack Marincovich recalled his younger days in Clifton:

> I remember watching my grandmother, she was a lot better knitting the net than my grandfather was. . . . And there'd be some other fishermen, you know, they were particular about the gear and they wanted certain people to knit their gear because they did such a good job . . . it's an art really.[4]

Knitting net was also an intensely personal activity, according to Georgia Maki:

> I had my net, I had it fastened to the wall in the living room and there was a window on each side of me and I wasn't aware of it but different ones said they knew I was knitting because the windows were singing. They'd go by and hear the windows vibrating and the windows were singing so they knew I was knitting net. . . . There's a rhythm. You work up a rhythm.[5]

Although women were frequently involved in working on nets, they seldom acted as crew on board the boats. An early reference to a female crew member appeared in 1895: "One of the Astoria fishermen has introduced his wife into the mysteries of boat pulling. She is a strong, young woman, and has adopted a bicycle bloomer costume and together they make a strong team."[6] The fact that this incident made the newspaper indicates that it was an uncommon occurrence in those days. There were probably several reasons for this situation. Gillnetting was a grueling occupation, particularly in the days before mechanization, and its sheer physical demands would have eliminated many women (and men) from trying it. Further, in communities of mixed occupations, women stayed home to operate the farms and raise families while the men fished.

By the late 1940s and early 1950s women began to appear as crew, especially those whose families were grown. The increasing mechanization of the fleet enabled them to assist in the fishing operation, in particular in running the boat. Once birth control became widespread, the fishery became more open to women, who could defer child bearing and spend their younger years learning the operation. The reel, which made its debut in the 1970s, made it possible for many women to take part in fishing. Once the physically taxing hand-hauling of the net was replaced by winding the net onto a reel, families began to reassess who should take part. Fathers began to teach daughters how to fish and act as crew, and wives were more likely to accompany their husbands in order to cut down on the need to hire extra help and retain more of the fishing profits in the family. It must be emphasized that gender roles in the fishery were not clear cut, but often blurred. Women stepped into whatever role was necessary for the support of the household, including bookkeeping, marketing, and political activism, as well as the more obvious roles of acting as crew and mending or knitting nets.

The materials from which nets are made have changed during a century-and-a-half of gillnetting on the Columbia, but the basic principle of how the net works has remained the same. Hank Ramvick described the early nets and the principle behind gillnetting:

> In the early days we used heavy linen nets up to twelve ply. That's almost like a wet gunny sack in comparison to the modern gear we use now. . . . It's a series of meshes. The depth is according to the fishermen's own preference. And it hangs in the water in a diamond shaped pattern. And the fish enter that naturally, with their head, and they get caught there. The reason it's called a gillnet is . . . they're supposed to stick their head all the way through it and get caught by the dorsal fin but if the fish is too big he just gets caught by the head, by the teeth or behind the gills. I'm talking now about a straight net with no strings or trammels on it. If you have strings on a net you can fish smaller mesh and you can catch large fish because it puts so much slack in there when the fish just hit the net they start spinning and get all wrapped up in there.[7]

In order to "put up" or put together a net, web must be ordered, usually months in advance. Corks are tested, a leadline purchased or molded, and corks strung on the corkline before a fisherman is finally ready to begin putting the net on the lines. The edge of the raw web may need to be selvaged before a line can be hung on it. Hanging a net, as the procedure is called, calls for precise measurement. Needles are filled with the appropriate size twine and the bale of web is opened and set up. Some fishermen will mark an entire corkline with the intervals between hangings before actually hanging it, or will use a "hanging stick," a stick cut to the desired length, to ensure that each hanging is accurate. Each hanging is comprised of a knot, with a cork placed every so many hangings, depending on the formula the fisherman is using. It generally takes about twenty hours to hang a 250-fathom corkline, and slightly less for a leadline, although individual speeds create some variation. After the backwall is hung with both corkline and leadline, the fisherman may then string it to create some slack. Slack web allows the fish to entangle itself in the gear. Most fishermen will also put in striplines or riplines, which are lengths of heavier twine that prevent a net from tearing completely off the lines if it is caught on a snag. The breaking strength of a leadline is important, as a leadline which breaks fairly easily will enable a fisherman to pull his net off a snag, while a leadline which does not break easily may cause a net to be stripped of its leadline, which remains caught on the snag. A fisherman who is hanging two or more layers of web will take considerably longer to hang a net than one who is putting up a simple floater net.

Other features of the net are the hoops known as the tail or "snorter" which are attached to each end of the leadline, and the buoys which are attached to each end of the corkline. The buoys serve to mark the ends of the net in the daytime and have lights for nighttime visibility. Early nighttime buoys were small floating wooden platforms, like little rafts, with kerosene lanterns fixed in place. These gave way to kegs when dry cell batteries were invented, as well as to specially carved wooden diver buoys.[8]

While it is theoretically possible to put up a variety of nets, each suitable for a particular purpose, the cost involved and the inconvenience of changing nets frequently kept the amount of gear pared back. In the days of linen, the eight-inch mesh trammel floater was the standard all-around salmon net fished in the spring and fall. Most fished straight gear near the mouth of the river, in order to avoid hake and jellyfish. Further upriver, fishermen used combination nets with a 6½ to 7¼ inch backwall, and a 7¼ to 8¼ inch apron. In the fall, many fishermen went to Willapa or Grays Harbor or to the Oregon coastal rivers to fish. Those who stayed on the Columbia used the same net they used in May. Those who fished dog salmon in November often used a salmon diver, as dog salmon are a good diver fish. Those who fished smelt might put up a "helldiver," a diver of one-inch mesh by 100 meshes deep fished on the hardest part of the ebb. Shad nets, single-walled floaters of 5³⁄₈ to 5½ inch mesh, or sturgeon divers of nine inch mesh or larger, might also comprise part of the fisherman's gear. Steelhead and blueback nets were also common.

Major changes in gear occurred in the 1950s when nylon began to replace linen webbing. Fishermen changing to nylon gear used mesh sizes one-half to three-quarters of an inch smaller than in a corresponding linen net. Wooden or aluminum floats were phased out, replaced by plastic and foam. Synthetic lines replaced cotton. The synthetic fibres permitted daylight fishing. Fishermen were suspicious at first, however, about the longevity of the new nylon web. As Elmer Hurula remembered:

> The [nylon company] representatives said that nylon doesn't rot. And the first thing that I done when I got a hold of nylon, I took a little piece of it and buried it in the mud where the sun would shine on it and the rain would rain on it and then about two months later I'd feel of it and it was just as solid as it was when I put it there. And the following year it was still there and it still hadn't rotted. So that proved it for me. And others done the same thing. . . . [Nylon] would last and you didn't have to bluestone it or rack it . . . it also fished better. . . . It was easier because nylon was strong and you could have a lighter ply in it. . . . So therefore it was better fishing in the daytime because it was not that heavy of a twine.[9]

Synthetic gear is now the norm for the Columbia, most of it imported from Japan or Taiwan.

Web is made from two or more strands of twine twisted together. The holding ability, color, stretchability, and quality of material used, plus the knitting process itself, all affect web quality. Although synthetics have replaced natural fibre corklines and leadlines in many cases, some fishermen still prefer the latter. Natural fibres require more care and must be soaked in a saturate solution of anhydrous copper sulfate and water at intervals in order to kill the bacteria that cause the materials to rot. This sterilization process is known as "bluestoning." Trap web was tarred. Former congresswoman Julia Butler Hansen was brought up in the fishing community of Cathlamet and remembered:

> To preserve the twine on the fishing nets they were dipped into a tremendous vat known as a bluestone barrel. One of the most fragrant recollections I have of spring along the Columbia is the fishtrap nets being tarred and the odor of tar hanging over the entire river area. The "environmentalists" would go crazy now, but it was the smell of spring returning, for the salmon season, in those years, began in May.[10]

In constructing or "putting up" a net, the primary emphasis is on regulation of the net in terms of the buoyancy of the corks or floats. Floater corks are larger than diver corks, as they must provide more buoyancy. Corks or floats (the terms are used interchangeably here) were originally made from cedar and were coated with paraffin, varnish, or paint in at attempt to make them impervious to water.[11] However, invariably some floats became waterlogged, so other materials eventually replaced wood. Aluminum, brass, steel, and copper floats all had their adherents. Metal floats did not soak up moisture, but they did cause wear on a corkline and corroded in bluestone. The clinking of the metal floats could be heard over the water as the nets were laid out, so that aluminum floats were nicknamed "cowbells." Some fishermen were purists, preferring a matched set of diver corks, while others did not feel it made a difference.

The configuration of the bottom of the river is very important in putting up a net. For example, as a net is drifting downstream on the ebb tide, the bottom may be sloped so that the bottom of the net is actually dragging along going uphill. This configuration is known as a "climbing bottom" and is the hardest to keep clear of snags. In such grounds, a lot of floats are needed to keep the net stiff, especially if there are mud humps. Fishermen prefer sandy bottoms, as the presence of rocks will wear out a leadline quickly. Pete Peterson gave a graphic description of how difficult it can be to fish a rocky bottom:

> We went to Celilo Falls. . . . We started fishing with that linen net and of course everybody had nylon gear and our net was all

> hung with nylon hanging line, it was only good for about three
> drifts down over the Oregon bank and you'd wear the hang-
> ings right off on them rocks. Every drift . . . we'd be hanging
> net right over the top of the old hangings to keep from falling
> out of the lines . . . on the weekend closure we bought another
> net, nylon net, and then we hung that with rawhide shoestrings.
> And they don't wear out. The rocks don't bother the rawhide
> when it's soft, it gets wet and it's real soft and it'll last. But when
> you're not fishing over a weekend . . . you rack it in a tub of
> water and you leave that leadline wet . . . so it don't get stiff.
> Otherwise it gets stiffer than a plank, you wouldn't be able to
> handle the stuff.[12]

Mud bottoms slow a net down or may even stop the net from moving, as the leadline tends to dig in.

A combination net is one which has more than one wall of netting, and may be either a floater or a diver. The main wall of web is
called a backwall. On either or both sides of it may be another wall
of web with larger mesh size, known as a trammel. A double trammel net has a layer of web on each side of the backwall, while a
single trammel net has the extra layer on only one side. As one
fisherman explained: "You have to figure out which combination is
the pot of gold and will outcompete the others."

An adaptation found only on diver nets is the apron, a wall of
web that hangs from the corkline at a forty-five degree angle from
the backwall. It first came into use around the time of the first World
War. It usually has a larger mesh size than the backwall. In this
way, the fisherman multiplies his options regarding the size of fish
he will catch. For example, a seven-inch backwall will catch a fourteen to fifteen pound fish, while an eight-inch mesh apron will catch
a twenty pound fish. Philosophies vary as to which mesh sizes to
use. Using trammels on the backwall and the apron also multiplies
the opportunities to capture a variety of sizes of salmon.

A good net man sees the advantages and limitations of his
grounds and tailors his gear to fit his unique individual circumstances. Competing fishermen will pick various niches, such as the
stage of the tide they favor fishing on or a particular spot where
they want their gear to stop at low water, and then work their gear
accordingly. Information from other fishermen on the drift is vital
to tell if the net is competing effectively with others, but at the same
time, competitors do not wish to give away too much information

about their catches. As one fisherman put it, "It's a series of damnable compromises, sort of like a marriage." Thus, observations about small details become important clues as to whether the net is fishing properly. Much of diver fishing is a matter of inference, of putting together a mental picture of how well the gear is fishing by observation of the minutiae of each drift. A fisherman will check to see how much the leads on his diver are shining, which will indicate how much they are rubbing on the sand as the net drags along the bottom. Observing how quickly the corks of a diver sink as the net is laid out will also tell an experienced fisherman whether his net is weighted just right or is too light or too heavy. The location in the web of the fish caught is also important. Are they caught in the leadline, the corkline, the back or front of the apron? Each of these positions indicates how the net is working; a third of the fish should be taken on the inside of the apron. The amount of debris is also significant, i. e., a heavy net will "load up" with debris while a light one will get virtually none.

Before a fisherman hangs a net he must make a great many decisions. The individual must know which size or sizes of fish he is after, when he wishes to fish them, whether he needs a diver or floater net, and which combination of layers of net is most likely to be effective on his fishing grounds. He must know the formulas for weighting a net which apply to his grounds, and must also be aware of what the other fishermen on his drift are fishing in order to maximize his own effectiveness and be competitive. He must also take into account his own strengths and weaknesses, what his vessel is capable of doing, and the cost effectiveness of his operation. He must know a number of technical terms. A fathom is a standard linear measure of six feet. What, though, is a stretch fathom? What is the difference between hard laid, medium laid, and soft laid? Nets are not standard equipment but are uniquely tailored to the fisherman's individual personality and fishing grounds.

The other major part of the gillnetter's time, when he is not fishing, working on the boat, or putting up gear, is spent mending gear. Holes occur when debris gets caught in the net and may have to be cut out. Fish also make holes in the net. The holes may vary in size from a couple of torn meshes to a large portion of the net. In order to mend small holes, new web is knit in by hand using a mending needle and a mesh board. Large holes are trimmed first to eliminate ragged edges, and generally a patch is sewn in. The basic knot goes by at least three names—double weaver's knot, double sheet bend, or double cat's paw—and has been used by fishermen world-wide for thousands of years. The single weaver's knot, cat's paw, or sheet bend is used to tie the two ends of the twine together at the initial step of mending. A mesh board which matches the size of the mesh of the net ensures that each new mesh is uniform in size. Heirloom needles and meshboards carved from wood are treasured possessions. Mending is considered to be an art among fishermen:

> . . . there are people—like in any craft—who took a great deal of pride and . . . what they did, they did as well as they could do and they wouldn't be satisfied with doing a poor job of it. And I know my uncle, for example, he was always near the top but he just loved the craft. When he mended his net he split the knots, he didn't patch the hole and [say] "this is good enough." . . . He carved his own needles and he took care of his own engine and he had a lot of pride in coming in with good deliveries. And there was a lot of pride in being a fisherman and being a good fisherman, especially in the community . . . there are some people who just fish and others who love to fish, who really love to fish, it's a labor of love. And my dad always just says, "It's all for love." And I know that's true.[13]

It is clear that the various cultures which migrated to the Columbia in the latter half of the nineteenth century were well versed in the techniques involved in creating a gillnet.[14] Perhaps not all the ethnic groups that migrated west utilized all the techniques, but certainly the major strategies of placing nets at different levels of the water column and creating slack in the web by means of strings and trammels had proven useful elsewhere. On the Columbia however, freshet conditions, the variation in depth of the river, the variation in the size of the fish, underwater debris, and geographic differences in the fishing grounds themselves from the mouth to Celilo Falls, forced an experimentation with the old ways that pushed the technology to its limits. Occasionally even today a fisherman will retrieve a wooden crosspiece in his net, the bottom of a home-made anchor made from tree branches lashed around a rock. Trap fishermen sometimes used rocks to hold down the bottom of the trap. These vestiges of Stone Age technology indicated a need for economy, especially during the Depression years. They also represented the layers of knowledge built up over the centuries, indeed millennia, by generations of fishermen who observed, experimented, innovated, and passed on their knowledge.

How did fishermen learn to work with nets and make innovations? Due to the need to have a large "data bank" of knowledge about grounds, tides, weather conditions, and fish migration patterns, fishermen frequently learned the fishery from a relative. Families passed on knowledge from one generation to the next, and fishermen as a group integrated potential fishermen into the group from childhood. Hank Ramvick's family started when children were very young:

> I was born into a fishing family and I started going with my dad out in gillnet boats and on the launch before I could walk. He used to pack me down there. He packed me back. So I started quite young. So naturally, I just evolved into a fisherman . . . and that's the way it was with most of the kids I grew up with . . . whose fathers were fishermen . . . we all started out real early. . . . [My] family's been involved in fishing . . . for I would guess 1000 years.[15]

Eldon Korpela recalled his family's fishing history:

> My father was Emil Korpela. And around the time I was in the second grade he took me out fishing. My first job was to steer the boat when he picked up the net. . . . My father . . . gillnetted for probably 35 years. . . . Same thing with my grandfather and my dad's brothers. They were full-time fishermen.[16]

Community focus oriented children towards the water and fishing. Cecil Moberg reminisced about his childhood in Astoria:

> Along the waterfront in Astoria, clear from Alderbrook all the way to Smith Point, we had net racks. Where the fishermen pulled their nets up . . . they had rails . . . they pulled the leadline over one rail and the corkline over the other and the web therefore was spread out in the sun. They dried their nets every week. And each fisherman had his own net rack . . . there were guys would fight if you got on their net rack . . . just like a cow going into its own stall.
>
> But you know the kids in those days always were down at the dock on Saturdays. You could always get a job helping a man to put his net on the rack and maybe clean up his boat . . . and gee, you could sometimes make as much as 50 cents, which

was a lot of money. You'd work all day for 50 cents. That was good pay for a boy around 12 years old.

They had these big lunch buckets, I can recall them, and was that a pleasure when the guys would come in on Saturday from fishing, they would let us kids go down and finish up their lunch buckets. And we'd go and get pie or cake, some of it was pretty stale, but it was fun just the same.[17]

An ancient technology, going back to the Bronze Age, reappeared whenever fishermen molded their leadlines. Leadline now comes ready made in the form of a core of flexible lead inside a woven line. At one time, however, fishermen had to mold lead weights onto a cotton line. In essence, a camp stove replicates a primitive smelter. Lead is melted in a cast-iron frying pan, and a ladle is used to pour lead into a brass mold which has been closed around a core of cotton line. The lead hardens in seconds, the mold is cut loose, and a new length of line is inserted. The drift's particular formula determines how far apart the leads are molded. Trim leads may be molded onto the line, or split leads may be molded separately and hammered onto the line when needed. Ross Lindstrom learned his technique from another fisherman:

> I had a guy walk by one day and he told me, "Pound some more lead on that net." And I looked at him and I thought, "Gee, that's a strange thing to say." I said, "How many?" He said, "Plenty." So that's all he said to me and he'd never said anything to me before in the way of helping me .... So I thought, "Well, I'll try it." So I put a lead on every tenth [lead] and the net worked quite a bit better and the next day I had it on the rack and I put one in between them. And he saw me putting the second batch on and he said "That's enough." That's all he said. Well, these guys, you learn from, you know.[18]

The hissing of the stove, the pale brass-colored sheen on the molten lead, the click of the lead mold cutting off the leads, and the thud as the weights hit the ground are all phenomena which used to be common on the Columbia River but are increasingly rare now. Burning old lead line in order to salvage and recycle the lead is an even less common activity. Few are left who have the knowledge and skill to perform this chore.

In sailboat times the boatpuller rowed and the skipper laid out the net over the gunwhale. The fish were picked up by underrunning and the net was pulled in over the side when the drift was over. The introduction of a roller helped immensely in this operation:

> In the early days we had what they called a skunk roller. It was made of brass. It had two upright rollers and a small roller and they were about 4 inches in diameter. . . . If the tide was crazy or it was blowing, the hard job was to pull that net together so that you could get hold of it. But when . . . somebody invented that skunk roller–it was a marvelous invention . . . it made the work so much easier.[19]

With the introduction of the gasoline engine a great many changes occurred in the boats, which in turn affected the nets:

> The boats were . . . about 26 foot with an eight foot beam and the engines were one cylinder mostly . . . some of the engines like the Union, the five horse Union, it didn't sound like it had any power at all. It just kinda went "wooo." It had . . . like a cough exhaust. But the old six (horsepower) Hicks, it was a boom, boom, boom. You could just hear the power in it. And the Regal–I could always tell my Dad's boat because the Regal had a sharp exhaust . . . and my dad's boat was a fast boat for only being a seven horse. But in about 1920 they . . . started converting these two man boats to one man boats. . . . The old two man boats were stern pickers. One man stood in the stern and pulled the net in. Course if it was blowing real hard then you both had to go in the stern. . . . Pulled the boat to the net, that's what you did. . . . And then when we went over to the one man boats, then you had the engine in the stern, the cabin on the stern, and the net in the bow. And you had controls in the bow so that you were able to bring the boat with power to the net.[20]

With the development of the bowpicker, the net was piled in the forward section or bow of the boat. As the boat ran forward, the net slid along a narrow deck along the side of the boat and out over the stern. Keeping the corkline on top of the leadline was critical in order to ensure that no turns occurred which might affect the net's fishing ability. When the drift was over, the fishermen pulled the net in over a roller in the bow of the boat, picked out the debris and fish as the net came in, and piled the net ready to be laid out again. A brief summary of this operation was given by a fisherman who began in the days of sailboats: "You just pick the net up, and if you got any fish in it, well you've got fish, and if you haven't, well then, you're skunked."[21]

In today's reel boats the net is laid out directly from the reel, situated in the bow or stern, and picked up from the same position. The change to the reels hastened the switch to synthetic twines, as the racking and bluestoning processes needed to keep natural fibers in good condition are harder to accomplish with a reel. Reels also created the necessity for grommeted floats which could withstand the higher pressure generated when pulling a net onto a reel. Fishermen have tended to move away from using trammels, which tend to backlash on the reel. (A backlash occurs when a portion of the web becomes entangled with a portion still on the reel while the net is being laid out.) The use of a levelwind, a development of the 1970s, can help minimize these to some degree. Despite mechanization, there are still fishermen who claim they could lay out a net faster by hand in the old bowpickers than they can with today's reels. Fishermen will generally concede that gear maintenance is higher with reels than on the old type of bowpicker, sometimes fondly referred to as a muzzle loader, due to the increased strain and pressure on the net.

Superstitions arose in the interplay of fish, nets, boats, and the fishing operation. The antiquity of many of the fishing superstitions on the Columbia can only be guessed at, but one curious story appeared in an interview with Don Riswick: "An old fisherman that I used to fish with . . . used to tell me some stories. One of them, was . . . in the moonlight, tides when there is a full moon, you can run along the sand and see the fish standing on their nose in the sand sleeping."[22] This same superstition was found in the 1870s among the cod fishermen of Norway.

Whistling in the boat was forbidden, a superstition shared with many ocean fishermen, as the underlying belief is that "You're whistling up a blow [storm]."[23] Some fishermen claimed that one had to urinate on a net to make it fish well, others claimed that a woman or young girl had to urinate on it, while others believed that having intercourse on a net made it fish better. It is doubtful that any of these fertility rites saw widespread practice, although the custom of breaking a bottle of wine across the bow of a new boat as it is launched for the first time is still a common practice. Some fishermen would not take a woman out fishing with them, although this superstition appears to have waned in the past twenty years, as many fishermen now take their wives to act as crew. Slav fishermen are reported as being unwilling to lend anything, claiming it brought bad luck. A belief common to the entire fleet, no matter what the individual ethnic origin, is that one does not remove the cover of the fish locker until the first fish is in the boat. Many fishermen retain the custom of taking the first salmon of the spring season home to eat, a kind of "first salmon ceremony" somewhat similar to that practiced by many of the region's Native American groups:

> I still keep the first one . . . there has to be a kind of spiritual relationship between the animal and yourself. Otherwise I think it'd drive you insane . . . because you really are killing and you have to have kind of—an importance to what you're doing and say, "Well, you're going to a good end. And nourishment and part of the cycle of continuing life."[24]

Much of the technical knowledge about fishing is retained only in the oral tradition. The how and the why of it are endlessly fascinating to fishermen. The feel of it and the sound of it and the smell of it all have their part to play in remembering a non-written technology. The constant repetition of stories and experiences is an additional mnemonic device to ensure that important details are retained, although one fisherman's wife grumbled, "If I discussed how I washed every dish, I sure wouldn't have many listeners." Nonetheless, it is an intensely oral tradition which survives and enables the fishery to be passed on.

Chapter Four
Underwater Logging

If the commercial fisherman could be likened to the cowboy of the Pacific Coast, the Columbia River snag diver held the maritime world's position equivalent to the old west's gunslinger. Wilmer Johnson commented, "Divers were real gutsy guys. . . . They just really knew what they were doing and they didn't worry about nothin'."[1] A rhymed advertisement in the *Columbia River Sun* of August 22, 1929, captured the essence of the diver's status:

> There is a town near the sea
> That always will be
> A city well worth your attention.
>
> You'll like the folks there,
> They're so jolly and square,
> There's fishermen, farmers and loggers.
> But there's one who lives there
> Whose work don't compare
> With the ones I have already mentioned.
>
> He goes down in the sea or the sound
> And brings up lost treasures
> That without divers
> Would never be found.
>
> Now the loggers and dairymen
> Are sturdy and true
> And the fisherman weathers storms while fish catching.
> But if your net should sag
> And tangle up on a snag
> Just phone the diver, John Patching.
>   Phone Clatskanie 13F4[2]

Children in fishing communities along the Columbia played at
being snag divers and fishermen, the marine equivalent of cow-
boys and Indians. Some went to the trouble of making mock diving
helmets, using them in the local creeks and sloughs. Although now
the stuff of legend, it is no exaggeration to say that early snag diving on the Columbia River was extremely difficult and dangerous,
requiring qualities of tenacity and sheer physical courage.

Snags were present from the earliest times on the Columbia.
Trees, root wads, shipwrecks, rock piles, and other debris cluttered
the river bottom:

> We've pulled old seining barges . . . seining houses, scows and
> one drift in Vancouver got a steam engine, 16 ton steam engine
> off their drift. You know, the river's a good place to hide any-
> thing. We've got ship's anchors, TV antennas, refrigerators,
> freezers, stoves, but mostly logs. It's mostly sinkers that have
> escaped from the log rafts and a lot of stumps and tree limbs.
> In some areas like the mouth of the Lewis River, the mouth of
> the Cowlitz, you get a lot of this stumpage type of snags.[3]

If the snag-littered locations happened to be good fishing grounds,
the snags either had to be removed or avoided.

Snags were not confined to the Columbia River. The same decision, whether to remove or avoid them, must have faced fishermen up and down the west coast during the nineteenth century.
With the exception of the Columbia, all other gillnet fisheries seem
to have preferred to try to avoid snags by fishing around them.

An examination of British Columbia gillnetting history indicates the presence of snags. Skeena River fisherman Walter Wicks
wrote about his early days:

> After three weeks "outside fishing" [in the deep water outside
> the river's mouth] . . . we would follow the salmon into the mouth
> of the river where fishing became even more back-breaking as
> we would then be operating in strong tidal waters. Sand bars,
> reefs and sunken logs in the river bottom were obstacles which
> often tore our nets to shreds. Then we were forced to return to
> our home cannery, sometimes a distance of twenty miles. Here
> we had to haul the net on the rack for repairs, sometimes los-
> ing two days fishing.[4]

Another Skeena River fisherman, Herbert Ridley, agreed: "Lots of
snags in Skeena in spring. They use a big snag scow to pull them
before fishing starts."[5]

However, fishermen did not remove snags in British Columbia. The government did. In 1881 the dominion government appropriated a thousand dollars for snag removal and the marking of the main channel on the Nass River. A cannery owner, Mr. Croasdaile, received the contract, hoping to bring steamers of less than ten-foot draft to his cannery on the Nass.[6] Beginning in 1884 and continuing until recent times, a series of snag vessels, the *Samson* I through V, removed snags from British Columbia rivers, primarily as an aid to navigation.[7] However, the benefit to fishermen was also well appreciated:

> For years there has been an informal partnership between fishermen and the Samson. Fishermen tell the Samson's captain about obstructions, then two fishing vessels take a length of cable apiece, drag until they encircle the sunken object, then pass the cable to the Samson, which hauls it in and on to the deck. No money changes hands.[8]

In the California gillnet fisheries knowledgeable fishermen used snags as a means of eliminating inexperienced competitors who were not aware of their locations or did not have the skill to avoid them: the novices lost gear and fishing time when they got caught.[9] This tactic succeeded also on Willapa Bay and Grays Harbor in Washington, although attempts to organize snagging occurred from time to time there. A snag fund existed on Willapa in the latter part of the 1930s and early 1940s, organized by the bulk of the fishermen in the area. But due to low prices for fish, the attempt to organize failed.[10] Similarly, fishermen occasionally cleared one or another of the tributaries of the Columbia, when a fishery existed in a particular stream, such as the Grays River,[11] but such efforts were sporadic. On Puget Sound snags were less of a problem due to the depth of the water and to the large open areas available to fish.

The alternatives in a gillnet fishery are to either pull snags or leave them in. Pulling them out clears the ground for fishing without damaging one's net. It entails expense and labor, however, and there is always the danger that someone who has not assisted in the snag-pulling process will try to encroach on the grounds. Leaving snags behind may discourage the competition, but it can entail considerable loss of gear and fishing time. The evidence indicates that there were a number of variables implicit in the decision to leave snags or pull them. If there was a lot of open water for fishing, so crowding was not a problem, there was no need to remove snags to make room for extra boats. This is the case on Puget Sound, and was the case on the Columbia in its earliest years. If a fishery were mobile, so that the fishermen migrated with the fish, following them along a particular route, snags appear to have been left behind. The Sacramento and British Columbia fisheries appear to be cases of such an adaptation, although some snags, especially those hazardous to navigation, were removed in British Columbia. If the fishery were a "pulse" fishery, of limited duration in time, such as existed on Willapa or Grays bays, snags were generally left. Only on the Columbia did the combination of long seasons, crowding, the need for extensive grounds, and high productivity combine to provide the impetus to make snag pulling a cost-effective means of improving access to salmon. The Columbia was so large and its salmon runs so immense and varied, that the fishery could be called a "gauntlet" fishery, with different communities along the river each taking a portion. In effect, it was possible for a fisherman to stay in one community for the various seasons and make a living, so "homesteading" a fishing area by clearing snags became a reasonable option.

The earliest accounts indicate that fishermen first attempted snag-diving on seining grounds in order to remove obstructions that hindered the smooth passage of expensive seine nets.[12] Gillnet fishermen organized in 1876 as the Columbia River Fishermen's Beneficial Aid Society specifically to pull snags in the lower river near Astoria. The rapid development of the fishery in the 1870s caused crowding on the grounds. In addition, the danger of getting several snags in a net which might then cause a fisherman to be swept over the Columbia River bar during his exertions to free himself remained an intimidating possibility. In 1899 Matt Korpela wrote to relatives in Finland that the "main reason for this dangerous fishing was money. Among the fishermen a saying originated: Salmon head is worth a dollar, but a man's head is worth nothing." Pulling snags reduced these problems and enhanced the fishery. When the Beneficial Aid Society lapsed, the Columbia River Fishermen's Protective Union (C.R.F.P.U.) took over the snagging duties. Newspaper accounts of the late nineteenth and early twentieth centuries indicate that snagging was a major function of the Union in the lower river:

> The Union last evening decided to take steps to see that the gillnet drifting grounds are kept clear of fishtraps and other obstructions. The secretary was instructed to ask permission from the U. S. engineers to pull the old trap piles, especially in the vicinity of Sand Island and to also request the Department to remove an old beacon from the Prairie Channel as it is a menace to gillnet operations.[13]

Minutes of the C.R.F.P.U.[14] during the 1880s and 1890s indicate that snags were pulled both in the lower river below Tongue Point and also further upriver on known drifting grounds. One of the main snag-removal chores consisted of removing trap piling left after trap fishermen had finished with their gear for the season. The stationary pilings proved an impediment to the more mobile gillnet fisheries, particularly if they had been broken off underwater due to some mishap. Considerable animosity grew between the two groups as increasing numbers of traps and gillnets competed in close proximity, especially near the mouth of the river. An unidentified clipping from April 24, 1891 reported the friction: "A number of fishermen are complaining about some unused trap poles which obstruct and make navigation dangerous near Desdemona Sands. As these traps are no longer in use no lights are kept on them and it is impossible for fishermen to see them until they are right on top of them."[15]

By 1884 the Columbia River Fishermen's Protective Union was lobbying the U. S. Army Corps of Engineers to remove traps in the lower Columbia, citing them as a hazard to navigation. The 1890 Rivers and Harbors Act did permit occasional removal of traps blocking navigation. This law was strengthened in 1899 when the Refuse Act required trap fishermen to obtain permits to drive piling in the Columbia.[16] At the same time, the War Department required gillnetters to obtain permits to pull snags on the drifting grounds. Although trap fishermen were supposed to pull their pilings after each season, in practice many did not. The increasing ill feeling between the two groups culminated in what became known as the "trap wars." One of the more original and certainly the most

dramatic account of the trap wars appeared in a serialized novel by
Paul Delaney, *Toilers of the Columbia*:

> The trouble had been under discussion for years. It had en-
> tered politics and was the means of arousing the animosity of
> the two states [Oregon and Washington]. The officers on the
> south side of the river stood by their fishermen and those on
> the north side were equally as loyal. It was an inter-state affair
> and needed but the firing of a gun to awaken a large citizenship
> and plunge the two states into most serious complications.
>
> Many of the fishermen on both sides are ignorant foreign-
> ers, desperate characters by reason of their calling and the
> hardships of a fisherman's life, and when once aroused to arms
> would lose their reason. Bloodshed and riot were now expected
> in their reddest form. . . .
>
> The trouble had been too long brewing to give up after one
> slight engagement. The fishermen on both sides felt that a prin-
> ciple was involved and they were there to settle it by might.
> The gillnetters declared that the traps were gradually destroy-
> ing the run of fish while the trappers claimed that the gillnets
> were doing greater harm to the industry than the traps. The
> men had spent their lives fishing, the support of their families
> depended upon it, and it was truly a vital issue with them.[17]

Although trap fishing ended by law in 1934 in Washington and 1948
in Oregon, trap pilings are still found in the river and must be pulled
in order to fish an area.

In addition to the difficulties between trappers and gillnetters,
controversies arose between seiners and gillnetters, although these
were more muted. An early account talks of sabotage of a seine,
and while gillnetters were not mentioned as being responsible, the
competing interests of the two fisheries invite speculation that they
were involved:

> Fitzpatrick is having trouble with his seines up above
> Skamokawa and a few days ago sent a diver down to investi-
> gate. The diver found a couple of boxes in 30 feet of water fitted
> with knives which had been ruining the seines whenever they
> passed over them. The knives were three inches wide and about
> seventeen inches long.[18]

Seining grounds were for the most part controlled by the packers and could produce large volumes of fish. The packers had them
cleared of debris in order to be fishable, and naturally it was a temp-
tation to use the cleared grounds to fish a gillnet:

The seine, you see, had the deeper water all cleared. All we cleared was all the stumps that come down from the high water of the year before. With team and wagon, take them off from there and when the water got high in the spring you had the best drift in the world. All flat for 3/4 of a mile, flat across there. . . . But we couldn't even sell our fish unless you owed McGowan's money because they was getting five ton a haul in the fall there with that seine.[19]

While the packer fished the area in the fall with the seine, and the gillnetters fished in the spring, this ground was considered so valuable that the packer tried to discourage any attempt to make it into a drift. A similar story, this time from the packer's point of view, occurred in 1926. The Columbia River Packers Association owned a seining ground near Eagle Cliff. The foreman of the Eagle Cliff Cannery, H. J. McGraw, contacted the head office in Astoria in January. Gillnetters who were fishing on the seining ground had caught a snag that had troubled the seining operations in the previous year. The foreman wrote:

It being low River I got the Diver and [had] it [the snag] taken out. I picked up a crew of fishermen that volunteered their services as it would also benefit them. Some of them wanted to help pay for the Diving but I would not let them pay anything so they could have any claim on the drift during the Seining season.[20]

An encouraging response came in the mail from headquarters: "You did perfectly right in not collecting anything from the men for the diving, as we want to keep the ground so they do not have any claim on this for a gillnet drift."[21]

By the 1890s diving techniques had improved to such an extent that divers could descend to deep levels and clear grounds previously unavailable. A record-setting dive by Fritz DeRock received notice in the *Cathlamet Gazette* in 1895:

Fritz DeRock, diver for Quinn and Hanthorn [seining ground] last week went down in 90 feet of water and cleared all the snags that were located. When DeRock was at a depth of 90 feet it required three men pumping air. This is the greatest depth any diver has gone down in this locality.[22]

Snagging operations conducted in the estuary area below Tongue Point benefitted not only the fishermen who fished

permanently in the area, but also those who came during certain
seasons, such as August. By the later 1890s snag associations or
snag unions had formed further upriver to clear specific areas of
river bottom. According to oral tradition, the earliest of these was
the Warrior Rock Snag Association, begun in 1899, coincidental
with the new requirement by the War Department that a permit be
obtained before snagging. Organization by the fishermen might
have been a formal response to this new requirement. It may also
have indicated a shift from the floater to the diver net.

Other snag unions formed which cleared specific areas of river
bottom. The fishermen who expended time, money, and labor in
the endeavor gradually asserted a right to fish the area. This right
became known as the "drift right." The term "drift" took on several
meanings. It might mean the physical stretch of water/river bottom where a particular group fished, such as the Gold Mine, or the
Channel. It meant the act of drifting with the tide, so that a fisherman might say, "I made two drifts last night." It also meant the
group of fishermen themselves, so that a person might say, "I need
to talk that issue over with the drift."

Fishermen saw the need to organize formally, so they developed bylaws and kept minutes of their meetings. At times a snag
union would form, clear a drift, and then incorporate formally under state laws at some later date. An example was the Three Tree
Point Drift, which fishermen cleared in the early years of the century, according to oral tradition. The Woody Island Fishermen's
Co-operative Association incorporated in 1928,[23] asserting that:

> Whereas, the above named parties, together with their associ-
> ates, have, since the year 1916, expended large sums of money
> and labor clearing and preparing said drifts [including Three
> Tree Point] for the use of gillnets; and Whereas, it is to the
> mutual benefit and advantage of the members of this associa-
> tion that said gillnet fishing drifts be cleared of all obstructions
> such as snags and other foreign matter which interferes with
> the operation of a drift net; and, Whereas, a considerable ex-
> pense is necessary in preparing, clearing and caring for said
> drifts from time to time for the mutual benefit and protection of
> the fishermen who occupy and use the above named and de-
> scribed drifts, NOW, THEREFORE, the objects of this associa-
> tion are (1) to promote, care for, improve, and protect said drifts
> herein before described; (2) to acquire, purchase, sell and deal

in personal property as may be necessary for the proper care and maintenance of said drifts.

The Altoona Snag Union had incorporated in 1922. It is clear from a reading of the various records owned by different drift associations on the river that by the 1920s more formal organization occurred in order to maximize the benefits of clearing the fishing grounds. The Oak Point Drift Company bylaws, created at the first meeting of the association in 1924 with twenty-one members, asserted that "Those working on snagging during the season have right to lay out net first, others must wait." By 1931 the rule had changed: "Every shareholder must get a man to work if he doesn't come when it is his turn for snagging."[24]

In sailboat days, snagging generally followed a pattern. A boat drifted a heavily leaded net called a snag net over the fishing grounds. When the net caught on a snag it stopped moving, and a "hard-hat" diver went down with a cable, which he fastened to the snag. At the surface, a snag scow with a winch held the other end of the cable. At a pre-arranged signal, the winch began to turn, pulling the snag up. Alternatively, if no snag scow were available, the fishermen fastened a mast between two boats, attaching the cable to it. As the tide rose the steady pull of the boats gradually sucked the snag out of the river bottom. Eddie Rasmussen described the process:

> You get 'em up and down as tight as you can, get her and then get the two boats on her working, going ahead and around sideways and all ways, you can work quite a snag out of the ground. Because those boats can lift quite a bit, I don't know how many ton you can lift, having this cross in the middle.[25]

He also commented on the amount of sheer effort it took to keep a drift clear:

> Your road's never clear . . . for a hundred years it wouldn't be clear. Because there is new stuff coming in and the grounds are changing, buried stuff would be coming up. One that we had an awful lot of trouble with here, it was a big hemlock and you put the scow on it and I don't know just how much we could pull with that scow but we pulled her clear down, water on the deck and let her lay there. Didn't have any luck pulling it out. And we hooked some boats on it and started working it. When

it broke loose that darn thing was floating that high out of water, she just popped up there, heck if she'd come up under a boat she would have busted the bottom out of her. And [hemlock and spruce] fill up so much gas in 'em and they get a buoyancy, up they come . . . a hemlock . . . will come to the top and float in the water and sink again. So you don't know where the heck it's at. There were twenty-three of us when we started [to clear our drift] but a lot of 'em got disgusted and quit and it wound up there was 13, 14 that stayed with it.[26]

The pre-power days of snagging involved tremendous amounts of physical labor. Ben Jolma recalled that "Before we got air compressors a man had to hand-pump air hour after hour to keep the diver breathing. We had to use Norwegian power [colloquialism for manual labor] to haul up the snags by turning a capstan manually."[27] They used olive oil to lubricate the air pumps, as it had no odor to cause nausea. Divers provided their own boats and air pumps. Eventually gasoline-powered pumps replaced hand-cranked ones.

Snaggers occasionally used dynamite to dislodge stubborn snags, particularly old trap pilings. Tall tales about its use (or misuse) are part of the oral history of the Columbia. A fisherman named Jack Zumwalt fancied himself a powder monkey, but set off a charge of dynamite too close to his boat. "You could see the sunset at Three Tree Point under his boat, she came so far out of the water," claimed one of his drift-mates later. "The blast blew all the caulking out of the seams, and we had to lash two boats, one on each side of his boat, to get it home," said another. The more usual method was for the hard-hat diver to take a line down to a snag, such as a trap-piling. Then his co-workers attached a charge of dynamite to a boomstick ring. When the diver had fastened the line to the snag and was safely back in the boat, the ring slid down the corkline to the bottom. A long fuse ensured that the charge did not go off until it had reached the bottom.

Paying the diver and purchasing cables and snag net materials were responsibilities of the drift, which kept ledgers to record cash and labor outlays by individual fishermen. Individuals were responsible for boat expenses, such as fuel. Each drifting ground was different, some taking immense labor to clear while others were comparatively easy. Wallace Island Drift fell in the latter category. A fishermen who helped clear it in the early years claimed "It was the best five dollars I ever spent." Three Tree Point Drift, on the other hand, was one of the most difficult. The water was 108 feet deep. A diver could go down only at slack water, or on a very slow tide, when an anchor and cable was put down for him. Only one or two snags could be pulled per tide. The drift could only be kept clear in the days when fishing went on year round, as removal of snags was a constant task.[28] Three Tree Point Drift is an example of a fishing area at the outer limit of what was technologically feasible in the 1930s.

The transition to scuba diving gear in the late 1950s made the diver more mobile. Ross Lindstrom combined the skills of both gillnetter and diver, and described the snagging operation from the diver's point of view:

> Well, if you like to swim, it's really no different than swimming except you're just pulling yourself down a net. And if you understand and know what a net can do you're not afraid of the net because it's harmless unless you wiggle and get into it. And in all the years I dove I only got stuck once and I got a little bit careless and I got a mesh around the regulator on the back of the tank and I backed up and when I felt it come tight I just reached up and turned it loose, and I said to myself, "That will never happen again," and it didn't . . . when you take diving instructions now you're taught about all the bad things that can happen. And we never were. All we were taught was "You're in charge and it's up to you to make sure that you get out of the mess you get in if you get in one, don't get in one and if you do don't lose your head." And it didn't seem to matter what kind of a pickle we came up against [snagging] . . . we would always go to [Billy Whitten's] dad and say, "Hey, we're in a bind." And we'd tell the guys on the drift, "Well, we're gonna quit for the day, we're going home and talk to the college professor. We'll be back. We'll pull it tomorrow." And they'd always think, "Well, you know, this is just a dodge. They're not going to be able to do nothing." Next day we'd come back, phutt, out it went. So I learned from a guy who didn't teach me to be afraid.[29]

A comparison of snagging expenses compiled by the Columbia River Packers Association indicated that cost was a big factor in the transition from the old style "hard-hat" diver to scuba gear. Ross Lindstrom expressed the same viewpoint:

> I went to Portland to buy my diving equipment and the guy said to me, "Can you clear your ears?" And I said, "What do you mean?" "Well," he said, "What do you know about diving?" I

said, "Not a thing." He said, "How are you gonna learn?" I said, "On the job. It's on the job training, give us the equipment we need." And in those days I bought all the diving equipment I needed for, I think, $150 or $180 . . . it's pretty darn cheap."[30]

Today's snagging operation begins sometime before the fishermen actually get on the river. Snag permits must be obtained from either the Washington Department of Fisheries or the Oregon Department of Fish and Wildlife. The diver is generally booked months in advance, to ensure that he will be available on the best tides. The best tides are in the morning, when there is the least likelihood of wind. The tide must be big enough to move the heavy snag net, but not too wild, making it difficult for the diver to work. A run-out tide is preferred. The snag net must also be prepared. It is a variant of the diver net, but is normally not as long, being about 125-150 fathoms in length. The shorter net is easier to handle and faster to pick up. It is designed to deliberately catch on a stationary snag, or pick up a loose one such as a hemlock sinker. The mesh size is generally fourteen inches or larger to avoid catching fish. The net is leaded and corked like a diver net would be for the particular grounds being worked, or it may be heavier. Wooden or aluminum corks stand up best to the hard usage.

On the morning tide, the boat with the snag net aboard lays out the net. A bow-reeler is best for handling a snag net, as there is not so much strain on the gear as there is in a stern-picker, especially on the hard tide. The bow-picker is best for tending the diver, as it is low and easy for the diver to climb in and out of. There is also plenty of room for cable and equipment. Once the snag net has caught on a snag, the boat with the diver goes to that location. A boat picks up each end of the snag net as close to the snag as possible, as all slack web must be tight before the diver goes down, to avoid tangling. The diver then goes overboard and follows the net down to the snag.

The Columbia is not an easy environment for divers, as there is no visibility and all work is done by feel. The diver takes a cable down with him. When he reaches the snag he tugs on the cable a certain number of times in a prearranged signal, to indicate that the boats with the net can slack the net so that he can disentangle it from the snag. The net drifts clear and is picked up. The diver fastens the cable to the snag and signals the boat that the snag now has a line on it. The fishermen in the tender boat pull up the slack in the cable and tie it to a cleat in the bow. Then they turn off the engine. The diver comes up the cable and hands his weight belt and other gear to the tender and then comes aboard. The fishermen start the engine and run the boat ahead into the current. The tender takes the cable from the bow and walks it back to the stern, where he waits until the boat is right over the snag before he fastens it to the stern cleat. The shorter the pull the better. The boat is then allowed to swing around so it faces stern-first to the current. The current can then do part of the job of pulling out the snag.

A steady pull on the snag will most frequently bring it out. The diver and tender stand in the bow to act as a counterbalance. Pulling and towing a snag are done as smoothly as possible to avoid breaking the cable and to ensure that the snag does not break loose, as well as to avoid damage to the boat. Once the snag is out the boat tows it to a dumping spot where it will not be a further hazard to fishing or navigation.

If the snag union owns a snag scow, it is maneuvered around the drift by means of two fish boats, one on each side of it. When a snag is located, the scow is taken over to it. The diver passes the cable to the snag scow, which has a winch on it. Don Riswick described the operation:

> We had a snag scow that they had built. It was just like a logging operation and we would use our net to catch the snag and then the diver would go down and choke the log or whatever it was [i.e. put a choker or cable on the log] and then you'd put the winch on it . . . several times we hauled in ship's anchors that were up to 5 or 6 ton. Just about pull the old snag scow under.[31]

Fishermen snag their drifts several times a year, generally before fishing seasons. They may also pull a snag during fishing season if it suddenly shows up on a drift. Or they may elect to try to "jump" a snag if it is inconvenient to pull it during a portion of the fishing season. "Jumping" a snag is done by tying a rag to mark the corkline of the net at the approximate place where the snag keeps appearing when the net is drifting. A buoy is fastened to the corkline by means of a long rope so that the buoy floats when the net sinks to the bottom. When the net is almost on the snag, which the fisherman has marked so he knows its location, the buoy is pulled up so the net is lifted up and over the snag harmlessly as the net continues to drift. The line is then released and the net sinks back to the bottom.

Not all snagging operations follow the same procedure each time. The diver may place tongs on a snag partially buried in sand where it is not possible to fasten a cable. He may also put on a "safety," a marker made up of corkline and buoys, so that fishermen can locate the snag again if they happen to break it off, without having to lay out the snag net again. Occasionally a drift will decide to pull a snag such as a whole tree with the snag net still on it. This procedure can put the diver at considerable risk, as the tree can roll over and trap him. The net may also catch on the boat propeller. A snag union may occasionally hire a tug to pull a particularly heavy or difficult snag.

Fishermen sometimes remove a snag without a diver present, by "towing a cable." They attach a cable to two boats, 100-150 feet apart, towing the bight of the cable slowly through the water so it drags along the bottom. They lengthen the cable by tying anchor line to each end, so that as much of the cable remains on the bottom as possible. The bight of the cable will catch on a snag, which will break loose due to the weight of the boats dragging on it. Alternatively, if the weight of the boats does not loosen the snag, they can in effect lasso it by crossing below it and putting one end of the cable through a shackle attached to an "eye" spliced in the other end, forming a slip knot. This technique is known as "reeving" a snag. After towing the snag away, the fishermen pull the pin out of the shackle to release it.

Transforming the river bottom to more closely approximate ideal fishing terrain also occasionally occurred. In some places, fishermen towed a cable between two boats to try to smooth out the bottom, particularly in an area with a lot of mud humps. Humps or banks of clay were a persistent problem on some drifts, as they caused the leadline to dig in and inhibited the net from drifting. Towing a cable evened out the bottom, somewhat like grading a road. The Cathlamet Channel Drift at one time went so far as to use water pipe held down with sandbags, which formed a kind of grate to allow the nets to jump mudbanks.

The snag unions that formed upriver cleared specific areas of river bottom, areas known to be productive fishing grounds that might support several boats. Sometimes a snag union cleared several drifting grounds to accommodate a substantial number of boats. The fishermen who expended time, money, and labor in the endeavor gradually came to be considered to have an exclusive right to fish the area, particularly on the ebb tide. This right became known as the "drift right." Snagging operations conducted in the estuary area below Tongue Point benefitted not only the fishermen who fished there, but also those who came from upriver during certain seasons. The area, was, for the most part, considered to be open water. The Columbia River Fishermen's Protective Union still coordinates the snag pulling in this area, using the Lower River Snag Fund to pay expenses:

> Sometimes we'll put a notice in the paper that we're gonna have a snagging such and such a day and where it is. And like somebody that fishes on the other side of the river, why it's up to him to get a bunch of guys together and clear that area . . . we have a snag fund set up. . . . It's $50 a year. . . . and out of that fund we pay for the diver. . . . And we have two snag nets which are 38 feet deep.[32]

At one time packers also contributed to snagging operations, matching contributions made by their fishermen.[33] A side benefit of snagging is the public service provided by removing hazards from navigational channels. The U. S. Army Corps of Engineers has commented publicly on this aspect of snagging, as the debris removed might damage the intake of dredges.[34]

Faced with recurrent snag expenses, fishermen developed the strategy of attacking the source of the problem. When logs dropped out of log rafts as they were being towed to markets and came to rest in the drifting grounds, fishermen attempted legal action[35] against offending companies, asking for individual damages due to lost fishing time spent clearing their drifts and also for costs incurred in removing the logs. Fishermen also sought help from public officials in trying to remedy the problem of recurring debris. Particularly in the decades since 1970, gillnetters have voiced their concerns at public hearings in a variety of forums.[36] The Columbia River Estuary Study Taskforce held a hearing in 1987 in order to update its 1979 studies of the Columbia.[37] Gillnetters attended to voice their concerns regarding logs from log rafts, among other things. Litigation and public input in planning and regulation are relatively recent techniques as fishermen attempt to keep drift areas fishable.

It would be a mistake to think that gillnetters developed the technology of pulling snags in isolation from other factors. Snag pulling evolved side-by-side with early logging practices. The expansion of the fishery reflected happenings in the woods in the pluralist communities along the river. Residents moved into and out of fishing, farming, and logging, depending upon the seasons and economic trends. Logging techniques became part of the common vocabulary. Farmers cleared their land using logging methods. Settlers built their homes and businesses with lumber logged and sawed locally, often from their own land. They surfaced early roads with cedar "puncheon." Snagging developed by means of a transfer of technology in mixed communities. Don Riswick described a snagging scow as one "which had all the logging equipment aboard it."[38] Eddie Rasmussen stated that his father worked in logging camps and gillnetted,[39] typical of many others in this region.

Snagging, logging, land-clearing, and road-building all entailed applied physics–how to move something from point A to point B. The techniques were entirely pragmatic. Terminology such as "block purchase" and "rigging chain" were used interchangeably in the woods, on the farm, and on the water. Reciprocal arrangements, whereby logging companies provided cable and other supplies for snagging in return for fish for the cookhouse, were common.[40] Fishermen recognized that "many of the best snag men were guys who worked in the woods in the off seasons."[41]

Snagging, organizing and clearing a drift, banding together to take action regarding dangers to the drift, all presuppose a certain amount of social organization. Cooperation, pooled financial resources, and common assumptions regarding goals and objectives are all explicit or implicit in snagging, and in the development of the drift right. To understand the function of the drift right in the Columbia River fishery, it is necessary to examine the social organization of the gillnetters.

Chapter Five
Our Drift Was First

Fish behavior dictates where a person fishes. On the Columbia, the various species of salmon, shad, sturgeon, and smelt all exhibit their own characteristic behavior patterns. Cecil Moberg discussed his observations from many years of fishing for salmon:

> Fish run in cycles and they're gonna come back to the same place. Fish are just like a cow. They go right back. A cow won't go in anybody else's stall and a fish, if he's turned loose in a certain creek, he's going back there. And he's gonna come the same way back. He has that instinct and he comes back. . . . And certain tides . . . the same time of year . . . you go back to those times.[1]

Because fishermen learned which places were best to fish, they tended to congregate there and return every season:

> My grandfather says to my father and my father passes on to me. . . . It's all timing, it was all timing within five minutes. You don't lay out before four hours and five minutes and you don't lay out after three hours and fifty minutes, because at precisely four hours and five minutes the fish will drop off of the sands and into the deep hole where your net is. . . . And the fish haven't changed their pattern just because we have different boats and different gear. . . . The fish still follow the same prehistoric or earlier habits of when they move off the sands into the channel and down.[2]

Selection of fishing grounds depended upon the presence of fish and absence of snags. Knowledge of the grounds and of fish behavior were key factors in a fisherman's success. However, pressure from too many other fishermen competing for the same space, especially below Tongue Point, created such crowding stress that fishermen were hampered in laying out their nets: "If you don't know the ground well, then of course you're just making a guess at it. And down below [at Astoria] those nets get so thick there that you don't try to lay it up and down or across ways or any way, you just lay out wherever you can find a hole to get it out in."³

Too many fishermen in too little space, plus the availability of diving technology, led to pulling snags on drifting grounds in the lower river, thus expanding the available fishing area. Similar pressures in upriver parts of the Columbia led to snagging on productive fishing grounds, aided in some instances by the Fishermen's Union. The ability to clear snags from the river bottom brought the development of the diver net, which made it possible to fish more effectively for the more valuable salmon that came during freshet conditions. As investment in various fishing grounds grew, the desire for maximum returns from the individual's contribution of time and money increased competitive pressures. Resolving conflicts entailed organization of community access to the local fishing grounds, organization which developed into the drift right.

Fishermen banded together in snag unions or drift associations to clear debris from the river bottom. The venture necessitated cooperation and some financial outlay to pay for the necessary equipment and diver. In return for the time, labor, and money invested to make an area fishable, the groups gained access to the fishing ground in the form of a "drift right." Each fisherman owned a right, which could be bought, sold, and inherited, depending upon the rules set by the drift association.

The preceding description simplifies the concept of the drift right, but as this form of organization has evolved over time, great variation has occurred. The Columbia River had several things in common with gillnet fishing in other locales during the fishery's formative years, but the concept of the drift right does not appear elsewhere. There were drift areas on the Sacramento, the Fraser, and on some coastal streams, for example, but these appear to have been stretches of water where fish came and were fished, geographic locations rather than organized territories. An account of the Sacramento in 1929 stated that

> After the net was laid out in the water, the fisherman would grasp one end of it and drift down the stream. At intervals the fisherman went along the net and picked out the salmon. When the net and boat had drifted the length of a particular fishing

ground or "drift" the fishermen "picked up" the net and went to some other place to try for more salmon. The use of gill nets has changed but little since the early days.[4]

The Klamath River had a similar system in place in early days.[5]

Early drifting grounds on the Sacramento had names, such as the Schwartz Fishing Grounds. Some social organization existed in the form of rules as to who could drift when:

> The distance they float, of course, varies with the grounds and the seasons. According to a law among fishermen, a second net is not to be placed in the water until the first one has floated down a certain distance, and although the fish are all caught running up the stream, the second, third and even fourth net frequently catches more than the first. They generally begin fishing at about half ebb tide.[6]

The fishery was mobile, as fishermen followed the salmon in their migration upstream.[7] However, the predominantly Greek and Italian fishermen of the Sacramento valued seniority, so that older fishermen had the right to lay out their nets first, leaving the younger men until last. This system encouraged the younger men to switch from gillnetting to trolling, especially with the advent of the gasoline engine, in order to make a living. This tactic gradually shifted the focus of the fishery to the front end of the run, until the bulk of the catch was taken before the fish ascended the river.[8] These pressures worked against any possibility of organizing drifts.

Willapa Bay in Washington state apparently had a snag association in the latter part of the 1930s and into the 1940s.[9] Most fishermen belonged, paying dues to a snag fund. There were drift rights on the Naselle River which empties into the bay. Seasons in both these locations were abbreviated and targeted primarily lower-value fish such as chum salmon. Snagging is no longer conducted there, as the expense is too great, and drift rights are no longer in force.

At one time, gillnetting took place in many coastal streams, part of a mixed economy.[10] As Clark Spurlock noted, "The great majority of the gillnet fishermen operating in the rivers along the coast have homes along the stream and may supplement their income from fishing by farming or logging in other seasons."[11] Some fishermen fished rivers such as the Willamette or Columbia and migrated to coastal streams when circumstances warranted.[12]

Fishermen may have removed snags on a sporadic basis, but no organization for such purposes seems to have existed.

In British Columbia there is evidence that recognition of the problems of crowding took place very early. The *Canadian Parliament Sessional Papers* in 1882 reported that the British Columbia Inspector of Fisheries had tried to establish a fair distance between fishing stations on the Nass River "to prevent, on a stream where the channel is comparatively narrow and the facilities limited, a system of crowding which would be generally obstructive."[13] The effect was to restrict fishing grounds on the Nass for the cannery in the immediate vicinity. There seems to have been no attempt on the part of the fishermen to organize into drift associations, however, with their formal rules and snagging practices. Canneries owned much of the gear, so there was little incentive on the part of the fishermen to protect it. The government pulled obstructions to navigation, which might also affect gear. Mechanization of the fleet, particularly in the north, occurred two-to-three decades later than on the Columbia. British Columbia fishermen appear to have relied more heavily on canneries and government assistance in their operations than was the case on the Columbia. Recently, the influx of Vietnamese fishermen into the British Columbia gillnetting fleet has resulted in ethnic tensions related in part to the traditional organization of British Columbia fisheries. Deborah Phelan, an information officer with the Department of Fisheries and Oceans, commented on the situation:

> In an industry that has developed through tradition, resolution is not just a simple matter of writing up a set of rules. . . . Many commercial fishing techniques are not regulated but are governed by an unwritten code of ethics and common principles— something like a code of honour. Lack of familiarity with the practices of this code creates contention and misunderstanding within the community.[14]

To resolve such tensions, a task force on cross-cultural relations in commercial fisheries has held meetings between the various fishermen's organizations.[15]

In summary, west coast gillnetters recognized and sought out productive fishing grounds from earliest times. Rules, ethnic custom, and alteration of the grounds themselves by snag-pulling controlled—in greater or lesser fashion—fishing access. Only on the

Columbia, with its immensely productive runs, did routine snagging of fishing grounds prove financially feasible on a permanent basis. The investment of money and labor provided the impetus to both develop and refine the concept of the drift right over the years.

This hypothesis was corroborated by the observations of Bill Puustinen, a gillnetter on the Columbia since 1917, who witnessed much of the early history of drift rights:

> It must be this need for co-operative snagging which was first used for cleaning fishing drifts, then later became the base for forming independent drift rights secured under the need for saving most fishing then for those who cleared the drifts. This was a very natural sequence. As this type of drift management really became more prominent, mostly upriver on the more limited fishing locations, it was then easy to go and organize a semi-legal compact with stated responsibilities of that drift's management by members of such compacts.[16]

During the first two decades of the twentieth century, drift areas were cleared at a great rate, leading to the frequently heard claim that "Our drift was first." Although no written records noted the dates of these early drifts, oral tradition does provide some information. The Warrior Rock Snag Association formed in 1899. The Sunny Sands drift near Puget Island was cleared by 1904 and the Shoofly by 1907.[17] By 1908 fishermen were using the Gut Drift near Skamokawa.[18] Wallace Island Drift existed by 1910;[19] the Coffeepot Drift by 1910 or 1911.[20] Con Harlow and Joe Budnick started the Jim Crow Drift in 1911-12.[21] There is some conjecture that Con Harlow had drift rights on the Willamette River and brought the idea to the Brookfield area when he moved there. Fishermen cleared the drifts a little at a time:

> At first when we got started [snagging] . . . we could only go down[river] . . . a couple thousand feet, that's all we had to start with. But we was still making enough that there was darn good prospect of a good drift out of it, which it did wind up to be. But as long as we was making a little profit on doing it, well, that's what we done.[22]

Rather than chasing fish, the fishing strategy employed became one of preparing one's fishing ground in the belief that the investment would pay off in terms of catch. By staying in one place a fisherman could get to know its changes and variations intimately, and the patterns and variations of the fish runs frequenting it. Ross Lindstrom commented on the psychology behind fishing in one area over a long period of time:

> It's a different way of fishing than in an open fishery because you're stuck where you are. You're stuck, psychologically, to that spot but by the same token you've got the comfort of know-ing that you're going to be able to fish there 'cause you keep it clean and it is a place where you can drift and not do a lot of damage to your gear.[23]

This strategy presupposed that there would be fish on the grounds. State regulations helped in this supposition. Although Washington and Oregon did not coordinate fisheries management for many years, the advent of closed seasons congruent for both states, beginning in 1909 and becoming more prevalent after ratifi-cation of the Columbia River Compact in 1918, meant that fish could migrate upstream during closed periods. The closures served to spread the salmon harvest over a longer stretch of river,[24] ensuring that those upstream had the possibility of good catches. Rather than hunting for fish, or trying to be more aggressive than one's fellow fisherman in order to out-compete him, the strategy became one of knowing the grounds, regulating the net, and being in the right place at the right time. Cecil Moberg gave his views on fish-ing one's own ground:

> You have a feel for gillnetting. You just have a feeling and I know that most of your good fishermen fish hunches. You al-ways fish a hunch. I think you've fished that much that you have a hunch and by golly, I wonder, low water tonight now. They should be here. That's where they should be. And one thing about a good fisherman. He never leaves his ground. A good fisherman stays with the ground he knows because the fish are gonna come there. You don't go to the fish, you let the fish come to you. Any guy that's chasing fish is always a day late. You cannot catch the fish that are in the cans. That's the old theory. You fish for the fish that are coming to you. . . . If you stay on the grounds . . . you may miss them one night, but when they do come on your ground you're gonna get your share.[25]

Fishermen quickly perceived that the cleared areas provided a better place to fish. Some fishermen, however, who were not members of snag associations and consequently did not pull snags, still expected to be able to fish the same grounds. Tensions arose when "outsiders," or those who had not pulled snags or paid dues, tried to fish among those who did. Many of the early drifts were reserved strictly for drift members on the ebb tide, when they used diver nets, but were open to all on the flood, when they used floaters. As cash outlays and time investments grew, individuals began to feel more possessive toward the various drift areas. Drift association members resented as "outsiders" those transients who moved from area to area. It was also increasingly evident that the most desirable fishing grounds would only provide a living for a limited number of boats. As the old method of "first come, first served" on the open drifts became increasingly less tenable, fishermen sought means to restrict access to the grounds. These means might include intimidation or more formal organization of the drift with rules to govern who had the right to fish there. Toots Peterson gave as an example the Alderbrook Drift:

> It was a dog eat dog situation out here, you'd make a drift and last of the tide you'd pick your net up and run back up and drop the anchor again [to hold a turn] for the next tide so you practically lived in the boat out there. And everybody got more or less disgusted with it so they just got together and drew numbers and you go out on your number when your time was up. And it worked out real well. . . . All the fishermen that were fishing out here at the time were invited to join.[26]

Intimidation might take the form of "corking," that is, laying out a net close to somebody so that he would not have the opportunity to catch any fish. As Ted Jackson explained: "Somebody comes here [on the drift] and has the whole river to himself but he lays right in front of you real close so you don't have much of a chance to catch a fish because he's right there so close. So then the next day I usually paid him back [by corking him]. Nobody said a word. They all knew what I was doing."[27]

Eddie Rasmussen described another means of eliminating unwanted competition from the drift:

> Some of them would want to come in and make running tide drifts [with a floater net on the ebb tide] which didn't pan out because they [the floaters] drift faster than the diver and there'd be nets getting tore up when they started that. If they went and drifted on top of you, then you'd have a right to cut their nets to

save your own. . . . We went and we got the snag net. And that was made to take a lot of hard knocks and pulling, heavy twine and heavy lines and we'd just lay that out and let 'em drift on top of it and get a couple of boats on it and reef it out underneath 'em. And with that catching up in their web they'd have a lot of big ragged spots in their nets. . . . That worked better than anything.[28]

Drifts organized formally in order to provide a more orderly means of access to cleared fishing grounds. When a group of fishermen organized to form a drift, they considered each member to be a partial owner and to have a share. Since their inception, fishermen recognized drift rights as a "gentlemen's agreement" between all fishermen, whether or not they all had drift rights. Not all fishermen subscribed to this view, however, and conflict still continues. An insight into the conflict may be found in Richard Anderson's novel, *Down River*, a story about a man who decides to go fishing and buys a gillnetting outfit from another fisherman. The following scene occurs when Henry, the new fisherman, is out snagging for the first time. The other person in the scene is "Judge," a lawyer who fishes part-time:

Turning that pump [for air for the diver] Henry didn't know whether or not he could hold out. He was surprised when the lawyer handed the life line to someone else and came over to ask if he wanted a rest. It was the first time that day anyone had spoken to him other than to suggest that he turn faster.

Judge took over and Henry rested against the winch. After awhile he said: "I see now what they mean when they talk about a drift right. It's a lot of work snagging out a drift."

"Yes," the lawyer agreed. He was losing his wind.

"I'd want to run out anybody who tried to muzzle in, now that I've worked on it. But still it's not like buying a piece of land. Something you can see."

Tormented, the lawyer replied, "That's where you're wrong. When you buy a piece of land, you can't buy the land itself. You can't put the land in your pocket and walk away with it. All you can do is buy the right to keep as many people off the land as you want. It's the same thing here."[29]

The argument for fishermen hinged on the ideas of exclusivity and equality. The labor movement, of which the Columbia River Fishermen's Protective Union (C.R.F.P.U.) was a part, fostered the notion of equality among the fishing brotherhood. So fierce was this egalitarianism that at the September 4, 1888 meeting of the Union's central board, the following discussion took place:

> The Chair then stated that the Johnson called Sand Island Johnson, a member in good standing, and who had the misfortune to lose a leg, was desirous of asking aid from the Union, if the Union would furnish him with a leg. He then could be able to support his family. After some discussion whether money could be appropriatcd to do so or to loan the money.[sic] A member asked for information what would be the amount necessary to purchase one. Leland then mentioned that he knew of an artificial leg being bought for $165. A motion was made that the Sect'y be instructed to purchasc a wooden leg and the same be rented out to Johnson for an indefinite period for the sume [sic] of one dollar, thus making the same, the leg, virtually the property of the Union.[30]

Bizarre as this decision may seem now, it speaks overwhelmingly to the mindset that believed firmly that all should be treated equally and no one, not even a person who needed a prosthetic device, should have or be perceived to have an advantage not enjoyed by every other fisherman.

This tension, between the belief in egalitarianism and the need to guarantee that fishing grounds be cleared of snags and that those who cleared them should have a preferential or exclusive right to fish there, led to clashes. Corking matches between rival fishermen assumed legendary proportions. But fishermen busy corking each other were not catching salmon. In addition, fishermen on the same drift were not above trying to out-maneuver each other regularly for the choice position, leading to clashes between driftmates. To regulate this competitive urge, minimize conflict, and ensure cooperation, drift users developed rules of behavior.

Foremost among these rules were regulations to determine who was permitted to lay out a net and when, and to govern snagging operations. The "draw" was a form of lottery, with fishermen drawing numbers written on scraps of paper or poker chips out of a hat. The Eagle Cliff Snag Association bylaws show that as of March 14, 1934 the organization decided to create three drifts out of the cleared areas of their fishing grounds, and that each fisherman would draw for all three drifts at Wallace Station at 5 p. m. The Oak Point Drift Company bylaws stated that as of April 9, 1939 drift members were to lay out their nets from the towhead twenty

minutes apart. In some areas a number of drifts banded together
to form one large cooperative. Each fisherman had a drift right in
the cooperative and could fish on any drift within its purview. A
general set of rules pertained to the entire group, and particular
rules served to satisfy the quirks of individual drifts. Rules have
become increasingly complex since the early years of organization.
The rules for laying out a net for the Skamokawa Snag Association,
for example, now cover two-and-a-half legal size typewritten pages.
Of the Milkmaid Drift's eighteen rules, thirteen govern when and
where to lay out and the rotation of fishing order.

There are varying patterns in the drawing of numbers. Usually fishermen draw two sets of daily numbers, along with Sunday
numbers, which are valuable because the season usually opens each
week on Sunday, and more salmon are likely to be present. Many
drifts have rules to the effect that at least three fishermen must be
present at the drawing. During the Great Depression, one group of
fishermen on a drift decided to go fishing during the closed period,
as times were tough. Despite the illegal nature of their activities,
they still met together at the towhead to draw numbers!

The following chronology provides a framework for understanding the development of the drift right:

1876—formation of the Columbia River Fishermen's Beneficial Aid Society to snag drifting grounds in the lower river;

1879—formation of the Columbia River Fishermen's Protective Union, which snagged drifting grounds;

1899—Warrior Rock Snag Association formed at St. Helens,
Oregon;

1890-1920—development and expansion of use of diver nets
and snagging of drifting grounds in Columbia River above Tongue
Point;

1920-1950—increased documentation of drift rights and drift
meetings, increased consideration of drift rights as property to be
bought, sold, and inherited;

1950-present—increased environmental pressures on fish runs
cause changes in productivity of drift rights, leading fishermen to
explore other grounds and to increase their role in environmental
monitoring.

Although written documentation concerning the exact period
when the concept of the drift right emerged does not exist, a

significant ad appeared in the April 24, 1919 *Columbia River Sun*: "Fishing rights on a good diver drift for sale. See Peter Wik, Cathlamet."[31] The fact that a drift right could be advertised for sale indicated that it had value. It also indicated that drift rights were firmly enough established as a form of "property" right that they were considered to be an asset to a fishing operation. Ads appeared frequently in the 1920s in newspapers all along the river. In 1938 a probate record for the estate of Hans Christian valued his two drift rights at $125, his two gillnets at $60, and his boat at $250.[32] Probate records appeared in various county courthouses after this date, all indicating drift rights to be a substantial part of the fishing operation. Although possibly coincidental, it is interesting to note that drift rights start to appear as property in such records shortly after the demise of fixed gear. In more recent years, drift rights have figured in property settlements in divorces.

Drift rights could not be conveyed at the whim of the owner, however. As they were a communal right, the drift association frequently insisted on having the right of first refusal on any transactions concerning a membership. The drift might refuse to allow a person to sell a right, preferring to buy the right in order to reduce the number of fishermen on the drift. Alternatively, a drift might create an extra right if it needed an extra person to help with snagging. Harold Viukhola recalled his early efforts to purchase a right:

> I had an awful time getting started fishing here but I finally got me a drift right. They wouldn't sell one [and] you had to have a drift right to fish on a drift. Well, I had to pay rent on one for fifteen years and then finally . . . I was able to buy [a] drift right for . . . $150. . . . If you were going to buy one now you couldn't get one for $4500 and if the drift . . . figures there's enough fishermen here already they don't want to sell you one anyway.[33]

Hank Ramvick reiterated the considerations in whether a drift association would buy or sell a right: "They sometimes buy out a fisherman that's gonna retire or gets sick or wants to get out of the business and they in turn will sell it back to another fisherman. Sometimes, not always. There's such a thing as getting too many boats in one drift, too. You're just cutting your own throat when that happens."[34] Some drifts would not permit one of their members to lease out his rights to another fisherman unless he were ill and could not fish himself. Some drifts had regulations that a right had to be fished once every two years (the period varies) or it became invalid.

To function as an organization, formal meetings of the drift occur several times each year, usually before each fishing season and at such other times as necessary. The drift captain chairs the meeting. Members of the association elect a captain for an indefinite period, usually as long as possible, since nobody wants the job! The drift captain is essentially an administrative figure who attends to payment of expenses incurred in maintaining the fishing grounds. He also schedules the diver for snagging and keeps track of issues regarding drift maintenance such as repair of snag nets, snag scow, and other items. There may also be a drift secretary who keeps minutes of meetings. Many drifts have minutes dating back to the 1930s, and even the 1920s. Keeping records is necessary to track who has paid snag dues, what rules are currently in force, and what decisions have been made in the buying and selling of rights. Occasionally litigation occurs, and accurate and complete records may be needed in court. Bills of sale and leases are also part of the records of many drift associations. Although each member of a drift has one vote, and although policies are, in theory, formulated on a majority-rule basis, in actual fact, consensus is usually the norm.

Ethnic homogeneity existed on many drifts. Cecil Moberg described a number of drifts near Astoria:

> You come up what we call the south side and there was the Smith Point Drift or Smith Channel. That was a diver drift. That was mostly Finnish fellas fishing down there. . . . And then as you went on . . . there was the Shoofly, Middle Channel, Taylor Sand, Seal Channel and Blind Channel. . . . The Black Spar Buoy was out there. That was mostly upper town Finnish fellas fished from that drift. And over on Blind Channel was mostly Greeks and Slavonians and the Booth's Cannery bunch. And then as you went on up the river . . . just out from Tongue Point there was a big flat . . . which was called Skunk Flat. . . . And then right above Tongue Point was the Prairie Channel. . . . And then as you got right up above the Skunk drift was the Tongue Point drift, the red light drift. And that was a bunch of fishermen, they were mostly Swedes, on that drift.[35]

Rules pertaining to drift rights took on aspects of the ethnic communities that developed them. Slavic drift rights, for example, were often inherited. This rule applied particularly to the Jim Crow Drift, which at first could be inherited by any son. However, the rule eventually changed so that the oldest son stood first in line to inherit. If the oldest son did not want the right it could pass to the next son. On this particular drift, this rule developed in order to cut down on the number of boats fishing. Scandinavian drift rights were usually inherited by the widow, who might sell with the permission of the drift association. She might also choose to have someone fish the right for her, although not all drifts permitted this option. Communities of mixed ethnic heritage or of American/British origin also followed this pattern. Finnish drift rights were more communal in nature, with the rights reverting back to the drift itself, which might or might not choose to indemnify the widow, usually with a token amount. A drift right might belong to a particular community, so that only a resident could fish on the grounds. Conflicts arose when men came back after serving in the military and tried to resume their rights, or when a community member moved away and still tried to fish in the area. In some cases where crowding became acute, the drift right died when the fisherman did, in order to reduce the number of boats.

Community and ethnic ties reinforced the drift as a major source of social interaction for fishermen. Socialization among drift members on the net rack, in the local coffee shop, or in each other's homes, provided information about fishing on the common grounds that could potentially be very useful. Not that such information was easy to obtain! Under-communication of fishing secrets served both to reduce the likelihood of one's competitor trying to use the same techniques, and also to avoid the appearance of being "better" than someone else.

Because the sharing of catch information is an important index in the evaluation of the fish-catching ability of one's own gear, few fishermen feel they are able to dispense with it. However, there is some tension in providing information that may aid a competitor. Inquiries about a competitor's catches are usually prefaced with remarks about the tide, the weather, and a very bland statement of what the inquirer caught. Balancing the "need to know" with the fierce competition on the fishing ground is difficult. At the same time, the cohesiveness of the group is important in order to be able to work together for the common good in snagging operations.

Group cohesiveness and keeping information within the group serves the function of discouraging transients from moving in.[36]

Fishermen were well aware of the value of the drift right. In addition, the salmon packing companies recognized the superior productivity possible through cooperative effort. They frequently loaned money to fishermen to purchase rights on areas known to be good salmon grounds. The Columbia River Packers Association (C.R.P.A.) kept records on who owned the various drifts and their production, and on the drift's production as a whole. The C.R.P.A. even assisted fishermen in relocating from their drift areas above Bonneville Dam after its construction, as their grounds were becoming less productive.[37]

Despite their knowledge of the productivity of the various drift areas, the companies appeared to have very little interest in actually purchasing rights for themselves. Occasionally rights did fall into their hands. A fisherman who died without heirs and owing money to the company might have his estate transferred to the company in payment of debts such as gear. Canneries extended credit to their fishermen for major purchases, the fishermen securing their loans with their drift rights as collateral. The packers also acted as go-betweens with agencies such as the Coast Guard when situations threatened orderly fishing on a drift right. Such an incident occurred during World War II when the Coast Guard attempted to shut down the river near Vancouver in order to hold launching trials of a new vessel.[38] The C.R.P.A. intervened on the fishermen's behalf, as it did not want to lose the production of the Vancouver and Milkmaid Drifts.

The recognition of the value of drift rights and their productivity was counter-balanced by a curious ambivalence on the part of the fish packing companies.[39] Despite the fact that they owned traps, seines, and fish wheels, they demonstrated little interest in owning drift rights to lease to fishermen. It should be noted, however, that most drift associations had rules regarding leasing which would have excluded the packers from such an attempt. The few rights that came into the hands of the salmon packers were either sold back to the drift or to another fisherman with the drift's approval. Rather than attempting to purchase drift rights and lease them out, companies vied with each other to attract the best fishermen, who, coincidentally, were those who had the best grounds. John

McGowan, once president of Bumble Bee Seafoods (formerly C.R.P.A.), gave an account of the situation:

> A cannery wanted to know what a fisherman's production record had been before they would back him . . . for nets and a boat. Or just money to tide his family over the winter to coming of next spring of the Columbia River season. And, you know, you'd get this information from other fishermen who knew these people . . . and if they were average to good producers, honest guys, you would back them because certainly if you didn't somebody else was going to anyway. And there was a lot of competition between the companies, between certain companies that competed directly against each other for fishermen in certain areas. In Ilwaco where I grew up, we were constantly competing with C.R.P.A. and of course, I was on the other side in those days. I was working for P. J. McGowan and Sons. . . . C.R.P.A. in those days was our blood enemy. . . . They were constantly trying to persuade our best producers to come on over to C.R.P.A. and we were working on some of their guys and this was just an ongoing thing.[40]

As gasoline engines became more powerful, fishermen became more mobile and were able to select fishing areas in several parts of the river, depending upon the species sought and the season. A fisherman who owned drift rights in Clifton, for example, might also purchase a right further upriver, perhaps on the Reeder Drift, about four miles below the mouth of the Willamette. He could then transfer between his fishing grounds, each of which was good for a different species and season, maximizing production options. Fishermen selected drifts in areas according to individual preference, although company backing and the presence of fishermen from one's home drift were influential. However, there was no set pattern of migration from one drift to another. Francis Seufert recalled fishermen coming to fish in the Dalles/Celilo Falls areas as being either transient fishermen who fished the Willamette and coastal streams, or Astoria fishermen, known for their big boats.[41] The former were mobile, and even in the 1930s trailered their boats from place to place. The latter ran their boats upriver and fished only the Columbia. By the 1950s fishermen from the lower river owned most of the upriver diver drift rights. They arrived, snagged, and then fished the drifts in the spring when catches were over in the lower river. Lower river fishermen used the upper river spring drift rights because of season closures and run timing. Usually, escapement over Bonneville Dam had been achieved by the time of the traditional openings on May 1 or June 15, but there were still substantial numbers of fish in the areas of the upper river drifts. These drifts thus produced large catches for a few days and then tapered off. These drifts were cleared primarily for these big opening catches, which would last for approximately a week or two of actual fishing. The peak of the runs had already passed through the lower river, so fishermen moved upriver to maximize harvest.

With increased mobility and the possibility of moving with the fish from place to place, problems arose for those fishermen who had snagged their drifts and did not want transient floater fishermen to use their grounds. The issue was territoriality. Fishermen from other parts of the river could fish on a drift if they had a drift right. If they were floater fishermen from another area, they were not welcome. Floater fishermen justified their use by noting that in the August seasons everyone migrated down to the mouth of the river to fish, an area considered to be open water. This strategy, however, increased competition for the floater fishermen who traditionally used the area. Fishermen proposed a variety of solutions, but the issue has never truly died. As recently as 1990 conflict reached such a level that a bill was introduced in the Washington state legislature to provide for a registry of drift rights to deal with the problems created by transient fishermen, particularly those from the Puget Sound region. A plea for respect of the "written and unwritten rules of conduct" ended with the following sentence: "The greatest order and productivity in all fisheries often arises from the unwritten rules, the rules by which fishermen govern themselves and ultimately the destiny of those fisheries."[42]

A court case running directly counter to this opinion occurred in 1990. While recognizing the potential for chaos in the fisheries, overcrowding, and "economic detriment to those holders of drift right," the court decided that regulation of these issues was the responsibility of the Department of Fisheries:

> The Department, by allowing plaintiffs to carry out snag clearing for many years may have allowed plaintiffs to operate under the impression that their drift rights were legally enforceable. By this opinion that impression comes to an end. The problems presented in this case must be resolved by

departmental rules and regulations. . . . Only the Department
is in a position to establish the orderly promotion of gillnet fishing on the Columbia River.[43]

It is to this conflict, involving individual responsibility, community custom, court decisions, and state mandates, that the next
chapter is addressed.

Chapter Six
Turf And TURFS

Rather than looking for the exact date of a technical innovation, I have considered it more fruitful to ask what problems each innovation solved, and what problems each in turn created. Technical problems and solutions also impinged on the social order, which in turn had to adapt to new realities. Up to this point, this book has focused on the minutiae of gear, boats, drift rights, and snagging technology on the Columbia River. But the Columbia River is not unique in having a system of rules, customs, and territories developed by its fishermen, although it is unique among the west coast salmon fisheries. Such concepts, however, exist worldwide. The United Nations Food and Agricultural Organization (FAO) has dubbed them TURFS—territorial use rights in fisheries.

The FAO defined TURFS as "community held rights of use (or tenure) and exclusion over the fishery resources within a specific area and for a period of time. Accompanying these rights might be certain responsibilities for maintenance and proper management of the resource base, as well as restrictions on the exercise of the rights of use and exclusion."[1] Examples of places where such rights exist include Brazil, Sri Lanka, Papua/New Guinea, Ivory Coast, Newfoundland, the United Kingdom, and the United States, where the Maine lobstermen's territories are well known.[2] There is a growing interest in learning about these territories, as well as in utilizing them in contemporary fisheries management to resolve such problems as overcrowding and overfishing.

The fishermen who relocated to the Columbia from Europe came from areas with TURFS already in place. The United Kingdom, for example, ordered its salmon fisheries by custom, particularly in Scotland[3] and Wales, where the river fishermen "administered a river through set rules of privilege and rights that had been passed down from time immemorial. They were oral laws passed down from father to son in closely knit, riverside communities."[4] While customs varied from country to country and river to river, the concept of a fishing territory was certainly not unknown among immigrant fishermen.

Fishermen originally used the idea of a fishing territory in the area below Tongue Point as a solution to overcrowding. As the diver net developed, making it possible to fish on the ebb tide during the freshet, the economic feasibility of paying for the development of fishing grounds further upriver by pulling snags became apparent. The area above Tongue Point developed in this fashion, with fishermen in adjacent small communities working on fishing grounds close to their place of residence. They exploited a specialized economic niche, which enabled them to remain in their home towns instead of migrating elsewhere to fish. It also enabled them to more easily pursue their pluralistic economic adaptations. A 1952 study of Wahkiakum County fishermen described their way of life:

> Most of the fishermen have their homes, boathouses and nethouses in sheltered sloughs or river estuaries. . . . Many of the sloughs have dikes around them and frequently the fishermen have their homes within the diked area, with their boathouses and nethouses located conveniently in the slough. These latter fishermen often combine fishing with farming, if land is available. A good example of this is the fisher-farmers of Puget Island, who supplement their yearly farm income by approximately $2,000 by fishing during the best parts of the seasons. This combined activity is also carried on (although not so extensively) in other parts of the county. Many other fishermen work in logging or at odd jobs in between fishing periods.
>
> Many of the fishermen, however, still depend on the river for their main source of income. . . . The drift is an important thing to the fisherman. . . . Most of the year the fisherman is using his diver net there, and at other times he is working to keep the drift clean. He prospers depending on whether he "belongs" to a good or bad drift. . . . It is said that a man "belongs" to a drift, that is, he uses his diver net there and must share the responsibility of keeping the area clean. . . . An unwritten code of honor prohibits fishermen from using any drift except the one or ones that they belong to. New fishermen are admitted to the drift by consent of all members when one of the old members drops out.[5]

TURFS become more nebulous "where stocks are mobile and there is no clear relationship (identity) between the biological unit (stock) and the socio-economic unit (community.)"[6] Stationary resources, such as clam or oyster beds, are much easier for a community to exert ownership over than are mobile species, such as anadromous salmon. Nonetheless, the Columbia River fishing territory known as the drift right certainly qualifies as a TURF under the FAO definition. The right is not an individual right but is held communally. The community may be an extended family, a fishing village, ethnic group, or legally incorporated body. The drift right encompasses a very specific stretch of river for the duration of the various fishing seasons. Maintenance of the river bottom in order to provide access to fish is the pivotal point upon which membership in the drift rests. The bill of sale cited below connects labor to ownership:

> I, Robert Gianelli, in payment of $62.00 (Sixty-two dollars) do sell my labors on the Clifton Drifts to the fishermen fishing those drifts now, therefore I forfeit all my privileges of fishing these said Clifton drifts.
>   Signed, Robert Gianelli

Fishermen devised rules and codes of conduct around potential areas of conflict, prescribing a pattern of etiquette to minimize inter-personal strife and maximize economic returns. However, conflict most frequently arose around the issue of exclusivity.

This issue pertains to TURFS worldwide. According to the FAO, "in addition to the right of use a minimum degree of exclusivity (that is, the right to exclude others) is necessary. . . . The rights of use and exclusion defined over a given territory are held by a community or a collectivity with socially integrating forces."[7] Or, in the common phraseology of the Columbia, "Drift rights are a gentlemen's agreement, but you've got to have a way to deal with the folks that aren't gentlemen." The Washington court decision which stated that responsibility for an orderly fishery rested with the Department of Fisheries specifically denied fishermen the right to exclude others from fishing drift rights, while recognizing the potential chaos that could arise from the ruling. The irony of the courts deciding in favor of what fishermen viewed as chaos and against what they viewed as orderly conduct was not lost on them.

The worldview that individual rights stem from government and court interpretation of the law ran directly counter to the fishermen's view of a community-developed body of custom and rules built up over a century of fishing the same grounds. In the fishermen's view, drift rights are not entirely exclusive because they are regularly bought and sold, and anyone has the right to clear a new drift in an unused area. Indeed, if a drift area fails to produce fish over a period of time, perhaps due to changes in bottom configuration, the only alternatives for the drift members are to buy rights elsewhere or to clear new grounds. Exclusivity can be a reward for labor, but it also has the potential to be a trap. If the fish do not appear on the cleared grounds, one cannot ethically invade another drift area.

In its decision, the court specifically mentioned that the Washington Department of Fisheries had the responsibility "to establish the orderly promotion of gillnet fishing on the Columbia river."[8] It chastised the department for giving fishermen the false impression that they had rights, based on the department's permission to pull snags in drifting areas. In fact, fishermen on the Columbia pulled snags long before there was such an entity as a state fisheries agency. Both the Washington Department of Fisheries and the Oregon Department of Fish and Wildlife have paid drift associations to pull snags in order to be able to conduct test fishing on their drifts. In Washington the test fishing contract specifically states that the test fisherman "must be completely familiar with the area's gill net drifts, and possess drift rights where necessary."[9] The conflicting view of access to fish based on custom and community standards, versus the state and court view of access to fish being a privilege dependent upon the law and government regulation, are fraught with inconsistencies such as these. The failure to find a common ground was nowhere more evident than in the following comment by a fisherman prior to the court decision: "Even if the decision goes against us [i. e. against drift rights] nothing will change. You have to have drift rights to carry on a fishery here, and the courts and the law can't change the river."

The field of the social sciences holds some empathy for culture and custom. As stated by Michael Orbach:

> [Unwritten rules] may exist either in place of or as a supplement to more formal legal strictures concerning the resource. It is often more important to develop a clear understanding of

these implicit rules than it is to understand a law as it appears on the books, for it is the former which guide much of the fishermen's behavior and consequently the fate of the resource.

... the fishermen, the governmental and scientific communities, and the general public will all benefit from a better understanding of the issues and viewpoints involved in fisheries management at all levels.[10]

This lack of understanding is evident on the Columbia River, and has not served the salmon well. Recent listings of salmonids under the Endangered Species Act, and the threat of further listings, must force a reexamination of the roles of all the above participants.

Much has been written about the "tragedy of the commons"[11] in the fisheries of North America and elsewhere. Stated simply, when resources such as fish are held "in common" among all citizens, there is no incentive for conservation. All the impetus goes towards exploitation for individual gain. There is much argument in the academic literature as to whether problems arise due to fish being common property, or because there is open access to fish. Rather than enter that controversy, it may be more helpful to use the "tragedy of the commons" theory as a lens to examine the current situation on the Columbia.

Due to actual and potential listings of various Columbia River salmon under the Endangered Species Act, management agencies have restricted fisheries throughout the Northwest. Endangered runs return mingled with strong runs of salmon, and there is no way as yet to identify and separate the weaker stocks. Managers have had to set harvest levels so as not to exceed the prescribed rate for the weakest stock present in a mixed-stock fishery. Despite the fact that it has been in place for some years, weak stock management, as it is called, has not succeeded in saving a number of threatened runs. Such runs have failed to thrive due to habitat loss, dams, and other environmental considerations. In a last-ditch effort to keep some of these remnant runs alive, fisheries all along the west coast of North America face drastic cut-backs in allowable harvest. The Columbia River gillnet fishery is one of several affected by this crisis.

Is the Columbia River gillnet fishery an example of the tragedy of the commons? It is but one means of access to the salmon of the Columbia. There are ocean troll fisheries from Alaska to California that also provide salmon for the consumer. Sport fisheries provide recreational access. Tribal fisheries supply salmon for the market and support tribal ceremonial and subsistence needs. A variety of agencies regulate these multiple points of access, including state, regional, and federal fisheries agencies. They manage salmon harvests by determining the numbers of fish needed for spawning escapement and the numbers of fish available for harvest, then allocating the latter among the different user groups, depending upon the time and place the salmon appear in the different fisheries. In addition to such space and time constraints, agencies may also mandate the types of gear used and limit access to the fisheries by controlling the numbers of fishers who may participate. Limited entry, as the last-named technique is called, as yet affects only commercial fisheries. There is no limit to the number of sport or tribal fishers who may partake in the given fisheries.

Management agencies have viewed the Columbia River gillnet fishery as a "management tool" useful for catching salmon unharvested by other fisheries, thus ensuring no waste. In the big years of 1986 and 1987, for example, when a large number of fish returned to the river, tired fishermen often remarked that they were just "doing their job," i. e. catching fish. The big years, however, also attracted opportunists who saw the chance to make big money and wanted to fish the traditional drift rights without pulling snags. Since the state only limits the numbers of licences and not access to particular fishing grounds, the situation was ripe for conflict. Such conflict is far less likely to occur during seasons of low abundance because there is no incentive for marginal fishermen, or those from other areas, to fish the Columbia.

Due to the expanding nature of sport and tribal fisheries, with the resulting pressure to allocate further resources to them and away from commercial fisheries, the right to exclude others from the fishing grounds assumes greater importance as gillnetting becomes more marginal. In 1992 the Washington Department of Fisheries attempted to resolve some of these allocation issues by proposing to reduce commercial licences still further.[12] Faced with a declining resource, it had several choices: produce more fish for all to share; impose limited entry on sport fishers; attempt to induce the tribal governments to establish limited entry among their own fishers; curtail commercial catches; maintain the status quo. By choosing to try to reduce the numbers of commercial fishermen, the department chose to limit public access to salmon for those citizens who purchase them in the market place.

Limiting public access to a wild species is certainly not new in the United States. Wild game species are now available only to sport hunters, except for animals raised on game farms. In the case of wild game, there were other cheap, readily available food substitutes, such as beef, pork, and chicken, so that its usefulness as a staple in the diet diminished, except for those for whom subsistence living remained a fact of life. It is debatable whether the more expensive and less available farmed salmon (generally Atlantic salmon) can fulfill this role *vis à vis* wild Pacific salmon.[13] Yet there has been surprisingly little public debate over the quiet transfer of access to the fisheries resources of the State of Washington.

Within the past five years the Washington Department of Fisheries has publicly stated its goal of making Washington the "Sport Fishing Capital of the Nation."[14] In order to accomplish that goal, the department has made numerous policy decisions, some of which directly affected commercial fisheries.[15] An example on the Columbia is the department's management of sturgeon, which led it to curtail incidental catches by commercial fishermen. More restrictive bag and size limits have been imposed on the individual sport angler, but, simultaneously, the department has actively sought access points for the sport fishery in the form of boat launches that it could develop to accommodate more anglers, in effect expanding the sport fishing fleet, which now takes over 85 percent of the allowable catch. Since potential boat launch sites often occur in areas where large numbers of commercial fishing families live, the department's policy has been viewed as an encroachment on the fishing community.

The pressure to reduce incidental catches of sturgeon is also an assault on drift rights. Sturgeon are taken incidental to salmon harvest. A fisherman may be out catching salmon and catch several sturgeon in the net as well, which then are sold. Current management strategy tends in the direction of reducing or eliminating this catch entirely. This trend affects both where the fisherman may fish, as some drifts are better sturgeon grounds than others, and how to design his net in order to minimize incidental catch.

For the fisherman who has made it part of his overall fishing strategy to maximize his incidental sturgeon catch, the department's policies have spelled disaster and are viewed as a direct intrusion on a TURF. The issue of exclusivity again arises, but this time on a state-wide, or even coast-wide, basis. Those being denied access to the fish are the consumers and their surrogates, the commercial fishers. That the fishing fleet sees itself in this role is quite evident from the bumper stickers on their pickups: "Oregon's Fisheries—Catching Your Seafood for You," and "Commercial Fishermen Fishing for America." That consumers are less aware of their position is evident by their lack of participation in natural resource public policy decisions affecting them.

The more a fisherman assumes the role of a hunter in seeking out fish, the less one finds in the form of fishermen-imposed rules regulating boundary maintenance, seasonal reoccupation of specific fishing grounds, and inheritance patterns. Contrast this fishing strategy with the Columbia River fisherman who opts for the more passive stance of waiting for the fish to swim to his grounds. Such an individual is in a very vulnerable position. The diver net is fine-tuned to a very specific area of river bottom and must produce over a relatively short period of time as the salmon pass through that area. Because of these limitations, fishermen formulated norms to offset the disadvantage of not being able to follow the fish migrations.

Drift rights are an example of the attempt to divide fish equitably as the fish move from one fishing territory to the next. Viewing drift rights as a form of riparian right, they provide for a division of the resource with a minimum of conflict. Each group of fishermen has its respective fishing area and the fish in that area are not considered to be common property among the entire fleet, but rather belong to the specific drift until they are either caught or move on. By contrast, in more mobile adaptations such as trolling, fish are considered common property until actually caught. The shift in focus is between that of occupying an ecological niche in the marine environment to a preoccupation with fishing as a business enterprise, although each adaptation contains elements of both.

The salmon themselves are caught up in a tragedy of the commons, due to the expanding nature of some fisheries and the contracting nature of the resource. However, the Columbia River gillnet fishery does not truly represent a tragedy of the commons, except that not enough fish escape other user groups to permit all licence holders on the Columbia to make a living. This is a situation over which the fishing families of the Columbia have no control, since state and federal agencies have the authority to regulate only harvest. In the agencies' view, the right of fishery is a common right. In the eyes of the gillnetters, particularly those with drift rights, the right of fishery is a TURF, rooted in custom and community. The following statement voted on by members of the Columbia River Fishermen's Protective Union (C.R.F.P.U.) in 1987 exemplifies their thinking:

> The Columbia River Fishermen's Protective Union in no way seeks to deny any bona-fide license holder from access to the Columbia River gillnet fishery. We would like to recognize, however, the fact that a substantial number of our membership have invested considerable time and money in maintaining certain areas of the Columbia River for the purpose of fishing while minimizing gear damage. Such areas are known as drift rights and have served for more than a century as a method of organizing much of the fishery.
>
> Such rights with the benefits and responsibilities they entail are regularly bought and sold between both local and nonlocal fishermen. The C.R.F.P.U. supports the concept of drift rights as a historic part of our fishery.[16]

An overwhelming majority of the members supported the statement.

The Columbia River is a textbook example of the four stages of development that riverine fisheries undergo, as delineated by Thayer Scudder and Thomas Conelly.[17] Stage one represents primarily subsistence fisheries, carried out during the trade and exploration era almost entirely by the native population. Stage two brings in incipient commercialization, with increasing numbers of early settlers involved in salting salmon. Stage three shifts to primarily commercial fisheries, which began on the Columbia with the success of the canning technology. Stage four deals with the increasing marginalization of formerly traditional fishing communities, due to lack of control over water tenure, credit policies, and management strategies. Scudder and Conelly state:

Whereas colonial regimes acknowledged the legal rights of communities, kinship groups and individuals to at least some of their customary land resources, these same regimes almost universally ignored or actively opposed customary rights to major bodies of water with the result that traditional communities had no legal basis on which to exclude outsiders.[18]

On the Columbia, those outsiders originally comprised commercial fishermen from other areas trying to encroach on traditional fishing grounds. They now include other fisheries, such as tribal and sport, which are trying to limit the number of fish available for commercial harvest. The Boldt/Belloni decision of the 1970s, which rested on treaty rights to "fish in common,"[19] is yet another example of the law and courts veering from the fishers' commonly accepted social norm of the TURF. Judge George Boldt ruled that the term "in common with," used to define the rights of tribal and non-tribal fishers in early treaties, meant that each group was entitled to an equal share. This decision applied to the Puget Sound region, but Judge Robert Belloni later concurred with the decision, thus extending it to the Columbia River. Ironically, different fisheries have been segregated even more under the decisions, on the basis of when and where each group may fish, especially on Puget Sound. On the Columbia, conflict has been minimized as specific territories are available for tribal fishers above Bonneville Dam and non-tribal fishers below Bonneville. As there is no encroachment on each other's territory, there has been little impetus toward direct confrontation, although allocation conflicts frequently arise.

Allocation decisions apportion salmon originating in the Columbia to users many miles away, thus preventing them from returning to their natal stream and limiting the amount available for in-river harvest. Under the Endangered Species Act, the runs of salmon in jeopardy may be returning with large numbers of non-endangered salmon, but agencies are required to restrict access to the latter in order to protect the weaker runs. In either case, the result is the same for the Columbia River gillnetter. Not only does the individual's catch diminish, along with the fleet in aggregate, but the ability to maintain the fishing grounds also diminishes, due to less available cash to invest in snagging. In addition, with less time on the water, the steady daily grounds' maintenance that normally occurs during a fishing season ceases. The ability to manage the grounds and access to the grounds erodes, with very little ability on the part of the fisher to change the situation. As social scientist Patricia Marchak put it:

> The fisher lacks management rights normally associated with property. There is a disjuncture between rights of access and of management that lies at the heart of the fisheries problem . . . . Since fishers cannot control licensing and since they are not permitted to manage a communal property, our attention should be focussed on the management of licensing access to fish, rather than on the licensed fisheries. This means that instead of talking about the "tragedy of the commons," we should be concerned with the tragedy of mismanaged state property.[20]

On a broader basis, private property rights frequently impinge on public property rights in fisheries, particularly in habitat issues. Logging of watersheds which may destroy spawning beds for salmon; irrigation and water rights which may contribute to inadequate flows for fish passage and exposure of salmon redds; dams which produce hydroelectric power but also hinder the downstream migration of juvenile salmon and upstream migration of the adults— all juxtapose the competing users of the Columbia.[21] The authority of the state fisheries and wildlife departments is very limited in dealing with such private property issues, despite their mandate to protect fish. The Pacific Fisheries Management Council did not even have a habitat protection statement during the first decade of its existence, and has virtually no power to enforce its current policy. Such private property rights may invade a fisherman's TURF by affecting the return of the fish, even though the owners of the facility in question may be miles away from the gillnetter's home territory.[22]

According to Linda Lampl, "Fishery conflicts, therefore fishery issues, are born at the intersection of . . . differences in values."[23] The values that are evident in salmon fisheries are a recognition of the salmon's desirability as food; as a source of income, either by direct sale of the fish or by some secondary enterprise; as a source of recreation; as a subject for study; as subsistence food; as a focus of religious and spiritual values; and as an indicator of the quality of the environment and life itself in the Northwest.

What is not so evident is the value gillnetters attach to a traditional way of life, and to a traditional way of fishing.

In part, the gillnetters themselves are responsible for being overlooked, as the secrecy with which they have treated their fish catches in discussions with competitors has seeped into all aspects of their lives. The supra-ethnic identity of being a gillnetter, which served to unite the fishermen of the Columbia into a relatively cohesive group, brought with it the need to conceal information from outside competition such as the trappers and seiners, from fellow gillnetters who might move in on one's territory, and from non-fishing outsiders who might be tempted to begin fishing themselves. It made sense for immigrants, who may have entered the country illegally or whose citizenship might have barred them from fishing, to conceal their backgrounds from authorities.[24] In the countries of origin of a number of the fishermen, governments were despotic, giving the immigrants little reason to trust anyone in authority in their new country. Up until the 1970s, the large salmon packing interests reinforced the habit of not talking about the details of the fishery with the larger world, since the packers represented the fishery in legislative battles. Representatives of the companies typically encouraged fishermen by saying, "Leave the legal and legislative stuff to us. You concentrate on fishing." Individual fishermen and the Columbia River Fishermen's Protective Union also took part in such frays, but the subject of drift rights seldom arose in public forums. The implicit (and sometimes explicit) motto was, "What they don't know can't hurt us." The very writing of this book is a break with this custom, and a number of gillnetters have expressed their concern: "Be careful what you say. You never know when they'll turn it against us." Yet it seems to me that it may be more helpful to the salmon to say straight out that the fish have allies, that they matter to someone, and they matter because we have so much at stake in terms of our fishing grounds and communities, our families, and our identities. Without them, we cease to exist. Without us, will they cease to exist?

Given the present situation, is there a way to resolve the dilemma of a fishery operated by custom among its participants, and one regulated by laws that may not respect custom? In the literature relating to TURFS the suggestion often arises of using TURFS as part of an overall management system. "Co-management" is the term used to describe a management partnership between government and user groups.[25] Such co-management is already in place on the Columbia River between state, federal, and tribal agencies.[26] However, as Norman Dale has pointed out, "Non-native fishermen have not been full partners in co-management and the accompanying social learning in Washington and Oregon."[27] In the view of the courts, state agencies have the responsibility for fisheries management, and they and tribal entities have been litigants for many years. Co-management has evolved in Washington and Oregon, not because it was seen as a positive good, but because it was seen as the lesser of two evils, as a way to avoid litigation. No such inducement exists to involve non-tribal fishing groups, many of whom are even further thrust to the periphery by the co-management regimes between tribes and other agencies. Anthropologist John Cordell expressed a pitfall common to many fisheries, including the Columbia:

> Too many authorities still look down from terra firma on local fishing traditions as primitive, inefficient and unproductive—lifeways that belong in the past. Few studies and proposals concentrate on what traditional fishing societies may need most of all to survive in future seafood economies and political systems: recognition of their customary rights and claims to resources and territories.[28]

Co-management schemes have worked well in Japan and Norway, and with a varying degree of success in a number of other countries.[29] One attempt to enter into co-management on the part of the fishermen of the Northwest arose with the creation of regional salmon enhancement groups, comprised of individuals from both the sport and commercial sectors who were dedicated to raising fish or improving habitat for salmon in order to improve the fisheries. While those involved in the groups do not have any management authority, they are to a certain extent influencing the future of their fisheries *vis à vis* the public agencies. Assessments on each licensee and other fund-raising mechanisms provide financial backing. Participants coordinate their efforts with regional biologists and local fisheries department personnel.[30] Would it be possible to use these groups as a basis to examine the concept of co-management? It is beyond the scope of this book to create a co-management scheme for the Columbia River, for by its very nature it will not succeed unless the users develop it themselves. However, as dissatisfaction with management agency actions and the outright failure of some runs of salmon force the issue, co-management is an idea that may prove useful in the salmon struggles.

Chapter Seven
The Theology of Gillnetting

The theology of gillnetting? The title could just as easily be "the morality of gillnetting." Enlarge it, and it encompasses "the morality of natural resource-based decision making" or "the theology of resource use." Currently, there are a number of land, timber, fish, and water use controversies nationwide that are particularly evident in the American West. The controversies usually revolve around public issues of who should have access to public resources and lands, for what purpose, and how much public control should be exercised. The arguments for and against are usually based upon widely different ethical norms, so that each group views itself as making ethical decisions within its own framework while seldom recognizing that perhaps other groups, though not using the same reference points, also view themselves as making ethical decisions.

The decision-making process regarding salmon harvest allocation provides a good example of how this ethical confusion has arisen on the Columbia. Each year the Pacific Fisheries Management Council decides who will fish and for how long. State agencies then implement these decisions. The 1992 El Niño, which caused poor ocean survival conditions for salmon, combined with the proposed and actual listings of various salmonids under the Endangered Species Act, complicated the process immensely. Because the troubled runs are intermingled with healthy stocks in what are called "mixed-stock" fisheries, the council severely limited access to fish runs in order to protect the weak stocks. The following observations are by no means a complete analysis of problems, but are intended instead to focus attention on where the various groups are "missing each other."

Rule morality[1] posits that rules or laws are for everyone's good and must be obeyed by all in order for society to function. Citing the Endangered Species Act as the rule which Congress established, the ethical decision would be to obey it. Justification for keeping the rule intact, despite its hardships, might be that the world is evolving to a higher state of environmental consciousness and that the Endangered Species Act is a means toward this end. Opposition to rule-morality thinking could argue that the Endangered Species Act determines that a species must be saved without sufficient reference to human context, and that human use is ignored. Hence, if the law itself is flawed, rule morality breaks down. Current language refers to these two views as a preservation ethic versus a conservation ethic, or with a shift in lexicon, as a preservation/conservation ethic versus a development or "wise use" ethic.

A second moral viewpoint, known as antinomianism, reacts against all law, against the tendency "to exalt legalism above human needs." At its extreme, a proponent of this viewpoint might state: "No one can tell me what to do with my land." However, a private owner may not feel obligated to care for the land, land which may contribute to critical salmon habitat. Translated to the world of fisheries, such a view might be that "everybody has a right to catch a fish," which tends to support superior moral rights of sport fishers. An alternative position is that "rights of access belong first and foremost to those most dependent on them."[2] This statement reflects the view of the gillnetters. Native American members of the Washat religion on the Columbia River go even further, believing that their right to catch salmon is more than a right, it is a sacred obligation which supersedes the law.[3]

Situation ethics claims that there is one absolute, that of love. The facts in each ethical dilemma must be determined, and a decision made according to what is the most loving action. The decision must be evaluated on its results. The Northwest Power Planning Council's "adaptive management"[4] policies seem to be based strongly on the situational model, although love may not be the underlying principle! A major weakness in this type of decision making on the Columbia River is that no one seems to agree upon the facts. The public and private power companies have openly scorned the fisheries management agencies' salmon mortality figures, and the latter do not tend to find the claims of the companies credible. Given that no one can agree upon the actual situation, the location of the cause of the problem continually shifts to other people, groups, agencies. At its worst, situational ethics leads to a political free-for-all with everyone acting in their own self-interest.

Ethical principles develop to deal with similar recurring situations. Due to the cyclical nature of the salmon's life cycle and predictable behavior, their management should be an easy area in which to develop ethical principles. The Pacific Fisheries Management Council has attempted to do just that by assuming the need for adequate escapement each year in order to perpetuate the runs. Biology, therefore, should be the basis for decision making. However, this principle has broken down in the face of legal decisions mandating catches to tribes which may impact escapement, and to natural conditions such as El Niño, where some runs cannot hope to enjoy adequate spawning escapement.

A final ethical ground for decision making rests in natural law. The Endangered Species Act assumes that all creatures have a right to exist. Not all parties involved in the life cycle of the salmon, however, subscribe to this view. It is frequently opposed by stating that "everyone has a right to make a living," an extension of the Constitution's stated rights of "life, liberty and the pursuit of happiness." Frequently the two views appear to be mutually exclusive. A search for equilibrium is seldom made by the parties involved, but rather by outside forces, such as state agencies, industry associations, or environmental groups.

With agencies, fishers, environmental groups, and those who impact habitat approaching the preservation of salmon with different goals in mind and fundamentally different sets of values and moral and ethical criteria for decision making, continual conflict occurs over even relatively trivial issues. In addition, the neglect of the fishing community by government, social service agencies, and religious organizations over past decades has ensured that its voice is least likely to be heard.[5] If public policy in the social service fields can so successfully ignore the fishing community, the situation is not much different in the area of environmental concern. Indeed, active environmental hostility towards those involved in natural resource-based adaptations appears to be growing.

In the summer 1991 issue of the *Amicus Journal*, the publication of the Natural Resources Defense Council, an article appeared called "The Reinvention of the American Frontier."[6] Its two authors described rural adaptations such as farming and logging as "extractive" industries, and sought to develop a "kinder and gentler frontier" by replacing them with retirement communities and tourism, viewed as non-extractive and therefore morally correct adaptations. A similar viewpoint was expressed in a letter to the editor of Longview *Daily News*:

> The ancient forests of the Northwest do not belong to the logging interests or even the people of the area any more than Niagara Falls belongs to New Yorkers or the Grand Canyon to the citizens of Arizona . . . .
> People all over want these trees saved. They are a vital part of the American soul and heritage. Please save these trees. For we won't come out to see stumps.[7]

Rural areas are usually characterized by traditional adaptations based on, in their view, renewable resources. The shift in terminology from such words as fishing, farming, and logging to "extractive industries" carries a negative moral weight, which in turn justifies the turning over of resources to the morally superior non-extractive users. The latent function of such thinking, however, is colonialist in nature. It is a classic case of urban exploitation of the rural hinterland. In this case, the hinterland is no longer permitted to export its raw materials, its wealth, to urban areas for processing as it could in previous eras. Rather, rural sources of income in the form of trees, fish, and land are transformed into a means of recreation for tourists. Is there not a disturbing echo here of how the original frontier was created, by means of a land grab from the aboriginal inhabitants of North America? Must frontier creation always involve a wresting away of resources from one owner/user by another? What are the social consequences of such decisions?

Robert Lee's study, *Social and Cultural Implications of Implementing "A Conservation Strategy for the Northern Spotted Owl*,"[8] listed four factors affecting people dependent upon the timber industry. These included job loss, a loss of trust in assured wood supplies (and the government who made the assurances), emerging class conflict, and the "dehumanization" inherent in attempts to degrade loggers.

Job loss is an obvious threat. Loss of trust in assured wood supplies is the death knell for many communities that were originally formed because of the promise of sustained wood production by the government and large timber corporations. The emerging class conflict takes place between rural loggers and those who see their decline as a positive good, a "sign that the world is evolving toward a higher level of environmental sensitivity"[9] and that they are an anachronism. Further dehumanization occurs when negative stereotypes turn up in the public press, in cartoons, in environmental organization literature. Lee points out that these stereotypes are classic cases of "blaming the victim"—"attributing to individuals pathological character traits that explain why they are suffering and justify negative consequences. (They are bad people and deserve to suffer.)"[10] As Lee points out, the political function of negative stereotyping is the dehumanizing of individuals "so that they can be exploited or treated unfairly."[11]

The situation described regarding loggers could just as easily apply to Columbia River gillnetters. Job loss is an obvious threat, since without fish or the consent of society to catch them, fishermen do not exist. Loss of trust in the agencies designated to manage and protect the salmon runs is at a crisis point, due to the agencies' evident failure to do either. Reduction of harvest was the management agencies' strategy to compensate for inter-dam and other salmon mortalities. The very real issue of overfishing that was so evident in the nineteenth and early twentieth centuries has now been transformed into a term used to mask the results of environmental degradation and hydroelectric development. In fairness to the agencies, it must be said that, for the most part, they did not have the authority to address these most critical issues. Now that the crisis is apparent to anyone who reads a newspaper, negative stereotyping of fishermen is a shield to deflect criticism from those who share the responsibility for habitat loss and damage to salmon runs.

Negative stereotyping has existed on the Columbia almost as long as the fishery. Witness this 1874 comment: "Were it not for the whiskey bottle and card table, the fishermen on the Lower Columbia might be a comfortable and prosperous class of men."[12] However, within the past decade, extremes in language go far beyond anything dreamed of in the nineteenth century. A drastic example appeared in a sportfishing newsletter that characterized gillnetters as "lower than child molesters." What is the result for the fishing community? To quote Lee again, "[Negative stereotyping] has predictable consequences for the victims. Self-blame, loss of self-esteem, and personal disempowerment undermine the ability of people to take pride in themselves and their capabilities, to fight back and to demand respect and equal treatment."[13]

The gradual erosion of the fishing community's psychological ability to defend itself, in conjunction with its previously successful tactic of silence and secrecy in order to preserve its lifestyle, have materially weakened its position *vis à vis* competing uses. One of the alternatives to natural resource-based adaptations is the development of tourism in areas of natural beauty. Washington state in particular has made an effort to promote the development of tourism in the latter 1980s and early 1990s.[14] However, the notion that tourism, recreation, and retirement are preservation uses that are morally correct and superior to "extractive" uses needs closer examination.

The moral issue of using wilderness is subject to extreme views. One side may say that no use should be permitted, while the other side may push for the development of all-terrain vehicle trails. Overcrowding of state and national parks is accelerating environmental degradation,[15] but denial of access to such places is almost unthinkable. In addition, private lands once available to recreational pursuits are being closed. *Oregon Wildlife* put it well:

> People who already own larger acreages [of land potentially useful for recreation] are also becoming less willing to share these lands with the public because of recurring problems with vandalism, littering and other illegal and irresponsible behavior. Access to many prime hunting areas may now carry a hefty price tag.[16]

This is the flip side of the success stories of the Texas and Montana cattle ranchers who lease access to their land to hunters.[17] Public policy in the past has tried to avoid access to recreational opportunities based on wealth, due to a strong American egalitarian ethic. As facilities become increasingly overtaxed, various forms of limited access are being proposed, with resulting ethical questions. More poignant was the comment from a resident of a small fishing community that has attracted increasing numbers of tourists due to its scenic beauty and historic charm: "Sometimes I feel as if we're living in a petting zoo."

Retirement communities are also not without their problems. Housing developments on rural lands, especially in waterfront areas, both restrict access to such areas and contribute to environmental damage in the form of storm water runoff, septic tank effluent, and loss of habitat. In addition, competition for such desirable property forces public agencies trying to purchase land for wildlife or recreational purposes to pay higher prices or forego acquisition altogether.[18]

The consequence of making the ethical choice to create a "kinder and gentler frontier," a New Frontier, without the rural adaptations upon which such areas have traditionally depended, brings its own ethical dilemmas. There is no guarantee that the New Frontier will be governed by a preservation ethic or that the land or resources preserved will be made accessible to all. In addition, rural communities looking for retirees to help retain their population base should note that many states give property tax breaks to seniors, based on age and income. In some states they are exempt from paying school and other special levies.[19]

Diminished resources for education in rural areas result in another export, this time of children. Children have been exported for some time, generally at college age. Some then return to rural areas to inherit family farms, or fishing boats, or to manage small family logging firms. A more recent export is children of grade and high school age. Rural schools face declining enrollments due to outmigration of families in search of jobs and declining funds due to waning tax dollars. These circumstances force schools to close down programs, driving brighter students to urban high schools, and compelling the less mobile to settle for a substandard education. The latter are then cycled into that other rural phenomenon, poverty, characterized by substandard medical care, lawlessness, hostility towards outsiders, and unstable family structures.[20] The mixed fishing, farming, and logging communities of the lower Columbia are already seeing the changes associated with diminished incomes. It is increasingly difficult to attract doctors to the area, so that some communities are now classed as medically underserved. Increases in the use of food stamps and medical coupons, not just among the unemployed but also the working poor, set new records during the early 1990s.

Aside from the cultural and social implications of radically changing rural America, based on moral precepts, there is also a global effect. The relationship between "extraction" and preservation needs closer examination. Will the demand for food, fish, or wood products cease? If not, where will they come from? They will come from Third World countries, already the source of much of the nation's clothing. Logging is already occurring in tropical rain forests and has moved to Russia. Beef is already imported from South America. Fish once caught in offshore and inshore fisheries by American fishers are now being taken by foreign vessels and processed in Asia. The jobs that were once the backbone of rural America are already being exported and this trend can only increase with the expansion of the New Frontier. Rural America is suffering from a decline in income as it tries to compete with Third World wage scales and put into practice the expensive environmental demands of our society. Those demands are not unrealistic. It is unrealistic, however, not to expect that someone will have to pay for them. The Third World countries that are gaining the jobs by supplying America's demand for cheap natural resources are not complying with the same environmental regulations. The hypocrisy of our society's demand for environmental concern is that we still want our commodities and necessities of life dirt cheap, so that the global ecosystem is sacrificed for the false security of the national one.

Ultimately, the question is indeed one of theology. *Newsweek*, not noted for its theological leanings, identified the issue in exactly that term:

> Those who make their living from the land are mounting their own counterattack. People for the West, a campaign launched by the Western State Public Lands Coalition, has established nearly 100 community groups to spread a pro-industry message. Many bristle at environmentalists who say they won't recognize the rights of those who mine and grow much of what the country consumes. The animosity is as much theological as it is political and economic. Many regard the harvesting of the land's resources as a calling with roots deep in Judeo-Christian tradition.[21]

The article called it "a war for the soul of the American West."[22]

The Judeo-Christian tradition also supports harvesting of the resources of the waters as a calling. New Testament tradition identifies at least seven of Jesus's disciples as fishermen. In addition, Matthew, the tax gatherer, would have been the person who granted permission to fish, and the one who collected taxes based on catches. A senior biologist with the Oregon Department of Fish and Wildlife commented recently in a private conversation, "I get the feeling that the people who are on the opposing sides of the Endangered Species listing for salmon are the environmental equivalent of abortion rights activists. Each side is convinced that it has the true faith." Must a pro-development stand negate all environmental concerns? Must a pro-environment stand eliminate all human considerations? There was a time when the Judeo-Christian tradition was the undergirding for a nation's philosophy of taming the frontier. Can this tradition be adapted to include environmental concern? Are there other traditions which are of more value in this area? Where is the place for the ethical decisions of the individual? How do the ethical decisions of the individual affect society? How does society choose to sacrifice one ethic for another?

In a 1991 workshop,[23] Lee stated that "Conservation of the ecological order is contingent upon conservation of the social and moral order."[24] In the moral order, those who exist within the "scope of justice" are treated justly. The recent campaign against high seas driftnets is an example of people being considered beyond the scope of justice. Washington congresswoman Jolene Unsoeld's letters to constituents have labelled the driftnet fishermen as "pirates" and insisted that they be halted. The possibility that the nets might be modified to eliminate by-catch was ignored. Despite the dramatic difference between high seas gear and U. S. inshore driftnets, such polemics make gillnetters everywhere uneasy, and with good reason. In 1992 proponents of a statewide initiative in Oregon that would have eliminated gillnetting on the Columbia used exactly the same terms to describe Columbia River gillnets as the opponents of high seas driftnet fisheries had used, calling them "curtains of death." The tactics used were not based on an understanding of the gear, but on targeting fishers so that they were placed outside the moral community.

A definition of a disaster is "collective stress that occurs when many members of a community fail to receive what is necessary and expected." The salmon listings under the Endangered Species Act (ESA) are just such a disaster for the fishing community, particularly along the Columbia River. Intimations of this situation have already been felt by gillnetters. Along with the ESA listings has come a concerted campaign by private and public utilities to denigrate commercial fishermen by negative stereotyping. No less a person than a chairman of the Northwest Power Planning Council stated: "I think gill nets have to go in the long run. We can't continue to allow gill nets in the lower river and expect people upriver to make sacrifices to save the fish."[25] Have we returned to the days when "a salmon head is worth a dollar, a man's head is worth nothing"? Somehow, there is a twisted sense of value and values in each of these quotations.

The numerous calls to eliminate gillnetting, either with or without compensation, and without setting the fishery into a frame of reference that includes other impacts on salmon such as dams, irrigation, dredging, development of watersheds, and environmental degradation, have tended to place fishermen outside the moral community and therefore outside the scope of justice. Quotations abound regarding harvest needing to "do its fair share," despite fisheries agencies figures indicating that over 90 percent of the endangered Snake River stocks in question are killed by hydroelectric facilities on the Columbia and Snake rivers.

The Northwest Power Planning Council held a public hearing on its proposed regional plan for helping the salmon runs in Longview, Washington, in the fall of 1991. Those attending were almost entirely from the commercial fishing community. The hearing officer publicly humiliated the fishing community representatives by querying them about technical details on water flows and regimes, subjects they were not familiar with. He ignored their real area of expertise, fishing gear. State actions, court decisions, and official conduct on salmon issues have steadily eroded the position of the fisher as a member of the wider moral community. "Time was when fishing was an honorable occupation," commented one fisherman's wife. "That's not true any more."

This shift in values has not been without its consequences on the fishing grounds. Gillnetter Bill Gunderson observed the changes taking place:

> Everybody [in past years] had a personality and they were thought of as human beings. And I've watched it, even this fall, it's rather savage. It's sort of barbaric. Watched people lay out

and they have no concern over who's there first or how close they come to somebody. The equipment allows, the technology allows them to pick up that net if they get into trouble . . . there's no sense of belonging . . . there isn't a sense of permanence. [In the past] there was a sort of guild without a written charter that if a boat, a man was broken down . . . you helped him out. It was just an unwritten law that there were certain ways that you should behave toward one another. And there was a sense of real community.[26]

The kind of humanity described by Gunderson existed in small, closely knit communities, often with strong ethnic composition, where extended families and kinship networks were important. Roles were clearly defined but within those roles there remained room for individual variation. There was a strong oral tradition so that people were connected with their past and the past of their neighbors and their community. The various communities were linked by a common occupation, gillnetting. The networks created in local communities expanded to include more distant communities, as Columbia River fishermen migrated to Puget Sound and Alaska in times of necessity.

When the Northwest Power Planning Council began development of a regional plan to protect Columbia River salmon, the hope existed that such a plan would be acceptable under the Endangered Species Act and achieve a regional consensus. Implied also was the hope of avoiding a debacle such as that which occurred with the ESA listing of the northern spotted owl. However, the process of developing this regional plan has proven to have astonishing similarities with that of the federal government in developing the spotted owl recovery plan. Both fishermen and loggers have suffered, particularly in the areas of negative stereotyping and blaming the victim. It may be that there is no way to deal with an endangered species listing without inflicting pain. But our society is deluding itself by blaming its surrogates, the fishermen and loggers, for a situation caused by its own appetite for electricity and wood products.

Due to the fluctuating and complex nature of the numerous conflicts on the Columbia River, almost anything that could be written is sure to be obsolete before publication. However, the overriding issues of marginalization and trivialization of a fishing community, and exclusion from the moral community at large, remain valid, despite the turbulence of everyday events and conflicts. Examination of several of the proposed solutions to problems encountered under the ESA illustrate the complexity of the issues and the further marginalization entailed.

One idea is simply to eliminate gillnetting on the Columbia River and come up with an alternative means for harvesting healthy stocks that will not impact endangered stocks. No such means has as yet been developed, although fish traps, currently illegal, appeal to some. Questions about who is to be allowed to use the new means of fishing access go unanswered. History tells us that gillnets were and are in use up and down the entire Pacific Coast and have outlived many other kinds of gear because they were adaptable, selective, efficient, manageable, and relatively cheap. Replacing them with gear that meets these criteria will not be simple, nor will it be instant. The Columbia River gillnet has evolved for well over a century to meet changing environmental and technical demands. Fishing communities have also changed and adapted to meet these demands. Mandating new, as yet unknown gear, has repercussions on that community.

A similar situation exists with the proposed leaseback programs, whereby a fisher's license would be leased for a period of, say, four years, and the fish he would have caught would be used to hasten replenishment of salmon runs in low abundance. The solution does not address the problems of keeping a boat operable during the interim. Nor does it address the social problems that occur when large groups of people in fishing communities are not working. Ancillary small businesses, such as gear stores, marine repair shops, and processing and buying facilities will be unable to function. The processing and buying facilities will have to locate new sources of fish to fill their markets in order to stay in business. Again, this solution does not address the community which is so vital a part of fishing.

**

This book is about a community, a community far removed from most people's world. It is a community that, despite changes, is still so tightly knit and isolated that even now, in the last years of the twentieth century, it is poorly understood. This isolation was caused originally by an accident of history, the fact that the fishery was at the western edge of frontier America, bypassed by most roads and railroads, reachable only by water. It is a community which has adapted to changing times by using the age-old techniques employed by fishing communities everywhere: develop new grounds, find ways to work together, find another fishery nearby to diversify into, find another little niche, such as a small farm or logging business, migrate for part of the year to a distant-water fishery. But what happens when there are no other fisheries to go to, when the rules collapse, when all the little economic niches are under siege, when everyone is trying to get into distant-water fisheries which now have limited entry and plenty of competition? What happens when fishing communities change into retirement communities and resort towns, sending the price of waterfront property so high that fishing families must relocate? What happens to the advocates for fish when fishing families can no longer afford to support organizations and representatives to ensure the survival of the salmon for their future? Diminished fishing seasons, with correspondingly diminished incomes, and the constant struggle for survival in allocation battles, particularly with the sport fishing lobby, have drained away much of the time, money, and energy that could have more profitably been spent on environmental issues affecting salmonids.

There are many issues that could have been addressed in this final chapter, all important and contemporary issues in gillnetting. The effect of dredging upon the life web of the Columbia River estuary could fill many pages. Recent studies documenting the effects of pollution on water quality point to serious problems.[27] Genetic issues concerning wild and hatchery salmonids are of great concern. The effect of hydroelectric projects would fill volumes. All of these issues are important in themselves. Their cumulative effect has stressed the salmon of the Columbia River to a point where recovery of the endangered runs is tenuous, and where healthy runs need only an El Niño or some other natural disaster to push them beyond the margins of safety. When all the slack is taken out of a system, the vulnerable components of that system need only a slight push to stress them beyond endurance. We as a society have stretched the natural and wonderful system upon which the salmon depend to that point, with a sort of blind optimism that somehow, despite evidence to the contrary, the fish will make it. Then nature "throws us a curve," as one gillnetter is fond of saying, and our society's folly becomes apparent. Along with it comes the collapse of the salmon fishery of the Columbia and the cultural and moral collapse of a community and a way of life.

The connection between the maintenance of biological diversity and cultural diversity is apparent in the following statement of principles from the First National Cultural Conservation Conference:

> Cultural diversity sustains and is sustained by biological diversity. Biological diversity is recognized as a critical measure of the health of ecosystems and is granted legal protection by NEPA [National Environmental Protection Act]. Cultural diversity should be recognized equally as critical to the continuing vitality of our national and global social and economic life.
>
> Human cultural diversity is a natural consequence of locally and regionally specific adaptations to the environment. There is no dichotomy between culture and nature: Therefore the protection and enhancement of cultural diversity will lead to the development of ecologically sustainable folkways.
>
> The cultural and ecological processes that connect local to regional and global levels of activity may either threaten or enhance the vitality of local bioregions: Therefore, it becomes a moral imperative to enhance as much as possible those processes and activities that contribute to cultural vitality, and, hence, diversity.
>
> Cultural diversity is continuously shaped, modified, and disrupted by global and regional economic, social and political forces that tend to favor uniformity: Therefore, it is necessary to understand and engage dominant power structures, social relations and paradigms.
>
> The empowerment of local culture groups is essential to the processes that encourage and sustain cultural vitality: Therefore, empowerment must involve advocacy, education, litigation and action-oriented research.[28]

The situation facing the gillnetters is one that faced their ancestors. They didn't come to America because they wanted to, but because they had to. They were forced out of their homelands by lack of access to fish. Many of the fishing families of the Columbia River now face the prospect of leaving the communities their ancestors created, where their families have lived for over a hundred years. They are being forced out, not because of anything they have done, but because the fish they depend on have been severely impacted by civilization in all its forms. Some are looking at Alaska or British Columbia fisheries as alternatives. Some have already left.

Among the early Finnish fishermen was a saying: "Beginning is always difficult, work is our joy, and industry overcomes bad luck."[29] Work is our joy! How many people in other occupational groups would say such a thing? Only with the recognition of the value of this unique community and a commitment by the wider society to both restore and nurture the salmon runs of the Columbia River can the Columbia River gillnetters continue to say, "Work is our joy." Within that wider society, each individual has ethical decisions to make regarding wise use of such basics as water and electricity, the things we take for granted which are life and death to the salmon. Without that individual decision of the heart, the salmon will go, and the gillnetters will also go. And the society which is left behind will be its own indictment.

Kent Martin fishes at fishdark. *Photo by Stan Chen.*

Epilogue
Drifting at Fishdark

It is nighttime and my husband and I are drifting in our gillnet boat, the *Floozie*. We are fishing for salmon on the Columbia River, perhaps for the last time. Due to endangered species listings of Snake River stocks, the likelihood of us being able to fish diminishes each season. There are still healthy runs of salmon, but they come into our part of the Columbia intermixed with the endangered.

We fall to reminiscing about past years, past seasons. "Do you remember when we fished at Three Tree Point, when the snowflakes were the size of silver dollars, drifting down in the hush and disappearing in the black water?" "Do you remember when we saw the fawn drinking from the river in Duncan's Cove?" "Do you remember when we found the stoneware beer bottle dating from the 1860s, lying on the beach at Bayview, in perfect condition?" We have it yet along with other fishing memorabilia: the sailmaker's kit, the two Swede stoves, the needles and mesh boards made by Great-grandpa.

The Fishermen's Union pennant flaps suddenly overhead in a twist of wind. To us, the gillnet is a tool, a tool upon which much time and effort is spent. The possibility that all of the tradition, the knowledge so carefully learned and painstakingly applied for so many years, will become obsolete is truly terrifying. Honesty and honor, however, leave no choice but to face that fear fully.

"Do you remember when we launched the *Floozie*?" "Do you remember the cherry tree that blooms each year in Turner's Canyon?" "Do you remember the custom and companionship of so many years, of going out together on the last day of the season to catch fish for giving away?" "Do you remember that faded poem in Swedish, given to Great-grandmother on her wedding day, the day she left Sweden, never to return?"

Like grasping a salmon it is, trying to understand this fishing life. So solid, so substantial, and you just think you have it firmly in your hand and it slips away and skates across the deck. And still we chase it, foolish but determined, searching always for rhythm in seasons, in customs, in boats, in gear, in the past, the present, but now without the future.

"Fishdark" is that period of time at dusk when fish are rising and moving. If it is raining, the pilots call it "raindark." If it is not raining, the sun goes down in reds and purples, and the water turns from bright blue to dark blue, steel blue, gold, green-gray, and finally black. All these colors are approximations, for the water gives color the qualities of clarity and subtlety that are beyond our language's capacity to describe.

We start the engine and wind in the net. A salmon comes aboard, with its watermelon smell. When the drift is done, we turn the boat upriver and head for home. "Do you remember the August nights on the Willapa, watching the shooting stars?" "Do you remember watching storms chase each other across Bristol Bay, so that it seemed that we were spinning with the universe?" "Do you remember, oh do you remember, the day when our daughters launched balloons from the boat, laughing in their delight as they let them go in the breeze?" And so we go drifting at fishdark. Remember us.

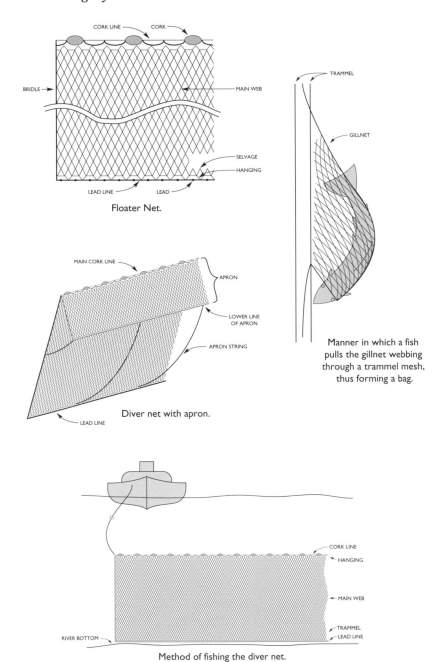

Floater Net.

Diver net with apron.

Manner in which a fish pulls the gillnet webbing through a trammel mesh, thus forming a bag.

Method of fishing the diver net.

From: Joseph Craig and Robert Hacker, The History and Development of the Fisheries of the Columbia River *(Washington, D. C.: Government Printing Office, 1940),* pp. 166-168.

Appendix: Buoyancy and Nets

Since buoyancy is the principle upon which a net's performance depends, a somewhat technical discussion of a fisherman's approach to dealing with this subject is provided here. In addition, a number of variant nets commonly found along the Columbia are described in somewhat more detail than was thought appropriate in the main body of the text. It must always be remembered that no one fisherman will do things exactly the same as another. A competent fisherman will have a grasp of the technological options available, and utilize them in order to maximize production on his individual grounds.

In order to determine how many leads or how much weight will keep the net hanging perpendicular in the water, fishermen conduct an exercise called "testing the corks." Spacing of the corks depends upon whether one is using synthetic or natural fibre lines. Synthetics do not absorb water the way a cotton line will, and therefore need more weight to hold them in the water. A piece of corkline equivalent to the length of corkline which would be used for ten corks is soaked in water and strung with ten corks. For example, if corks are centered thirty inches apart, 300 inches of corkline would be used. An equivalent amount of leadline is then taken and leads are added until the floats sink, with only one cork barely breaking water. The number of leads is then considered to be what the corks will carry. The lead mold is also important, as some will mold more than one lead on a line at a time, spaced an equal distance apart. Others will mold only one lead at a time. Lead molds vary in the thickness of line they will take and the size of the lead they make. Extra leads, called trim leads, may have to be molded or hammered on the line to achieve the right balance. Different drifts have different formulas. In some cases, as many as four leads may be added for every ten corks over what the corks will carry. On some drifts, fishermen just fish what the corks will carry. On a drift where the current is slow, a fisherman might fish even less than what the corks will carry. Water temperature also affects the buoyancy of the corks. The stage of the river (low river, high river) also makes a difference, as does the species of fish sought. A heavy net is most effective for fishing silvers, while a light net catches chinook better. In creating a combination net to catch both silvers and chinook, a fisherman aims for a middle point.

A different technique for spacing corks and regulating weight appeared in Skamokawa in the early days of diver fishing. This method, known as "hanging combinations," was considered to be more precise than the regular methods. To illustrate: suppose that one has ten corks on a corkline, with forty hangings eight inches apart. The length of line is therefore 320 inches. Ten corks pack forty-five leads, so that if one divides 320 inches by 45, a trim lead must be added to the line at every seventh regular lead. The Skamokawa method went on the premise that if ten corks pack forty-five leads, one has only forty hangings to put them on; 320 divided by 40 is eight, so that one would have forty leads, each eight inches apart. Five leads would be left over. Therefore a trim lead would be placed every eighth space.

A combination net has more than one wall of webbing, and may be either a floater or a diver. The main wall of web is called a backwall. On either or both sides of it may be another wall of web with a larger mesh size, known as a trammel. A double-trammel net, therefore, has a layer of web on each side of the backwall, while a single-trammel net has the extra layer on only one side. When the fish strikes the backwall, it may be too large to become gilled in the smaller mesh of the backwall, but it will force the backwall through the trammels to form a pocket with the layers of web and become entangled. Different sized meshes catch different sized fish. For example, an $8^{1}/_{4}$-inch mesh will catch a twenty-two pound chinook, while the smaller coho gill in a $5^{3}/_{4}$-inch mesh. A one-inch mesh is sufficient for smelt, in contrast with sturgeon which need a nine- or ten-inch mesh. State agencies may regulate the size of mesh in order to allow non-target fish to escape. An eight-inch mesh will capture chinook salmon, for example, while allowing the smaller steelhead to go through. The single-trammel backwall has the advantage of being better for daylight fishing, especially in semi-clear water. There is also less upkeep in terms of mending, and it is easier to remove sticks and other debris from these than the double-trammel net.

A variant on the aprons discussed in the body of the text is the balloon apron. A balloon apron has a trammel on one side, the inside, next to the backwall. The web thus balloons up in the water. The fish approaches the backwall and may sense an eddy near it. It backs away and swims upwards, trying to find a way over the obstruction, and gets caught in the apron. To be effective, the apron should be fishing shallower than the backwall, although this varies among different drifts. Some nets have single-trammel aprons, with the trammel on the outside, while some even had double-trammel aprons, with trammels on both sides. The latter are very heavy to use and difficult for the fisherman to regulate, pushing the gillnet technology to its furthest limits. Another feature that was occasionally used was a slacker, which can best be described as an apron on an apron.

Smelt fishermen developed a unique net known as the "bobber net." It is fished in areas where smelt have bogged down, that is, have ceased moving upstream, generally due to cold water conditions. It is employed when a diver net cannot be used due to snags, or when smelt are not on the bottom of the water column. It is slightly negative in buoyancy, so that it will sink, and has bobber strings attached to the corkline on one end and to a ring of floats, such as bleach jugs, on the other. The floats or jugs are thrown out as the net is being laid out in the water. The strings are the length which corresponds to the depth the fisherman wants the net to fish. This kind of net is fished on the slow ebb and sometimes on low water. Occasionally a floater net was fished for smelt but it was large and a large shed or dock area was needed to shake the smelt out. If the net became loaded down with smelt the weight could sink a boat. The smelt drag is another form of gear occasionally fished by gillnetters. Developed in the late 1960s and early 1970s by the National Marine Fisheries Service, it is an effective piece of gear under cold water conditions when the smelt are bogged down in deep water. The dipnet fishery of the tributaries, however, remains the single most effective fishery for smelt, as large volumes can be dipped in relatively short periods of time and the difficulty of removing the fish from the net is avoided.

Shad nets were generally of $5^1/_2$ to $5^3/_8$-inch mesh in a single-walled floater. They generally provided an ancillary income to fishermen. Sturgeon nets were fished in deep holes where there were likely to be snags. As a consequence, they needed a very heavy leadline in order to prevent the net from moving much and getting torn. The net was laid out at low water when the tide had stopped moving, and was fished on the flood. It was picked up at high water. On very small tides it could be fished on the ebb. Sturgeon nets had large meshes, from nine to eleven inches.

The change from the Columbia River bowpicker to vessels that used a reel to lay out or pull in a net caused a number of significant gear changes. It hastened the switch to synthetic twines, as the racking and bluestoning processes needed to keep natural fibres in good condition were harder to accomplish with a reel. Synthetic twines, however, brought some problems with them. Under strain, the knots in the web may pull, creating warped or draw meshes. Alternatively, if the meshes do not draw, they may pull so tightly that the knot is weakened. Cotton and linen twine would abrade under strain, but synthetic twines tend to cut off in a sharp bend or knot if they are set too tightly. Sunlight can cause them to deteriorate, so keeping a net under cover when not in use will add to the longevity of the gear. Reels created the necessity for grommeted foam floats, which would best withstand the higher pressure generated when pulling a net onto a reel, and discouraged the use of plastic floats with their higher incidence of cracking and crushing. The levelwind was invented in order to guide the net evenly onto the reel, but even so, there is skill needed in winding net onto each side of the reel so that it builds up on each side and helps avoid backlashes. Trammel gear is becoming less common, as the trammels are more difficult to handle on the reel, and are being replaced by strings to build slack into the net.

Endnotes

Abbreviations Used in the Endnotes

CRFPU: Columbia River Fishermen's Protective Union
CRMM: Columbia River Maritime Museum, Astoria, Oregon
CRPA: Columbia River Packer's Association
OHS: Oregon Historical Society, Portland, Oregon

Notes for Chapter One

1. Interview with Oliver Dunsmoor by Jim Bergeron, Nov. 2, 1988, p. 6, CRMM.
2. *Grays River Builder*, June 26, 1936, p. 8.
3. *Ibid.*, p. 8.
4. "Power Applied to Lifting Gillnets," *Pacific Fisherman*, 29: 5 (April 1931): 37.
5. Interview with Arthur Peterson by Kent Martin, Dec. 7, 1989, pp. 4-6, CRMM.
6. For a good brief summary of conflicts among user groups, see Courtland Smith's *Fish or Cut Bait* (Corvallis, Ore.: Oregon State University, 1977), pp. 16-19. Also see Henry Wendler, *Regulation of Commercial Fishing Gear and Seasons on the Columbia River from 1859 to 1963*, vol. 2, no. 4 (Olympia: Washington Department of Fisheries, Fisheries Research Papers, 1966), pp. 19-31; and *Report of the Commissioner of Fish and Fisheries on Investigations in the Columbia River Basin in Regard to the Salmon Fisheries* (Washington, D. C.: U. S. Government Printing Office, 1894).
7. "Log of the Chenamus," April 26 and 27, 1844, John H. Couch Collection, OHS, Mss. 952B.
8. James Birnie Accounts, OHS, Mss. 920.
9. Joseph Craig and Robert Hacker, *The History and Development of the Fisheries of the Columbia River* (Washington, D. C.: U. S. Government Printing Office, 1940), p. 149.
10. William Wood, "H & B Seining Grounds," *Columbia County History*, 5 (1966): 39.
11. Craig and Hacker, *History and Development of the Fisheries of the Columbia River*, p. 165; Wood, "H & B Seining Grounds," p. 39; *Morning Oregonian*, May 26, 1890, p. 4.

12. Wood, "H & B Seining Grounds," p. 39.
13. Anon., "William Hume," *Columbia County History*, 12 (1973): 51.
14. Anon., "The First Salmon Cannery," *Pacific Fisherman*, 16: 3 (March 1918): 53.
15. *Ibid.*
16. Robert D. Hume, *Salmon of the Pacific Coast* (San Francisco: Schmidt Label and Lithograph, 1893), p. 15.
17. See, for example, the U.S. Fish Commission Report of 1872-73, pp. 589-629, for descriptions of obstructions to the ascent of salmon in east coast rivers. Likewise, William Kendall's study, *The Fishes of New England: The Salmon Family*, vol. 9, no. 1 (Memoirs of the Boston Society of Natural History, 1935), contains detailed notes of the fisheries and obstacles to the fisheries of the New England rivers. A more recent study is that by Anthony Netboy, *The Salmon: Their Fight for Survival* (Boston: Houghton Mifflin, 1973).
18. L. R. Williams, *Our Pacific County* (Raymond, Wash.: Raymond Herald, 1930), p. 92.
19. Arthur McEvoy, *The Fisherman's Problem* (Cambridge: Cambridge University Press, 1986), p. 70.
20. Emma Adams, "Salmon Canning in Oregon," *Bulletin of the U. S. Fish Commission*, (1885): 362.
21. McEvoy, *The Fisherman's Problem*, p. 70.
22. *Ibid.*, p. 75. See also "Early Chinese Fishermen," in *National Fisherman*, October 1988 (p. 4 of West Coast Focus insert); Robert Spier, "Food Habits of the 19th Century California Chinese," *California Historical Society Quarterly*, (March 1958): 79-85; (June 1958): 12.
23. U. S. Commission of Fish and Fisheries, *Report of the Commissioner for 1881* (Washington, D. C.: U. S. Government Printing Office, 1892), pp. 220-221.
24. Peter Crawford, "Cowlitz Journal," *Daily News* (Longview, Wash.) Oct. 13, 1952, p. 2, is a journal account of conditions on the Columbia River, written in 1866.
25. C. G. Atkins, "The River Fisheries of Maine," in George Brown Goode, *The Fisheries and Fishery Industries of the U. S.* (Washington, D. C.: U. S. Government Printing Office, 1887), p. 679.
26. "The First Salmon Cannery," p. 53.
27. Robert D. Hume, "The Evolution of the Salmon Popagation [sic] Problem," *Pacific Fisherman*, 6: 1 (Jan. 1908): 25.
28. *Ibid.*
29. *Oregonian*, March 10, 1868, p. 2.
30. Dale Johnson, "Alexander Abernethy; His Political Life and Times," *Cowlitz County Historical Quarterly*, 17: 4 (Feb. 1976): 2.
31. Hume, "Evolution of the Salmon Popagation Problem," p. 25.
32. Robert D. Hume, *A Pygmy Monopolist; The Life and Doings of R. D. Hume, Written by Himself and Dedicated to His Neighbors*, ed. by Gordon Dodds (Madison, Wisc.: State Historical Society of Wisconsin, 1961), p. 41.
33. *Tri-Weekly Astorian*, Nov. 29, 1873, p. 2.
34. *Report of the Commissioner of Fish and Fisheries for 1875-76* (Washington, D. C.: U. S. Government Printing Office, 1878), p. 811.
35. Reprinted in *Daily Astorian*, March 20, 1878, p. 2.
36. Anon., *The Fishermen's Own Book* (Gloucester, Mass.: Procter Bros., 1882), p. 119.

37. W. A. Jones, *Salmon Fisheries of the Columbia* (Washington, D. C.: U. S. Government Printing Office, 1887), p. 33.
38. Data from Columbia River Packers Association, Inc. summary from U. S. Engineer's Gauge, Portland, Oregon. Copy loaned to author from private collection.
39. Hume, *A Pygmy Monopolist*, p. 35.
40. As quoted in the *Cathlamet Gazette*, April 30, 1897, p. 4.
41. Clark Spurlock, "A History of the Salmon Industry in the Pacific Northwest" (unpublished master's thesis, University of Oregon, 1940), p. 75.
42. *Cathlamet Gazette*, Dec. 18, 1891, p. 3
43. Craig and Hacker, *History and Development of the Fisheries of the Columbia River*, also report on sturgeon nets, but do not make it clear whether the nets were of the diver or floater kind at this time.
44. *Ibid.*, pp. 205-206.
45. *Skamokawa Eagle*, Feb. 6, 1896, p. 4; July 23, 1903, p. 4.
46. *Ibid.*, June 11, 1908, p. 4.
47. Katherine Ytredal to the author, Oct. 23, 1976.
48. C.R.P.A./ Bumble Bee Seafoods Collection, 85.55.714, CRMM.
49. Anon. "Diver Nets on the Columbia," *Pacific Fisherman*, 18: 2 (Feb. 1920): 46.
50. As quoted in Smith, *Fish or Cut Bait*, p. 37.
51. W. H. Barker, "Reminiscences of the Salmon Industry," *Pacific Fisherman Yearbook*, (Jan. 1920): 67.
52. Charles Carey, *General History of Oregon* (Portland: Binfords and Mort, 1971), p. 696.
53. For the flax industry see John S. Hittell, *The Commerce and Industries of the Pacific Coast* (San Francisco: A. L. Bancroft, 1882), p. 284. In 1897 the Oregon Agricultural Station printed a report entitled *Flax Culture in Oregon*, an indication that the growing of flax was worthy of some attention. The entire issue of the *Oregon Magazine*, 26: 1 (1931) was devoted to the flax industry of Oregon.
54. C.R.P.A./Bumble Bee Collection, 85.55.1172, CRMM.
55. *Pacific Fisherman*, 15:6 (June 1919): 26.
56. Lillie Madsen, "Astoria Fishermen Find Winter Tasks," *Sunday Oregonian*, Feb. 2, 1930, section 6, p. 2.
57. Murray Wade, "Right Angles," *Oregon Magazine*, 26: 1 (Jan. 1931): 32.
58. C.R.P.A./ Bumble Bee Seafoods Collection, letter dated Jan. 6, 1927, 85.55.1170, CRMM.
59. Hugh Smith, "Notes on a Reconnaissance of the Fisheries of the Pacific Coast of the U.S. in 1894," *Bulletin of the U. S. Fish Commission* (1894): 245. Prior to 1893 fishermen were paid so much per fish, regardless of size, although it took two fish under twenty-two pounds to count as one full-sized fish. Once fish were purchased by weight, total poundage was important, rather than individual fish size, and fishermen could then choose to use smaller-meshed gear to catch smaller fish.
60. *Astoria Budget*, Feb. 13, 1922, p. 1.
61. *Skamokawa Eagle*, Feb. 18, 1922, p. 4.
62. Compare to John Cobb, "Pacific Coast Fishing Methods," in *Pacific Fisherman Yearbook*, (Jan. 1916): 20, and Carl Wick, *Ocean Harvest* (Seattle: Superior Publishing Co., 1946), pp. 70-72.

63. Interview with Elmer Hurula by Jim Bergeron, Nov. 23, 1988, p. 14, CRMM.
64. Information regarding gear changes was summarized in Henry Wendler, *Regulation of Commercial Fishing Gear and Seasons on the Columbia River from 1859 to 1963*, p. 25.

Notes for Chapter Two

1. For further information on the early Columbia River salmon trade see the following items: Alfred Lomax, "Hawaii-Columbia River Trade in Early Days," *Oregon Historical Quarterly*, 43: 3 (Sept. 1942): 328-338; Samuel Morison, "New England and the Opening of the Columbia River Salmon Trade, 1830," *Oregon Historical Quarterly*, 28: 2 (June 1927): 111-132; Hubert Howe Bancroft, *History of the Pacific States of North America*, vol. 25, *Oregon*, vol. 2 (San Francisco: The History Company, 1880), pp. 730-731; Clark Spurlock, "History of the Salmon Industry in the Pacific Northwest" (unpublished master's thesis, University of Oregon, 1940), pp. 102-111.
2. Copy of testimony taken in 1902 at Astoria in support of a claim of the Chinook Indian Tribe against the U. S. for land in the State of Washington near the mouth of the Columbia River, pp. 7-40. Typescript in Astor Library, Astoria, Oregon.
3. Jack Edwards, unpublished summary of canneries and packers on the Columbia River, p. 4. Typescript provided to author.
4. Astoria Customs House records given in the *Tri-Weekly Astorian*, Nov. 29, 1873, p. 2, show substantial shipments of salt fish along with canned salmon.
5. Robert Hume, *A Pygmy Monopolist; The Life and Doings of R. D. Hume*, ed. by Gordon Dodds (Madison: State Historical Society of Wisconsin, 1961), p. 3.
6. Jack Edwards summary, p. 6.
7. Matti Kaups, "Norwegian Immigrants and the Development of Commercial Fisheries Along the North Shore of Lake Superior, 1870-1895," in *Norwegian Influence on the Upper Midwest; Proceedings of an International Conference, University of Minnesota, May 22-24, 1975*, ed. by Harald Naess (Duluth, Minn.: Continuing Education and Extension, University of Minnesota, 1976), p. 24.
8. *Ibid.*, pp. 21-23.
9. J. L. McDonald, *Hidden Treasures or Fisheries Around the Northwest Coast* (Gloucester, Mass.: Proctor Bros., 1871), p. 8.
10. Anon., *The Fishermen's Own Book* (Gloucester, Mass.: Proctor Bros., 1882).
11. No publisher is given for this pamphlet, but there is a notation that the statistics were selected from the *Astorian* of January 6, 1877.
12. Anon., *Columbia River Illustrated* (Portland, Ore.: L. Samuel, Publisher, ca. 1880).
13. Cleveland Rockwell, "The Columbia River," *Harper's New Monthly Magazine*, 66: 391 (Dec. 1882): 3-14.
14. Vera Laska, *The Czechs in America, 1633-1977* (Dobbs Ferry, N. Y.: Oceana Publications, 1978), p. 31.
15. Akseli Jarnefelt, *Suomalaiset Amerikassa* (?, Finland: n. p., 1899).
16. For information on the various expositions held during this period, consult the annual reports of the U. S. Commissioner for Fisheries.
17. Erick Martin was the great-grandfather of the author's husband, Kent Martin. Erick Martin's father was Tollef Tollefson, a fisherman from Avaldness

parish, baptized February 10, 1799. Erick Martin's mother was Ane Margrethe Tobiasdatter, who had come to Stavanger from the town of Farsund in 1839. She was born about 1810, the daughter of Tobias Jensen, a skipper. Various spellings of Erick Martin's wife's name (Anna Marie Johansdatter) appear in the family records.

18. *Skamokawa Eagle*, Jan. 2, 1908, p. 4. John Strom was the author's husband's great-grandfather.
19. Howard Furer, *The Scandinavians in America, 986-1970* (Dobbs Ferry, N. Y.: Oceana Publications, 1972), p. 44.
20. Arnold Berwick, "Norwegian Mountain Farms Then and Now," *Sons of Norway Viking*, (July 1988): 252-255, 275.
21. Karl Dambeck, "Geographical Distribution of the Gadidae or the Cod Family, in its Relation to Fisheries and Commerce," U. S. Commission of Fish and Fisheries, *Report of the Commissioner for 1877* (Washington, D. C.: U. S. Government Printing Office, 1879), p. 555.
22. Anon., "An Account of the Loffoden Islands of Norway," *Ibid.*, p. 563.
23. See interview with Hank Ramvick by Jim Bergeron, Oct. 25, 1988, p. 2, CRMM. For a description of the cod fishery, M. Friehle's "An Account of the Fisheries of Norway in 1877" in the *Report of the Commissioner of Fish and Fisheries for 1876-1877* (Washington, D. C.: U. S. Government Printing Office, 1879), pp. 712-733, gives specific gear types and biological characteristics of the species sought.
24. Anon., "Emden Joint-Stock Herring-Fishery Association," *Report of the Commissioner of Fish and Fisheries for 1876-1877*, p. 759.
25. Alfred Apsler, "Puget Island, Smorgasbord Paradise," *Seattle Times*, July 31, 1955, p. 5.
26. Dr. Ivan Cizmic, "Croatian Emigration to the United States," as quoted by Mary Ann Petrich and Barbara Roje, *The Yugoslav in Washington State: Among the Early Settlers* (Tacoma: Washington State Historical Society, 1984), p. 3.
27. Carl Peyrer, "Fish and Fishery Laws in Austria and of the World in General," *Report of the Commissioners for Fisheries, 1873-74* (Washington, D. C.: U. S. Government Printing Office, 1876), p. 660.
28. *Ibid.*, p. 661. In 1869 in Silesia, a report stated: "In many waters, everybody is allowed to fish; in some, the community is considered to possess this right, without its being clear whether it possesses it as a corporation, or whether it merely means that any person belonging to such community has the right to fish; sometimes the mayor of a village is mentioned as the privilege-holder, or the clergyman, or some landed proprietor; the fisheries are mostly considered as belonging to the former proprietors of the lands, among them the cities; and, in other cases, the privilege is said to belong to the inhabitants of the banks and occasionally to these and to everybody."
29. *Ibid.*, p. 669.
30. Anthony Netboy, *The Salmon: Their Fight for Survival* (Boston: Houghton Mifflin, 1973), p. 136.
31. Laska, *The Czechs in America*, p. 31.
32. Petrich and Roje, *The Yugoslav in Washington State*, p. 3.
33. Carlton Appelo, *Brookfield* (Deep River, Wash.: Western Wahkiakum Telephone Company, 1966), pp. 24-27.
34. Wahkiakum County Probate Records, Roll 1, 1864-1910, Ref. 31, Wahkiakum County Courthouse, Cathlamet, Wash.

35. Interview with John Vlastelica by Jim Bergeron, c. 1988, p. 4, CRMM.
36. James Weaver, "The Sea Fisheries of Austro-Hungary from 1877 to 1883," *Report of the Commissioner of Fish and Fisheries for 1883* (Washington, D. C.: U. S. Government Printing Office, 1885), p. 1197.
37. David Nicandri, *Italians in Washington State: Emigration, 1853-1924* (n. p.: Washington State American Revolution Bicentennial Commission, 1978), p. 8.
38. *The Fishermen's Own Book*, pp. 117-118.
39. Sue Bysen, *Some Historical Highlights of the History of Pittsburg* (n. p.: n. p., 1964), pp. 3-4. See also a brief reference in John Kemble's *San Francisco Bay: A Pictorial Maritime History* (Cambridge, Mass.: Cornell Maritime Press, 1957), p. 100.
40. Achille Costa, "On the Fisheries of the Gulf of Naples," *Report of the Commissioner of Fish and Fisheries for 1876-77* (Washington, D. C.: U. S. Government Printing Office, 1879), p. 139.
41. *The Fishermen's Own Book*, p. 119; Charlene Perry, et al., *Martinez; A California Town* (Martinez, Cal.: RSI Pubs., 1981), p. 75.
42. Jack London, *Tales of the Fish Patrol* (New York: Grosset and Dunlap, 1905).
43. Carlton Appelo, *Cottardi* (Deep River, Wash.: Western Wahkiakum Telephone Company, 1980), tells the story of an Italian immigrant fisherman on the Columbia.
44. Michael Passi, "Fishermen on Strike: Finnish Workers and Community Power in Astoria, Oregon, 1880-1900," in *The Finnish Experience in the Western Great Lakes Region: New Perspectives*, ed. by Michael Karni, Matti Kaups, and Douglas Ollila (Vamilla, Finland: Institute for Migration, 1975), p. 94.
45. Carlton Appelo, *Deep River* (Deep River, Wash.: Western Wahkiakum Telephone Company, 1978).
46. Edgar Davis and Charlotte Davis, *They Remembered, Book II* (Ilwaco: Pacific Printing, 1983), p. 100. See also Merle Reinikka, *Ilwaco's Early Finns, Pacific County, Washington* (Portland, Ore.: Finnish American Historical Society of the West, Special Reports Series, 1992). Entire issue of vol. 20, no. 1, Jan. 1992 contains much original research on the life of B. A. Seaborg, which Merle Reinikka was gracious enough to share with me before publication.
47. Jarnefelt, *Suomalaiset Amerikassa*, pp. 208-209.
48. William Hoglund, *Finnish Immigrants in America, 1880-1920* (New York: Arno Press, 1979), pp. 7-15.
49. I am indebted to Merle Reinikka for obtaining a translation of Jarnefelt's *Suomalaiset Amerikassa*, p. 196, for me.
50. June Egstad, "Thompson Family History," June 1988, pp. 1-12. Typescript in author's possession.
51. Nicandri, *Italians in Washington State*, p. 31.
52. Courtland Smith, *Fish or Cut Bait* (Corvallis: Oregon State University, n.d.), p. 5.
53. *The Fishermen's Own Book*, p. 119.
54. For an indication of community ethnic background see the *U. S. Directory of Commercial Fishermen* (New York: U. S. Seafood Reporter and Commercial Fisherman, 1907), which contains listings of individual fishermen by community.
55. *Daily Astorian*, May 4, 1876, p. 2.
56. Reproduced in facsimile in *Columbia River Gillnetter*, 6: 1 (Feb. 1975): 4-5.
57. John Hittell, *The Commerce and Industries of the Pacific Coast* (San Francisco: A. L. Bancroft, 1882), p. 371.

58. *Daily Astorian*, May 27, 1879, p. 3.
59. *Ibid.*, p. 3.
60. *Columbia River Fishermen's Protective Union* (Astoria, Ore.: C. W. Snyder, 1890), p. 14.
61. *Ibid.*, p. 16.
62. Thomas Hatley, "Efficiency in Oregon's Commercial Salmon Fisheries: A Historical Perspective" (unpublished master's thesis, Oregon State University, 1975), p. 32.
63. Paul George Hummasti, *Finnish Radicals in Astoria, 1904-1940: A Study in Immigrant Socialism* (New York: Arno Press, 1979), pp. 200-211, gives a description of unsuccessful attempts to organize gillnetters.
64. J. Smith and A. Kornberg, "Some Considerations Bearing Upon Research in Canada and the United States," *Sociology*, 3 (1969): 342, as cited in Joan Vincent, "The Structuring of Ethnicity," *Human Organization*, 33: 4 (1974): 376.
65. Interview with Vlastelicia, p. 6.
66. *Columbia River Fishermen's Protective Union*, pp. 16-17.
67. *Ibid.*, p. 18.

Notes for Chapter Three

1. Interview with Kent Martin by Irene Martin, Dec. 30, 1992.
2. A description of the twine is found in Emma Adams's account, "Salmon Canning in Oregon," *Bulletin of the U.S. Fish Commission*, 5 (1885): 364. The best material for a salmon net is Barbour's twine, made at Paterson, New Jersey. Such is the strength of this twine that a single thread will sustain a strain of 160 pounds. The cord is made of Irish flax, imported dressed only, and therefore duty free. Brought over in the form of twine, an impost of 40 percent is levied. The cord must be exceedingly pliable, else the sensitive salmon will not enter the net. It is therefore made very slack-twisted, a single turn of the spindle being given to an inch of the thread. Twelve subordinate threads compose the twine. Two hundred pounds of twine construct an ordinary net forty-five meshes deep, each mesh nine inches square.
3. Merle Reinikka, personal communication with author, 1991.
4. Interview with Jack Marincovich by Jim Bergeron, Nov. 2, 1988, p. 8, CRMM.
5. Interview with Georgia Maki by Jim Bergeron, n. d., p. 43, CRMM.
6. *Skamokawa Eagle*, April 25, 1895, p. 1.
7. Interview with Hank Ramvick by Jim Bergeron, Oct. 25, 1988, p. 51, CRMM.
8. "It was made like a torpedo more or less and you spliced a line in on the front sharp end and then you hollowed it out and then so these two batteries would fit in it and you wired it up to a little socket on top and you had a glass over that socket and you used these little light globes–they were made for these small batteries, and then you had a boat iron over the glass and those batteries would last about three months. That was the light you had on the end of your nets." Interview with Cecil Moberg by Jim Bergeron, Oct. 24, 1988, p. 29, CRMM.
9. Interview with Elmer Hurula by Jim Bergeron, Nov. 23, 1988, pp. 19-20, CRMM.
10. Julia Butler Hansen, *Cathlamet Pioneer, The Paintings of Maude Kimball Butler* (Tacoma, Wash.: Washington State Historical Society, 1973), p. 36.

11. The father and brother of Cecil Moberg had the last float mill in the North-west. "My dad treated his first floats with coal tar . . . and it got hard, but they soaked water . . . you had to get them up every week and dry them in the sun. . . . [At their float mill] they treated them with paraffin. They . . . put them in a pressure tank and they put 100 floats in this tank and then they would put so many pounds of paraffin in there and with 100 pound air pressure, they'd put that paraffin in there. . . . And they never soaked water, no never soaked water after that." Moberg interview, p. 18.

12. Interview with Arthur Peterson by Kent Martin, Dec. 1989, pp. 19-20, CRMM.

13. Interview with Bill Gunderson by Jim Bergeron, Dec. 16, 1988, pp. 9-10, CRMM.

14. Bent Thygesen introduced the idea that the diver net may have developed along the lines of a similar net used on the Drammen River in southeastern Norway in 1784: "This fishery is carried out by two men in a boat. One rows, the other fishes. The man who does the fishing holds the net in one end by a rope about 20 feet in length, depending on the depth of the river, so that the net can reach the bottom. A wooden block with a rope of equal length holds up the far end. After first the block and then the net are thrown out, they drift with the boat on the current until the wooden block begins to move up and down. This is a sign that there are salmon in the net and it alerts the fisher-man to pull in the net." See "Cultural Crisis on the Columbia," in *Socio-Economics of the Idaho, Washington, Oregon and California Coho and Chinook Salmon Industry, Final Report to the Pacific Fishery Management Council by the Department of Agricultural and Resource Economics* (Corvallis, Ore.: Oregon State University, 1978), vol. A, p. 137. The following citations all support the view that placement of gear at different levels in the water column, and building in slack by means of trammels or strings, were adapta-tions found in the countries of origin of the Columbia River gillnetters: James W. Milner, "Report on the Fisheries of the Great Lakes; The Result of Inquir-ies Prosecuted in 1871 and 1872" in *Report of the Commission of Fish and Fisheries, 1872 and 1873* (Washington, D. C.: U. S. Government Printing Office, 1874), pp. 1-75; Captain J. W. Collins, "Gill-nets in the Cod Fisheries: A Description of Norwegian Cod-nets, etc., and a History of their Use in the United States," in *Report of the Commissioner of Fish and Fisheries, 1884* (Washington, D. C.: U. S. Government Printing Office, 1886); J. Geraint Jenkins, *Nets and Coracles* (London: David and Charles, 1974); and W. A. Carrothers, *The British Columbia Fisheries* (Toronto: University of Toronto Press, 1941).

15. Ramvick interview, p. 2.

16. Interview with Eldon Korpela by Jim Bergeron and Larry Johnson, n.d., pp. 1, 4, CRMM.

17. Moberg interview, pp. 27, 11.

18. Interview with Ross Lindstrom, Jerry Alto video, April 9, 1988, pp. 13-14, CRMM.

19. Moberg interview, p. 7.

20. *Ibid.*, pp. 6-7.

21. Interview with Edward Rasmussen by David Lee Myers, Nov. 18, 1975 (Olym-pia: Washington State Archives), p. 18.

22. Interview with Don Riswick by Jim Bergeron, n.d., p. 58, CRMM.

23. Interview with Cecil Moberg by Jim Bergeron, Nov. 10, 1988, p. 10, CRMM.

24. Gunderson interview, pp. 40-41.

Notes for Chapter Four

1. Interview with Wilmer and Stella Johnson by Kent and Irene Martin, n. d., Tape 60, p. 4, CRMM.
2. *Columbia River Sun*, Aug. 22, 1929, p. 8.
3. Interview with Ross Lindstrom, April 9, 1988, p. 8, CRMM.
4. Walter Wicks, "The Early Gillnet Fishermen," in *Pioneer Days in British Columbia*, vol. 2, ed. by Art Downs (Surrey, B. C.: Heritage House, 1975-1979), pp. 78-79.
5. Joan Skogan, *Skeena: A River Remembered* (Vancouver: B. C. Packers Ltd., 1983), p. 75.
6. Gladys Young Blyth, *Salmon Canneries: B. C. North Coast* (Lentzville, B. C.: Oolichan Books, 1991), p. 69.
7. G. E. Mortimore, "Samson V is Chugging Toward Oblivion," in *Vancouver Sun*, Oct. 2, 1980, p. A5. Other information regarding B. C. snag vessels was found in the *Mercantile Navy List*, 1937, 1947, and 1976, published in London, England, and the *List of Shipping*, 1976, published by the Canadian Department of Transport.
8. *Vancouver Sun*, Oct. 2, 1980, p. A5. The *Daily Columbian* (New Westminster), July 3, 1894 noted:

   > Snags are at all times dangerous, but this one is especially so, being nearly seventy feet in length, all of which, with the exception of some twelve feet, being submerged, and terminating four feet above the water line, in a formidable looking point, which would penetrate any steamer plying on the Fraser having the misfortune to run against it. . . . While on this subject do the authorities not intend to remove the many snags which have been brought downstream by the recent high water? Their name is legion and they seem to be deposited in every place that a fisherman can "throw" his net. They (the fishermen), being the chief sufferers, are moving in the matter, and a petition is being circulated amongst them for signature; but from the fact of the men being so scattered, and having to be reached by rowboat, slow progress is made. In the meantime, the great sockeye run is approaching, the advance guard being due in two weeks. So, to be of much benefit, the work of removal should begin at once; otherwise the destruction of nets will be immense. The Samson will have all she can do to clear away the offenders in the time intervening.

   Today the *Samson* V is a floating museum in New Westminster, British Columbia.
9. Personal communication, Kit Helsley to author, n. d.
10. Interview with Harold Oblad by Bruce Weilepp, June 17, 1988, CRMM.
11. Interview with Dean Badger by Irene Martin, April 5, 1986.
12. *Daily Astorian*, Nov. 6, 1877, p. 1.
13. *Astoria Evening Budget*, March 6, 1918, p. 1. Sample news items regarding snagging are found in the *Skamokawa Eagle*, April 30, 1896, p. 4; Oct. 11, 1906; June 11, 1908; and the *Cathlamet Gazette*, June 14, 1895, p. 6.
14. Various entries in the C.R.F.P.U. minutes indicate problems with snags such as trap piles, wrecks, and beacons. See Minutes, Central Board, April 15, 1887, pp. 12-13; Minutes, C.R.F.P.U. June 13, 1891, p. 278; May 21, 1892,

pp. 284-285; March 5, 1899, pp. 125-126; correspondence May 11, 1893, pp. 78-79; June 17, 1895, p. 187; June 23, 1895, p. 137. All located in C.R.F.P.U. office files, Astoria.

15. "Fish and Fishing," April 24, 1891, source unidentified, clipping found in scrapbook compiled by George H. George, CRMM.

16. William Willingham, *Army Engineers and the Development of Oregon* (Washington, D. C.: U. S. Government Printing Office, 1983), p. 192.

17. Paul DeLaney, *Toilers of the Columbia*, a novel serialized in the *Skamokawa Eagle*, Oct. 6, 1904 to Jan. 5, 1905. Chapters 13 and 14 contain the heart of the struggle. The whole novel may be read as a *roman à clef*, as a number of the figures are identifiable with figures in the fishery at the time.

18. "Fish and Fishing."

19. Wilmer and Stella Johnson interview, Tape 58, p. 7.

20. Letter from H. J. McGraw, Jan 21, 1926 to Columbia River Packers Association, in C.R.P.A./ Bumble Bee Seafoods Collection, 85: 55: 815, CRMM.

21. Letter from C.R.P.A. to H. J. McGraw, Jan. 22, 1926. In C.R.P.A./ Bumble Bee Seafoods Collection, 85: 55: 815, CRMM.

22. *Cathlamet Gazette*, Sept. 20, 1895.

23. Articles of Incorporation of Woody Island Gillnet Fishermen's Co-operative Association, Clatsop County Courthouse, Astoria, Ore.

24. Copy of drift bylaws in author's possession.

25. Interview with Edward Rasmussen by David Myers, Nov. 18, 1975 (Olympia: Washington State Archives), p. 10.

26. *Ibid.*, pp. 12-13, p. 7.

27. *Sunday Oregonian*, Aug. 14, 1977, p. D3.

28. Interview with Paul Starkey by Irene Martin, March 9, 1986.

29. Lindstrom interview, pp. 8-10.

30. *Ibid.*, p. 10. An inventory found in Cowlitz County Courthouse (Inventory and Appraisement, Estate of Roger Risley, No. 1724) indicated that in 1928 a helmet-type diving outfit was appraised at $200. At the same time, a twenty-four-foot boat with a five horsepower engine was valued at $150 and a pile-driver at $300 (Risley probate). While these values cannot easily be compared with those of today, it is significant that a diving outfit was inventoried along with such major capital expenses as a boat and pile driver.

31. Interview with Don Riswick by Jim Bergeron, c. 1988, Tape 35, p. 10, CRMM.

32. *Ibid.*, Tape 37, p. 60.

33. 1941 Agreement between the Fishermen of the Columbia River Gillnet Fishermen's Union; and the Salmon Packers, April 14, 1941, p. 1, both in author's possession.

34. *Sunday Oregonian*, Aug. 14, 1977, p. D3

35. Complaint filed in the Circuit Court, State of Oregon, Clatsop County, Aug. 5, 1970. In their original complaint Clifton fishermen sued Crown Zellerbach Corporation, alleging that:

> In the fall of 1969 commercial fishing in the area of the Clifton drift was opened on Sept. 15, 1969 under regulations of the State of Oregon; that at some time prior to Sept. 15, 1969, defendant moved a log raft consisting of a number of logs which did not have sufficient buoyancy to float through and over and across said Clifton drift and in particular through that portion of the Clifton drift designated as the Manhattan drift. That a number of logs were lost from the raft in the

Manhattan drift area. That the number and location of said logs were such as to prevent the use of gillnets in the area. . . . That upon determining that defendant would take no further action to remove its logs from said drift area, plaintiffs commenced the removal of defendant's logs; that plaintiffs finally succeeded in clearing said drift area of defendant's logs on October 10, 1969.

36. In 1985 the Wahkiakum County Planning Commission, at the request of the Westport Drift, asked the Wahkiakum Board of County Commissioners to request the Washington Department of Natural Resources to hold a public hearing regarding log storage areas along Coffeepot Island adjacent to the drift. Letter from Don Mathison, Planner, Wahkiakum County Planning Commission, Mar. 29, 1985 to Wahkiakum County Board of Commissioners, Wahkiakum County Courthouse, Cathlamet, Washington.

37. Ruth Kaste, "Gillnetters Complain About Sand Bars, Sunken Logs," in *Daily News* (Longview, Wa.), Aug. 22, 1987, p. A3.

38. Riswick interview, Tape 37, p. 59.

39. Interview with Edward Rasmussen by David Myers, July 30, 1975 (Olympia: Washington State Archives), p. 7.

40. A corroboration of these observations from the logger point of view may be found in *Logging the Way I Seen It*, a video production chronicling the lives of the Hobi family, loggers for several generations. Among other points, in the days of logging with bull teams, companies such as theirs shut down in rainy weather, often when fishermen were fishing, and worked in the dry seasons, hiring sailors, farmers, fishermen, and others as crew. The video makes the point that the axes, saws, peaveys, and jacks used in logging were common to several occupations. (Ken Eurick Production, 1991.)

41. Kent Martin to author, 1992.

Notes for Chapter Five

1. Interview with Cecil Moberg by Jim Bergeron, Nov. 10, 1988, p. 15, CRMM.

2. Interview with Bill Gunderson by Jim Bergeron, Dec. 16, 1988, p. 37, CRMM.

3. Interview with Edward Rasmussen by David Myers, July 30, 1975 (Olympia: Washington State Archives), p. 16.

4. G. H. Clark, *Sacramento-San Joaquin Salmon (Oncorhynchus tschawytscha) Fishery of California* (Sacramento: Division of Fish and Game of California, 1929), p. 11.

5. John Snyder, *Salmon of the Klamath River, California* (Sacramento: Division of Fish and Game of California, 1931), p. 8.

6. David Starr Jordan and Charles H. Gilbert, "The Salmon Fishing and Canning Interests of the Pacific Coast," vol. 1, section 5 of *Report Upon the Fisheries and Fishery Industries of the United States*, as quoted in *Report of the Commissioner of Fish and Fisheries, 1888* (Washington D. C.: Government Printing Office, 1892), p. 165.

7. *Ibid.*, p. 163.

8. There were a number of reasons for the shift to trolling, which are well documented in Christopher Dewers's "Technical Innovation in the Pacific Coast Commercial Trawling and Salmon Trolling Fisheries" (Ph.D. dissertation, University of California at Davis, 1985). However, I have never seen the

ethnic component documented anywhere and offer it here as a logical consequence of a fishing system based on seniority.

9. Interview with Harold Oblad by Bruce Weilepp, June 17, 1988, CRMM.
10. See plates of maps of the west coast fishing grounds in *Report of the Commis-
    sioner of the U.S. Commission of Fish and Fisheries, 1888*.
11. Clark Patrick Spurlock, "A History of the Salmon Industry in the Pacific North-
    west" (master's thesis, University of Oregon, 1940), p. 76.
12. Interview with Bill Finucane by Kent and Irene Martin, April 1991.
13. As quoted in William Ross, *Salmon Cannery Distribution on the Nass and
    Skeena River of B. C. 1877-1926* (Vancouver: University of British Columbia
    Department of Geography, Board of Education Essay, 1967), p. 44.
14. "Newcomers to the Fishing Fleet," in *Pacific Tidings*, 3:3 (Summer 1990): 7.
15. It should be noted that, unlike the Columbia River, there were ethnically based
    fishermen's associations in British Columbia.
16. Letter from Bill Puustinen to author, Jan. 30, 1987.
17. Interview with Sigurd Blix by Kent Martin, December 1976.
18. Interview with Burtell Anderson by Kent Martin, early 1970s; interview with
    George Emery by Kent Martin, 1974.
19. Interview with Elmer Hurula by Irene Martin, n. d.
20. Blix interview.
21. Interview with Gus Budnick by Kent and Irene Martin, Nov. 16, 1985.
22. Interview with Edward Rasmussen by David Myers, Nov. 18, 1975 (Olympia:
    Washington State Archives), p. 86.
23. Interview with Ross Lindstrom April 9, 1988, p. 3, CRMM.
24. Thomas Hatley, "Efficiency in Oregon's Commercial Salmon Fisheries: A
    Historical Perspective" (master's thesis, Oregon State University, 1976),
    p. 37.
25. Moberg interview.
26. Interview with Arnold "Toots" Peterson by Jim Bergeron, n. d., Tape 72,
    p. 46, CRMM.
27. Interview with Ted Jackson by Jim Bergeron, Nov. 1, 1988, pp. 63-64, CRMM.
28. Rasmussen interview, Nov. 18, 1975, p. 9.
29. Richard Anderson, *Down River* (Portland.: Binfords and Mort, 1950), pp.
    44-45.
30. Minutes of the Central Board, Columbia River Fishermen's Protective Union,
    Sept. 5, 1888, p. 105. C.R.F.P.U. office files, Astoria, Oregon.
31. *Columbia River Sun*, April 24, 1919, p. 4.
32. Superior Court of the State of Washington for Wahkiakum County. Petition
    for Sale of Personal Property in the Estate of Hans Christian, March 21, 1938.
    Wahkiakum County Courthouse, Cathlamet, Washington.
33. Interview with Ernest Niemela and Harold Viukhola by Jim Bergeron, n. d.,
    p. 29, CRMM.
34. Interview with Hank Ramvick by Jim Bergeron, Oct. 25, 1988, p. 49, CRMM.
35. Moberg interview, pp. 14-19.
36. I am indebted for much of this information to my husband, Kent Martin, who
    has written numerous papers on fishermen's social interactions during his
    studies at various universities.
37. C.R.P.A./Bumble Bee Seafoods Collection, 85: 55: 163, CRMM.
38. *Ibid.*

39. One curious phenomenon should be mentioned. In the Willamette Slough there were shad drift rights. These were the Lake Farm or Old Ship Drift, the Gilbert Drift, or simply the Willamette Slough Drift. Information on them must be inferred from a number of bills of sale and miscellaneous documents kindly loaned to the author by Hampton Scudder. The C.R.P.A. kept records of ownership and compiled catch records for these areas. They also financed the repurchase by the drift of several shad rights, indicating that they considered access to shad in this location to be a priority, as Willamette Slough was a well-known migratory path for the shad on their upriver journey. One right sold for $750 in 1950, a significant amount of money. Shad were a high-value product, the roe being especially prized. Although only conjecture, it is possible that the C.R.P.A. was interested in controlling the shad production on the river, and hence proved amenable to financing purchases of drift rights that would enable the company to increase its share of the catch.
40. Interview with John McGowan by Irene Martin, n. d., Tape 31, pp. 3-4, CRMM.
41. Francis Seufert, *Wheels of Fortune* (Portland: Oregon Historical Society, 1980), p. 58.
42. Letter by Bill Sibbett, *Columbia River Gillnetter*, 10:4 (Feb. 1988): 10.
43. In the Supreme Court of the State of Washington, *Gary Marincovich et al. v. Joseph B. Tarabochia et al.*, Motion for Summary Judgment, filed Mar. 8, 1990, pp. 7-8.

Notes for Chapter Six

1. Theodore Panayotou, *Territorial Use Rights in Fisheries* (Rome: United Nations Food and Agricultural Organization, 1984), FAO Fish Report No. 289, Supplement, p. 154.
2. James Acheson, *The Lobster Gangs of Maine* (Hanover and London: University Press of New England, 1988), p. 143.
3. Association of Scottish District Salmon Fishery Boards, *Salmon Fisheries of Scotland* (Farnham, Eng.: Fishing News Books, 1977), p. 14.
4. J. Geraint Jenkins, *Nets and Coracles* (London: David and Charles, 1974), p. 15.
5. James Eugene Brooks, "Wahkiakum County, Washington: A Case Study in the Geography of the Coast Range Portion of the Lower Columbia River Valley" (master's thesis, University of Washington, 1952), pp. 54-55.
6. Panayotou, *Territorial Use Rights*, p. 155.
7. *Ibid.*, p. 154.
8. In the Supreme Court of the State of Washington, *Gary Marincovich et al. v. Joseph B. Tarabochia et al.*, Motion for Summary Judgment, filed March 8, 1990, pp. 7-8.
9. Copies of both contract and check stubs relating to departmental usage of drift rights are in the possession of the author.
10. Michael K. Orbach, " 'Rights' to Fisheries Resources," in *Report of the Workshop on Extended Jurisdiction, May 10-11, 1976* (Woods Hole, Mass.: Woods Hole Oceanographic Institution, 1976), pp. 22-23.
11. Aside from the other works quoted in this chapter, I have found several other articles useful on the "tragedy of the commons." These include: Susan Hanna,

"The Eighteenth Century English Commons: A Model for Ocean Management," in *Ocean and Shoreline Management*, 14 (1990): 155-172; Bonnie J. McCay, "Sea Tenure and the Culture of the Commoners," in John Cordell, ed., *A Sea of Small Boats* (Cambridge, Mass.: Cultural Survival, Inc., 1989), pp. 203-227; and Elinor Ostrom, "Institutional Arrangements and the Commons Dilemma," in Vincent Ostrom, David Feeny, and Hartmut Picht, eds., *Rethinking Institutional Analysis and Development: Issues, Alternatives and Choices* (San Francisco: ICS Press, 1988), pp. 103-139.

12. Washington Department of Fisheries, *A Study of Washington's Commercial Salmon Fisheries* (Olympia, Wash.: Washington Department of Fisheries, 1991).

13. National Marine Fisheries Service, *Aquaculture and Capture Fisheries: Impacts in U. S. Seafood Markets* (Washington, D. C.: U. S. Department of Commerce, 1988), pp. 22-23. See also a survey included in *Salmon 2000* (Juneau: Alaska Seafood Marketing Institute, 1991).

14. Washington Department of Fisheries, *1988 Annual Report* (Olympia, Wash.: Washington Department of Fisheries, 1989), p. 1.

15. The October 1989 *Recreational Fishery Enhancement Plan*, for example, lists proposed methods of enhancing recreational fisheries, along with projected commercial fisheries impacts (Olympia, Wash.: Washington Department of Fisheries, 1989).

16. Certified election results in author's possession.

17. Thayer Scudder and Thomas Conelly, *Management Systems for Riverine Fisheries* (Rome: United Nations Food and Agricultural Organization, 1985), Fisheries Technical Paper No. 263, pp. 16-21.

18. *Ibid.*, p. 21.

19. Perhaps the best and briefest summary of the Boldt/Belloni decisions is Mason Morisset, "The Legal Standards for Allocating the Fisheries Resource," *Idaho Law Review*, 22:3 (1985-86): 609-627.

20. Patricia Marchak, "Uncommon Property," in *Uncommon Property; The Fishing and Fish-processing Industries in British Columbia*, ed. by Patricia Marchak, Neil Guppy, and John McMullan (Toronto: Methuen, 1987), p. 5.

21. A similar situation exists in a number of fisheries throughout the United States. Linda Lampl analyzed the redfish situation in "Fishery Allocation: To the Fish Catchers or the Fish Eaters?" in *Marine Resource Utilization: A Conference on Social Science Issues, May 4-6, 1988*, ed. by J. Stephen Thomas, Lee Maril, and E. Paul Durrenberger (Mobile: University of South Alabama College of Arts and Sciences, 1989), p. 104.

22. See Marchak, "Uncommon Property," p. 8, for a similar discussion regarding British Columbia fisheries.

23. Lampl, "Fishery Allocation," p. 101.

24. Licensing requirements at the turn of the century deliberately sought to eliminate the Slavic fishermen, many of whom were not citizens, by requiring citizenship in order to fish.

25. Evelyn Pinkerton, ed., *Co-operative Management of Local Fisheries; New Directions for Improved Management and Community Development* (Vancouver: University of British Columbia Press, 1989).

26. Pamela Madson and William Koss, *Washington Salmon: Understanding Allocation* (Olympia, Wash.: House of Representatives, Office of Program Research, 1988), p. 23.

27. Norman Dale, "Getting to Co-Management," in Pinkerton, *Co-operative Management*, p. 66.
28. John Cordell, "Introduction: Sea Tenure," in *A Sea of Small Boats* (Cambridge, Mass.: Cultural Survival, Inc., 1989), p. 3.
29. Svein Jentoft, "Fisheries Co-Management: Delegating Government Responsibility to Fishermen's Organizations," in Thomas, et al., *Marine Resource Utilization*, pp. 153-163.
30. Such fishermen's groups exist in Washington, Oregon, California, Alaska, and British Columbia. Although the enabling legislation differs considerably in each jurisdiction, permitting a greater or lesser degree of fishermen involvement or control, I believe that the rise of fishermen's involvement in habitat improvement and fisheries enhancement reflects both their anxiety over the status of the salmon runs and their frustration with state and other management agencies.

Notes for Chapter Seven

1. A useful summary of differing ethical frameworks is found in Earl Brill, *The Christian Moral Vision* (New York: Seabury Press, 1979), pp. 31-46.
2. Bonnie McCay, "Sea Tenure and the Culture of the Commoners," in John Cordell, ed., *A Sea of Small Boats* (Cambridge, Mass.: Cultural Survival, Inc., 1989), p. 224.
3. Barbara Dills, et al., *In Defense of Che Wana* (Portland: Columbia River Defense Project, 1987), p. 5.
4. Dulcy Mahar, "Point of View: Kai Lee," *Northwest Energy News*, 9:5 (Sept.-Oct., 1990): 17-18.
5. This neglect was documented on a national scale by Sarah Bittleman, *Commercial Fishers: An Endangered Species* (Seaman's Church Institute of New York and New Jersey, 1990), p. 1: "There are probably less than 5,000 active merchant seafarers in the United States today. However, there are approximately 230,000 commercial fishers! These commercial fishers are, far and away, the largest segment of seafarers in the U. S. today. Yet, with a few notable exceptions, religious and other social service agencies ministering to seafarers here in the U. S. largely ignore commercial fishers. . . . The likely explanation is the natural inclination . . . to direct their efforts towards the 'stranger amongst us' (the merchant seafarer), rather than towards the fisher/seafarer who is seen as a 'local' with the same problems as other workers e.g. a factory worker or farmer."
6. Frank and Deborah Popper, "The Reinvention of the American Frontier," *The Amicus Journal*, (Summer 1991): 4-7
7. *The Daily News* (Longview, Wash.), Aug. 31, 1991, p. A8. The letter was written by Graham R. Hodges of Liverpool, New York.
8. Robert Lee, *Social and Cultural Implications of Implementing "A Conservation Strategy for the Northern Spotted Owl"* (Seattle: College of Forest Resources, University of Washington, June 21, 1990).
9. *Ibid.*, p. 22.
10. *Ibid.*, p. 26.
11. *Ibid.*, p. 27.
12. *Morning Oregonian*, July 16, 1874, p. 1.

13. Lee, "Northern Spotted Owl," pp. 26-27.
14. *Team Washington News*, the official organ of the Washington Department of Trade and Economic Development, has, since its inception in 1989, printed numerous articles on the development of tourism in areas affected by ESA listing of the northern spotted owl.
15. Numerous citations could be given here. An example is a newspaper article, "Overuse is Killing Oregon Wilderness," *Daily News* (Longview, Wash.), Sept. 19, 1991, p. D3.
16. *Oregon Wildlife*, 47:1,2 (Jan.-April 1991): 28.
17. Popper, "American Frontier," pp. 6-7.
18. *Oregon Wildlife*, 47:1,2 (Jan.-April 1991): 28-29.
19. Information from Assessor's Office, Wahkiakum County Courthouse, Cathlamet, Washington.
20. Lee, "Northern Spotted Owl," pp. 31-32.
21. Bill Turque, "The War for the West," *Newsweek*, (Sept. 30, 1991): 23.
22. *Ibid.*
23. Workshop sponsored by the Lutheran Church of Western Washington, Sept. 27, 1991, Olympia, Washington.
24. Lee used this definition at the workshop cited above.
25. Jim Goller in *Update*, the newsletter of the Northwest Power Planning Council, 8:10 (Oct. 1991): 1.
26. Interview with Bill Gunderson by Jim Bergeron, Dec. 16, 1988, pp. 26-28, CRMM.
27. Lower Columbia Bi-State Water Quality Program, *Reconnaissance Survey of the Lower Columbia River: Draft Reconnaissance Report* (Bellevue, Wash.: Tetra Tech, 1992).
28. Benita Howell and Eugene Hunn, "Environmental Protection," in *Folklife Center News*, 12:3,4 (Summer-Fall 1990): 15.
29. Letter from Matt Korpela to his relatives in Finland, 1895, kindly furnished to the author and translated by Eldon Korpela, grandson of Matt Korpela.

Glossary

Apron: a wall of web which hangs from the corkline at an angle of about forty degrees from the backwall.

Backlash: the entanglement of part of the net under another part of the net on the reel.

Basket: a cage-like protective device used on gillnet boats to keep the web from getting caught in the propeller.

Bight: bend or curve in a rope.

Bluestone: anhydrous copper sulphate. Also, to soak a net in a saturate solution of anhydrous copper sulphate and water.

Bluestone tank: a large wooden tank used for soaking nets in bluestone solution.

Bowpicker: a fishing vessel used on the Columbia, where the net is pulled into the boat by hand and piled in the bow.

Bow-reeler: a fishing vessel used on the Columbia, where the net is wound into the boat on a reel on the bow.

Buoy: a marker for the ends of the net.

Climbing bottom: a portion of river bottom which is slanted upwards towards the downstream end.

Cork: a float on the top edge of a gillnet. There are about 500 on the average Columbia River gillnet, but this number varies in accordance with the length of the net and the distance between each cork. Also, an action taken by one fisherman to shut off the supply of fish to another fisherman's net, usually by placing one's net very close to someone else's, especially on the downstream side.

Corkline: the upper rope of a net which has floats strung on it.

Coyote: a short drift, usually where only part of the net is laid out.

Cusey: an unprofessional and uncraftsmanlike way of mending a net.

Dead slack water: see slack water.

Deadhead: a submerged, waterlogged log with one end floating upright near the surface of the water.

Diver: a type of net that is used mostly on the ebb tide. The net is shallow (twelve to fourteen feet), with a heavy leadline that causes it to sink and drift along the bottom of the river, fishing from the bottom up in the water column. Also, a person who dives for the purpose of affixing a cable to a snag on the river bottom.

Drift: to ply the river with a net, on either the flood or ebb tide. Also, a specific section of river bottom from which the snags and other obstructions have been removed. Each drift is named according to geographic location, historical event, or the ethnic background of individuals fishing there. Also, the organization of those who fish a given drift area.

Drift captain: the chief officer of the drift.

Drift meeting: a meeting of the organization for the purpose of considering matters at hand, such as snagging operations.

Drift right: an individual fisherman's share or membership in the drift. This membership gives the members of the drift exclusive rights to fish this area on the ebb tide. Although drift rights are considered to be only a gentlemen's agreement, a membership may be bought or sold—with the permission of the other members of the association—much as is a piece of real estate.

El Niño: weather phenomenon in the eastern tropical Pacific that tends to force warmer tropical waters north from the coast of South America, with lethal effects on salmon.

Fathom: standard measurement of six feet.

Firefly: a faint light on the buoy at the end of the net.

First boat: refers to the fisherman who draws the number one position, making him the first person to lay out his net on the drift.

Floater: a type of net that is fished mainly on the flood tide and slack water. This net is usually deep, thirty to fifty feet, and may be fished in any area on the flood tide and in those areas where no organized drifts exist on the ebb tide. The floater floats from the surface down in the water column.

Gaff: a metal hook attached to a handle which is used to pull a fish aboard when it appears it is not securely caught in the net.

Gillnet: a net which has floats attached to the top line (corkline) and weights to the bottom line (leadline) so that it will hang perpendicularly in the water. Fish swim into the net, become entangled, and are then removed from the net when it is pulled out of the water and into a boat. Also, to fish with a gillnet.

Hang: the act of stitching the web onto the corkline, leadline, or apron line.

Hanging: one stitch attaching the web to one of the lines.

Hanging bench: a bench at which a fisherman sits while hanging a gillnet on the lines.

Hanging twine: a heavier-duty twine used to attach the corkline and leadline to the web.

Hard laid (medium laid, soft laid): denotations of the tightness of the twist of the fibre in various kinds of twine.

Highliner: a fisherman whose catches are consistently far above average.

Hoop: the marker on the ends of the lead line—also known as the snorter.

Jackpot: term denoting any one or a combination of difficulties a fisherman might get himself into—e. g. net caught in the propeller, catching a snag or a jetty or ship channel marker.

Knit: to create web from twine.

Lay out: to set out one's net in the water.

Lead: molded pieces of lead attached to the bottom line of the gillnet. Also, the pattern followed by fish as they move along an obstruction such as a wall of fencing used to convey them into a fish trap.

Lead mold: brass mold used to make lead weights.

Leadline: a weighted line used on the bottom edge of the gillnet.

Leadline roll: a situation where the leadline rolls into the web, creating a tangle.

Levelwind: device that guides the net evenly onto the reel.

Mark: to affix the exact position of a snag or one's own position by lining up various geographical positions; to take a mark. Also, on a diver drift, that point on the drift where another boat lays out from the towhead.

Medium laid: see hard laid.

Mesh: the diamond shaped portion of the web of the gillnet.

Meshboard: measuring device used to ensure that meshes are of an even size when sewn into a net.

Needle: wooden or plastic tool filled with twine which is used for mending, sewing, or hanging a net.

Needle filler: a machine used to fill needles with twine.

Net guard: a protective device designed to prevent a gillnet from being entangled in a boat's propeller.

Net-house: see net-rack.

Net-rack: a building or structure with rails over which nets are pulled to dry, or to be mended; also known as a net-house.

Numbers: the order in which various fishermen on a drift lay out their nets and drift down the river. Numbers are drawn before the season opens, and at other times the drift deems necessary or desirable.

Pick: to pull the net into the boat after a drift is made. Also, to remove fish from the net.

Picking hook: small hook-like device used to ease the web off a fish when untangling the fish from the net.

Power roller: see roller.

Put up a net: to construct a net.

Rack: to spread a net to dry over rails in a net-rack.

Redd: a salmon nest in gravel, where the female lays her eggs.

Reel: large spool onto which the net is wound.

Riplines: lines placed at intervals from corkline to leadline which are strong enough to prevent a net from tearing completely off the lines if it is caught on a snag; also called striplines.

Roller: a mechanical or hydraulic device to aid in pulling the net into the boat; also called power roller.

Scratch fishing: generally poor to fair fishing; also called scratching.

Seine fashion: pulling a gillnet aboard but keeping the leadline, corkline, and web piled separately.

Selvage: last half mesh on the top and bottom edges of a piece of web, finished with heavier twine to prevent chafing.

Sew: to attach two pieces of web together.

Show: distance between nets drifting on the river.

Skunk: a drift which yields no fish.

Slack water: that time during which the tides are changing direction; also referred to as dead slack water.

Snag: a log or other obstruction on the river bottom. Also, to tear one's net on said obstruction. Also, the operation of removing snags or obstructions from fishing grounds. Known, too, as snagging, snag-pulling.

Snag assessments: dues or the share of money which each member must pay to finance the cost of snagging operations.

Snag boss: the individual who organizes and supervises snagging operations.

Snag scow: a large scow or barge equipped with winches, lines, and diving equipment for use in pulling snags.

Snagline: a wire cable used in the removal of snags.

Snorter: see hoop.

Soft laid: see hard laid.

Stern-picker: a type of boat where the net is pulled or wound into the boat over the stern.

Stretch fathom: measurement by which web is usually ordered, generally twice the length of the hung net, e. g. a 200-fathom net would be 400 stretch fathoms.

Strings: lengths of twine spaced evenly along the net from corkline to leadline, of a shorter depth than the net, in order to create slack web in which fish can more easily become entangled.

Striplines: see riplines.

Towhead: the point where the fishermen of a given drift wait their turn to ply their nets. The term originally came from the days of sail, when a steam launch would tow the vessels to the spot where they were to lay out their nets.

Trammels: a wall of very large meshes on one or both sides of a wall of smaller-meshed web, designed so that a fish striking the smaller meshed web will push it through the larger meshes, forming a pocket in which it becomes trapped.

Twine laid: denotes the lay of cotton lines.

Web: the netting portion of a gillnet—as opposed to the lines, such as corkline and leadline.

Bibliography

A simple listing of sources consulted for this book would not tell the real story of the actual research conducted over nearly twenty years. Accordingly, I want to do more than list titles. Instead, I want to point out sources of information and ways of searching which may be of value to anyone who wants to spend the time to explore a subject in depth. I am aware that not everyone has the luxury of time, and that I have been incredibly fortunate in this regard. However, I am convinced that some of the things I did which were most time-consuming were also the most rewarding and productive.

Foremost among these undertakings was the reading of a number of local newspapers, including the *Skamokawa Eagle*, the *Columbia River Sun*, the *Grays River Builder*, the *Frankfort Chronicle*, the *Cathlamet Gazette*, several decades of the various editions of the Astoria newspapers and the Portland *Oregonian*, and smaller portions of a number of other newspapers. Similarly, I read *Pacific Fisherman* and the *Bulletins* and *Reports* of the United States Fish Commission. No other sources could have given me a better overall background of the fishing communities of the late nineteenth and early twentieth centuries. I would never have known about Paul Delaney's serialized novel if I had not come across it in the *Eagle*. The various community news columns proved to me how strong the drifts were as a social organization, as many meetings were mentioned in them, as well as in advertisements. The *Bulletins* and *Reports* were invaluable in providing background about national and international events, and also provided many technical details that otherwise could not have been recovered.

I also explored the material available in the courthouses of half a dozen counties along the Columbia, searching for names of fishing families that I knew lived in the area. In this way I learned about how drift rights gradually came to be regarded as property, as they began to appear in wills and other property conveyances. I also searched the archives of museums from Portland to the coast, looking for material. The Columbia River Maritime Museum's collections were particularly rewarding in this regard, especially the Columbia River Packers Association/Bumble Bee Seafoods collection, which I had the pleasure of indexing. In addition, I spent a great deal of time exploring libraries in Oregon, Washington, and British Columbia.

Oral history has figured prominently in this book. My husband began interviewing old-time gillnetters in the 1950s when he was in high school, and retained all his notes. These have been a superb resource for me. The excellent work done by David Lee Myers and the Washington Oral History Project (now in the Washington State Archives in Olympia) provided voices from the 1970s. Jim Bergeron spearheaded the Columbia River Gillnetters Oral History Project, which provided the bulk of the interviews used in this book. There is a wealth of detail contained in these interviews, which may be found in the Columbia River Maritime Museum. It is my hope that others will refer to them, as they contain enough material for more than one book.

Various state, local, and county historical societies along the river publish journals and quarterly magazines. I read through complete runs of these, and found much useful information which led me to further research. Foremost among such publications is the *Oregon Historical Society Quarterly*, which has published some very fine work in the area of fisheries history, as has the *Quarterdeck Review*, published by the Columbia River Maritime Museum. *Cumtux*, published by the Clatsop County Historical Society, the *Cowlitz County Historical Quarterly*, the *Sou'wester*, published by the Pacific County Historical Society, and *Columbia County History* all proved useful. The National Sea Grant Depository Library publishes *Sea Grant Abstracts*, a good way of keeping abreast of current work in the field of fisheries. The library also provided me with a number of books and journal articles upon request.

Official documents, such as plans and reports from a variety of agencies, have made up a large portion of my reading for the past two decades. These include annual reports of the Oregon Department of Fish and Wildlife and the Washington Department

of Fisheries, and their British Columbia, Idaho, and California coun-
terparts; the Columbia River Intertribal Fish Commission; the Pacific Fisheries Management Council; the Pacific Salmon Commission; the Columbia Basin Fish and Wildlife Authority; the Pacific
States Marine Fisheries Commission; the Northwest Power Planning Council; and the Bonneville Power Administration— plus their
various newsletters and house organs, such as the Power Planning
Council's *Northwest Energy News*. Reports on hatchery and fish
run status, as well as pre-season data summaries, appear in various
agency documents annually or semi-annually. I have also followed
the legislative activities regarding salmon in both Oregon and Washington and at the federal level. I examined census records from
Wahkiakum and Clatsop Counties from 1860 to 1900.

I have included a number of fictional accounts about salmon
fishing in the bibliography. Since some of them date back to the
turn of the century, they now have historical value, both in terms
of their descriptions of the fisheries of their times and their authors' views of those same fisheries.

The following bibliography is a select one, including those
items which I have found most useful during the writing of this
book. A complete bibliography of Columbia River fisheries has yet
to be done, and would be massive. The material cited here concen-
trates mainly on the historical, social, and economic aspects of the
fishery, omitting much of the work by biologists that has been done.
I made this choice, not because the biological material is unimpor-
tant, but to make the bibliography a manageable size. Further citations in this area may be found by consulting the bibliographies
listed.

Bibliographies

Atkinson, Clinton E. *An Inventory of Research of Pacific Salmon Along the Pacific
    Coast of the U. S. and Canada*. Seattle: U. S. Bureau of Commercial Fisher-
    ies, 1963.
Columbia River Estuary Data Development Program. *A Literature Survey of the
    Columbia River Estuary*. Vancouver, Wash.: Pacific Northwest River Basins
    Commission, 1980.
Holmberg, Edwin K. *Salmonid Literature Compilation, 1960-64*. Seattle: Fisher-
    ies Research Institute, College of Fisheries, University of Washington, 1969.
Lamson, Cynthia and J. G. Reade. *Atlantic Fisheries and Social Science: A Guide
    to Sources*. Halifax, N. S.: Department of Fisheries and Oceans, September
    1987.

Landberg, Leif, Comp. *A Bibliography for the Anthropological Study of Fishing Industries and Maritime Communities.* Kingston, R. I.: International Center for Marine Resource Development, 1979.

McConnell, Robert J. *Sources of Biological, Chemical and Physical Information for the Lower Columbia River, River Mile 0 to 146, 1970-1990.* Lower Columbia River Bi-State Steering Committee, 1990.

Macy, Paul T. *English Translations of Pacific Salmon Literature (A Preliminary List).* Seattle: U. S. Bureau of Commercial Fisheries, Literature Research Unit, 1961.

Martin, Fenton. *Common Pool Resources and Collective Action: A Bibliography.* Bloomington: Indiana University, January 1989.

Martin, Irene. "A Bibliographical Essay on Wahkiakum County." *Washington Heritage,* 3:1 (1985): 8-12.

_____. *An Inventory of the Columbia River Packers Association/Bumble Bee Seafoods Collection.* Astoria, Ore.: Columbia River Maritime Museum, 1990.

Maxfield, G. H. *Pacific Salmon Literature Compilation—1900-59. Instructions and Index.* Seattle: Bureau of Commercial Fisheries, 1965.

Merdinyan, Mark E., Christine D. Mortimer, and Laine Melbye. *Bibliography: The Relationship Between the Development of Fishing Gear and the Study of Fish Behavior.* Narragansett: University of Rhode Island, 1979. Marine Memorandum 59.

Morgan, John B., Linda Marston, and Robert Holton. *An Annotated Bibliography of the Columbia River Estuary.* Corvallis: Oregon State University Sea Grant Program, Sept. 1979. Oregon Estuarine Research Council Publication No. 3.

Newell, Dianne and Logan Hovis. *Industrial Archaeological Survey of British Columbia Salmon Canneries Project, 1984-1985; British Columbia's Salmon Canning Industry: A Preliminary Annotated Guide to Bibliographical and Archival Sources.* Vancouver: University of British Columbia, 1985.

Orbach, Michael and Valerie Harper. *United States Fisheries Systems and Social Science: A Bibliography of Work and Directory of Researchers.* Washington, D. C.: U. S. Department of Commerce, National Marine Fisheries Service, August 1979.

Soderberg, Michael. "Selected Bibliography for the Columbia River Sailing Gillnetter Project." Astoria, 1987. Typescript, available at Columbia River Maritime Museum.

U. S. Department of the Interior, Water Resources Scientific Information Center. *A Selected Annotated Bibliography on the Columbia and Snake Rivers.* Olympia, Wash.: Department of Ecology, 1973.

Washington Department of Ecology. *Columbia Estuary Basin Bibliography.* Olympia, Wash.: Department of Ecology, April 1973. Basin Bibliography No. 8.

Unpublished Materials and Manuscripts

Birnie, James. Accounts. Oregon Historical Society, Mss 920.

Columbia River Fishermen's Protective Union. Minutes, Ledgers, Correspondence. Fishermen's Union Office, Astoria, Oregon.

"Copy of Testimony taken in 1902, at Astoria, in Support of a Claim of Chinook Indian Tribe Against the United States for Land in the State of Washington,

Near the Mouth of the Columbia River." Typescript, Astor Public Library, Astoria, Oregon.

Columbia River Packers Association/Bumble Bee Seafoods Collection. Columbia River Maritime Museum, Astoria, Oregon.

Doyle, Henry. "Rise and Decline of the Pacific Salmon Fisheries." Typescript, 2 vol., University of British Columbia Libraries, Vancouver, B. C.

Edwards, Jack. Binder of material regarding canneries on the Columbia River from a variety of sources. In author's possession.

Egstad, June. "Thompson Family History; A Welshman's Journey to a New World." 1986. Typescript in author's possession.

Korpela, Matt. Typescript of letter written to his relatives in Finland in 1895. Translation in author's possession furnished by Eldon Korpela, grandson of Matt Korpela.

Log of the *Chenamus*, Oregon Historical Society, John H. Couch Collection, Mss 952B.

Newspapers and Periodicals

The Amicus Journal
Anadromous Fish Law Memo
The Astorian
Bulletin of the U. S. Fish Commissioner
The Bumble Bee
The Cathlamet Gazette
The Chinook Observer
The Columbia River Gillnetter
The Columbia River Sun
CRITFC News
The Daily Astorian (a number of different editions were published under different titles)
The Daily News (Longview)
Folklife Center News
The Frankfort Chronicle
The Grays River Builder
The Nature Conservancy Magazine
Northwest Energy News
Ocean and Coastal Law Memo
Oregon Wildlife
The Oregonian
PCFFA Friday
Pacific Fisherman
Pacific Tidings
The Quarterdeck Review
The Skamokawa Eagle
The South Bend Journal
The St. Helens Mist
Salmon Country
Wana Chinook Tymoo
Yakima Basin Resource News

Theses and Dissertations

Brooks, James Eugene. "Wahkiakum County, Washington: A Case Study in the Geography of the Coast Range Portion of the Lower Columbia River Valley." Master's thesis, University of Washington, 1952.

Carty, James. "Washington—Oregon Fisheries Compact, With Special Reference to Legislative and Judicial Problems." Thesis, State College of Washington, 1949.

Casaday, Lauren W. "Labor Unrest and the Labor Movement in the Salmon Industry of the Pacific Coast." Ph.D. dissertation, University of California, Berkeley, 1937.

Dewers, Christopher. "Technical Innovation in the Pacific Coast Commercial Trawling and Salmon Trolling Fisheries." Ph.D. dissertation, University of California, Davis, 1985.

Hatley, Thomas A. "Efficiency in Oregon's Commercial Salmon Fisheries: A Historical Perspective." Master's thesis, Oregon State University, June 1976.

Hayden, Mildred Vera. "History of the Salmon Industry in Oregon." Master's thesis, University of Oregon, July 1930.

Helsing, Paul LeRoy. "Fish vs Dams: The Economics of Maintaining the Columbia River Basin Fishery." Ph.D. dissertation, Washington State University, 1972.

Hewes, Fordon Winant. "Aboriginal Use of Fishery Resources in Northwestern North America." Ph.D. dissertation, University of California, Berkeley, 1947.

Martin, Kent. "The Law in St. John's says . . . Space Division and Resource Allocation in the Newfoundland Fishing Community of Fermeuse." Master's thesis, Memorial University of Newfoundland, 1973.

Negri, Pamela. "History, Management and Interpretation of the *W. T. Preston,* a Sternwheel Snagboat." Master's thesis, University of Washington, 1982.

Richards, Jack Arthur. "An Economic Evaluation of Columbia River Anadromous Fish Programs." Ph.D. dissertation, Oregon State University, 1968.

Ross, William. "Salmon Cannery Distribution on the Nass and Skeena River of B. C., 1877-1926." Board of Education Essay, University of British Columbia, Department of Geography, 1967.

Spurlock, Clark Patrick. "A History of the Salmon Industry in the Pacific Northwest." Master's thesis, University of Oregon, 1940.

Books and Pamphlets

Acheson, James. *The Lobster Gangs of Maine.* Hanover: University Press of New England, 1988.

Adams, G. F. and D. P. Kolenosky. *Out of the Water; Ontario's Freshwater Fish Industry.* Toronto: Ministry of Natural Resources, 1974.

Alaska Seafood Marketing Institute. *Salmon 2000.* Juneau: Alaska Seafood Marketing Institute, n. d. (Addendum to this Report dated 1992).

Allison, Charlene J., Sue-Ellen Jacobs, and Mary A. Porter, eds. *Winds of Change: Women in Northwest Commercial Fishing.* Seattle: University of Washington Press, 1989.

American Fisheries Society. *Columbia River Salmon and Steelhead.* Bethesda, Md.: American Fisheries Society, 1977.

American Friends Service Committee. *Uncommon Controversy: Fishing Rights of the Muckleshoot, Puyallup, and Nisqually Indians.* Seattle: University of Washington Press, 1970.

Anderson, Randall. *The Columbia River Fish Management Plan.* Seattle: Washington Sea Grant, 1989.

Anderson, Richard. *Down River.* Portland: Binfords and Mort, 1950.

Andrews, Ralph W. and A. K. Larssen. *Fish and Ships.* New York: Bonanza Books, 1959.

Anon. *Columbia River Illustrated.* Portland: L. Samuel, Publisher, ca. 1880.

Anon. *The Fishermen's Own Book.* Gloucester, Mass.: Procter Bros., 1882.

Anon. *U. S. Directory of Commercial Fishermen.* New York: U. S. Seafood Reporter and Commercial Fisherman, 1907.

Appelo, Carlton. *Altoona.* Deep River, Wash.: Western Wahkiakum Telephone Co., 1972.

_____. *Brookfield: The Joe Megler Story.* Deep River, Wash.: Western Wahkiakum Telephone Co., 1966.

_____. *The Cottardi Station Story.* Deep River, Wash.: Western Wahkiakum Telephone Co., 1980-81.

_____. *Deep River: The C. Arthur Appelo Story.* Deep River, Wash.: Western Wahkiakum Telephone Co., 1978.

_____. *Frankfort.* Deep River, Wash.: Western Wahkiakum Telephone Co., 1965.

_____. *The Knappton Story.* Deep River, Wash.: Western Wahkiakum Telephone Co., 1975.

_____. *Pillar Rock.* Deep River, Wash.: Western Wahkiakum Telephone Co., 1969.

_____. *A Pioneer Scrapbook.* Deep River, Wash.: Western Wahkiakum Telephone Co., 1986-87.

Association of Scottish District Salmon Fishery Boards. *Salmon Fisheries of Scotland.* Farnham, England: Fishing News Books, Ltd., 1977.

Association of Northwest Steelheaders, Northwest Chapter. *Steelhead Trout . . . Game Fish or Food Fish.* N. P.: n. p., n. d.

Bailey, Conner, et al., eds. *Proceedings of the Workshop on Fisheries Sociology, April 26-27, 1985.* Woods Hole, Mass.: Woods Hole Oceanographic Institution, 1986. Technical Report WHOI-86-34.

Ballaine, Wesley C. and S. Fiekowsky. *Economic Values of Salmon and Steelhead Trout in Oregon Rivers.* Eugene: Bureau of Business Research, School of Business Administration, University of Oregon, 1953.

Bancroft, Hubert Howe. *History of the Pacific States of North America.* San Francisco: The History Company, 1880.

Barsh, Russel L. *The Washington Fishing Rights Controversy: An Economic Critique.* Seattle: University of Washington, Graduate School of Business Administration, 1979.

Beach, Rex. *The Silver Horde, A Novel.* New York: Harper and Bros., 1909.

Benson, Lucile B. *Summary of Community Survey of Wahkiakum County, Washington.* Olympia, Wash.: Department of Social Security, 1938.

Bittleman, Sarah. *Commercial Fishers: An Endangered Species.* New York: Seamen's Church Institute of New York and New Jersey, 1990.

Blair, Carvel Hall and Willits Dyer Ansel. *A Guide to Fishing Boats and Their Gear.* Cambridge, Mass.: Cornell Maritime Press, 1968.

Blyth, Gladys. *Salmon Canneries: British Columbia North Coast*. Lantzville, B. C.: Oolichan Books, 1991.

Brill, Earl. *The Christian Moral Vision*. New York: Seabury Press, 1979.

British Columbia Legislative Assembly. *Report of the Commissioner of Fisheries for the Year Ended December 31st, 1934*. Victoria, B. C.: King's Printer, 1935.

Brown, Bruce. *Mountain in the Clouds: A Search for the Wild Salmon*. New York: Simon and Schuster, 1982.

Brown, William, et al. *Improved Economic Evaluation of Commercially and Sport-caught Salmon and Steelhead of the Columbia River*. Corvallis: Oregon State University, August 1976. Special Report 463.

Brown, William G., et al. *An Economic Evaluation of the Oregon Salmon and Steelhead Sport Fishery*. Corvallis: Oregon State University, 1964. Oregon Experimental Station, Technical Bulletin 78.

Browning, Robert J. *Fisheries of the North Pacific*. Anchorage: Alaska Northwest Publishing Co., 1980.

Bullard, Oral. *Crisis on the Columbia*. Portland: Touchstone Press, 1968.

Bysen, Sue. *Some Historical Highlights of the History of Pittsburg*. N.P.: n.p., 1964.

Carey, Charles. *General History of Oregon*. Portland: Binfords and Mort, 1971.

Carrothers, W. A. *The British Columbia Fisheries*. Toronto: University of Toronto Press, 1941.

Chaney, Ed and L. Edward Perry. *Columbia Basin Salmon and Steelhead Analysis; Summary Report Sept. 1, 1976*. Pacific Northwest Regional Commission, 1976.

Chasan, Daniel J. *Up For Grabs: Inquiries into Who Wants What*. Seattle: Madrona, 1977.

Childerhose, R. J. and Marj Trim. *Pacific Salmon and Steelhead Trout*. Seattle: University of Washington Press, 1979.

Clark, G. H. *Sacramento—San Joaquin Salmon (Oncorhynchus tschawytscha) Fishery of California*. Sacramento: Division of Fish and Game of California, 1929.

Clark, John, ed. *The Frontier Challenge; Responses to the Trans-Mississippi West*. Lawrence: University Press of Kansas, 1971.

Clement, Wallace. *The Struggle to Organize: Resistance in Canada's Fishery*. Toronto: McLelland and Stewart, 1986.

Cobb, John N. *Pacific Salmon Fisheries*. Washington, D. C.: U. S. Government Printing Office, 1930.

College of Law, University of Idaho. Symposium on Legal Structures for Managing the Pacific Northwest Salmon and Steelhead. *Idaho Law Review*, 22:3 (1985-86). Entire issue.

Columbia River Fishermen's Protective Union. *The Columbia River Fishermen's Protective Union*. Astoria, Ore.: 1890.

Cordell, John, ed. *A Sea of Small Boats*. Cambridge, Mass.: Cultural Survival, Inc., 1989.

Craig, Joseph A. and Robert L. Hacker. *The History and Development of the Fisheries of the Columbia River*. Washington, D. C.: U. S. Government Printing Office, 1940.

Crutchfield, James A. and G. Pontecorvo. *The Pacific Salmon Fisheries: A Study of Irrational Conservation*. Baltimore, Md.: Johns Hopkins Press, 1969.

Cullenberg, Paula. *Gillnet Hanging*. University of Alaska Sea Grant College Program, 1987.

Davis, Edgar and Charlotte Davis. *They Remembered. Books I and II*. Ilwaco, Wash.: Pacific Printing, 1981 and 1983.

Delarm, Michael R., Einar Wold, and Robert Z. Smith. *Columbia River Fisheries Development Program Fishways and Stream Improvement Projects.* National Marine Fisheries Service, Feb. 1989. NOAA Technical Memorandum NMFS F/NWR-20.

Department of Agricultural and Resource Economics, Oregon State University. *Socio-Economics of the Idaho, Washington, Oregon and California Coho and Chinook Salmon Industry: Final Report to the Fishery Management Council.* Corvallis: Oregon State University, Department of Agricultural and Resource Economics, Sept.-October 1978. Two volumes.

Dikkanen, Siri. *Sirma: Residence and Work Organization in a Lappish-speaking Community.* Norway: The Norwegian Research Council for Science and the Humanities, 1965.

Dills, Barbara, et al. *In Defense of Che Wana.* Portland: Wheel Press, 1987.

Dodds, Gordon B. *The Salmon King of Oregon.* Chapel Hill: University of North Carolina Press, 1959.

Donaldson, Ivan J. and Frederick K. Cramer. *Fishwheels of the Columbia.* Portland: Binfords and Mort, 1971.

Elverum, Ken. *Gill Net Fishing on the Columbia River.* Salem, Ore.: Legislative Research, 1982. Research Monograph 82:94.

Fagan, John. *The Chinese Work Force at the Warrendale Cannery, 1876-1930. Paper Presented at the Society for Historical Archeology Conference, Jan. 7, 1983, Denver, Colorado.* Portland: U. S. Army Corps of Engineers, 1983.

Forester, Joseph E. and Anne D. *Fishing: British Columbia's Commercial Fishing History.* Saanichton, B. C.: Hancock House, 1975.

Fox, Maggie. *The Winter's Doctrine of Indian Reserved Water Rights and the Revival of Columbia River Anadromous Fish Runs, an Inter-Tribal Water Conference.* Portland: Columbia River Intertribal Fish Commission, 1980.

Freeburn, Laurence, ed. *The Silver Years of the Alaska Canned Salmon Industry.* Anchorage: Alaska Northwest Publishing Co., 1976.

Furer, Howard. *The Scandinavians in America, 986-1970.* Dobbs Ferry, N. Y.: Oceana Publications, 1972.

Gibbons, Diana C. *The Economic Value of Water.* Washington, D. C.: Resources for the Future, 1986.

Gilbert, Dewitt. *Fish for Tomorrow.* Seattle: University of Washington, 1988.

Gilmore, Janet. *The World of the Oregon Fishboat: A Study in Maritime Folklife.* Ann Arbor, Mich.: UMI Research Press, 1981.

Goode, G. Brown. *The Fisheries and Fishery Industries of the U. S.* Washington, D. C.: U. S. Government Printing Office, 1887.

Guthrie, Dan, ed. *Proceedings of Wild Trout, Steelhead and Salmon in the 21st Century, Portland, Oregon, July 19, 1986.* Corvallis: Oregon State University, 1989.

Hanna, R. Scott. *Compensation Valuation Study; A Study of Issues Related to Compensation to the Commercial Fishing Industry for Reallocations to the Aboriginal Fishery.* Vancouver, B. C.: EB Economics, 1992.

Hansen, Julia Butler. *Cathlamet Pioneer: The Paintings of Maude Kimball Butler.* Tacoma: Washington State Historical Society, 1973.

Haw, Frank, H. O. Wendler and G. Deschamps. *Development of Washington State Sport Salmon Fishery Through 1964.* Olympia: Washington Department of Fisheries, 1967.

Hill, James M. and Todd Olson. *Evaluation of a Low-Cost Salmon Production Facility, Annual Report FY 1988*. Portland: Bonneville Power Administration, 1989.

Hittell, John S. *The Commerce and Industries of the Pacific Coast*. San Francisco: A. L. Bancroft, 1882.

Hoglund, William. *Finnish Immigrants in America, 1880-1920*. New York: Arno Press, 1979.

Holbrook, Stewart. *The Columbia*. New York: Holt, Rinehart and Winston, 1974.

Howell, Philip, Kim Jones, Dennis Scarnecchia, et al. *Final Report: Stock Assessment of Columbia River Anadromous Salmonids*. Portland: Bonneville Power Administration, July 1985.

Hume, Robert. *A Pygmy Monopolist: The Life and Doings of R. D. Hume, Written by Himself and Dedicated to His Neighbors*, ed. by Gordon Dodds. Madison: State Historical Society of Wisconsin, 1961.

_____. *Salmon of the Pacific Coast*. San Francisco: Schmidt Lithograph and Label Co., 1893.

Hummasti, Paul George. *Finnish Radicals in Astoria, 1904-1940: A Study in Immigrant Socialism*. New York: Arno Press, 1979.

Jacobsen, Jon and Kevin Davis, eds. *Federal Fisheries Management; A Guidebook to the Fishery Conservation and Management Act*. Eugene: Ocean and Coastal Law Center, University of Oregon Law School, 1983.

Jarnefelt, Akseli. *Suomalaiset Amerikassa*. Finland: n. p., 1899.

Jenkins, J. Geraint. *Nets and Coracles*. London: David and Charles, 1974.

Jensen, William. *The Salmon Processing Industry: The Institutional Framework and Its Evolution, Pt. 1*. Corvallis: Oregon State University, May 1976.

Johnson, D. R., et al. *The Effects on Salmon Population and the Partial Elimination of Fixed Fishing Gear on the Columbia River in 1935*. Portland: Oregon Fish Commission, 1948.

Jones, W. A. *Salmon Fisheries of the Columbia*. Washington, D. C.: U. S. Government Printing Office, 1887.

Jones, Suzi, ed. *1977 North Coast Folklife Festival*. Salem: Oregon Arts Commission, 1977.

Kemble, John. *San Francisco Bay: A Pictorial Maritime History*. Cambridge, Mass.: Cornell Maritime Press, 1957.

Kendall, William. The Fishes of New England: The Salmon Family. *Memoirs of the Boston Society of Natural History*, 9:1 (1935). Entire issue.

Larkin, Peter. *Pacific Salmon: Scenarios for the Future*. Seattle: Washington Sea Grant, 1980.

Laska, Vera. *The Czechs in America, 1633-1977*. Dobbs Ferry, N. Y.: Oceana Publications, 1978.

Lee, Robert. *Social and Cultural Implications of Implementing "A Conservation Strategy for the Northern Spotted Owl."* Seattle: College of Forest Resources, University of Washington, June 21, 1990.

Lewis, Robert C. *Preliminary Economic Analysis of Management Alternatives for Limiting Harvest Efforts by Oregon Commercial Fisheries*. Portland: Oregon Fish Commission, 1973.

Liao, David S. and J. B. Stevens. *Oregon's Commercial Fishermen: Characteristics, Profits and Incomes in 1972*. Corvallis: Oregon State University Sea Grant College Program, 1975.

London, Jack. *Tales of the Fish Patrol*. New York: Grosset and Dunlap, 1905.

Lower Columbia Bi-State Water Quality Program. *Reconnaissance Survey of the Lower Columbia River: Draft Reconnaissance Report.* Bellevue, Wash.: Tetra Tech, 1992.

Lloyd, Timothy C. and Patrick B. Mullen. *Lake Erie Fishermen: Work, Identity, and Tradition.* Urbana: University of Illinois Press, 1990.

Lyons, Cicely. *Salmon: Our Heritage.* Vancouver, B. C.: British Columbia Packers, 1969.

McDonald, Marshall. *Report of the Commissioner of Fish and Fisheries on Investigations in the Columbia River Basin in Regard to the Salmon Fisheries.* Washington, D. C.: U. S. Government Printing Office, 1894.

McEvoy, Arthur F. *The Fisherman's Problem: Ecology and Law in the California Fisheries, 1850-1980.* Cambridge: Cambridge University Press, 1986.

McGee, W. J., ed. *Proceedings of a Conference of Governors in the White House, Washington, D. C., May 13-15, 1908.* Washington, D. C.: U. S. Government Printing Office, 1909.

McKeown, Martha F. *The Trail Led North; Mont Hawthorne's Story.* New York: McMillan, 1948.

McKinney, Sam. *Reach of Tide, Ring of History.* Portland: Oregon Historical Society, 1987.

McNeil, William, ed. *Salmon Production, Management and Allocation; Biological, Economic and Policy Issues.* Corvallis: Oregon State University Press, 1988.

McNeil, William and Daniel C. Himsworth, eds. *Salmonid Ecosystems of the North Pacific.* Corvallis: Oregon State University Press, 1980.

Madsen, Pamela and William Koss. *Washington Salmon: Understanding Allocation.* Olympia, Wash.: Office of Program Research, House of Representatives, August 1988.

Marchak, Patricia, Neil Guppy, and John McMullan. *Uncommon Property: The Fishing and Fish Processing Industries in British Columbia.* Toronto: Methuen, 1987.

Martin, Irene. *Index to the Grays River Builder (1936-1944) and the Skamokawa Eagle (1899-1934).* Prepared under LSCA Title I Grants, Washington State Library Commission, 1985.

————. *Skamokawa: Sad Years, Glad Years.* Longview, Wash.: Reprographics, 1985. 2nd Ed. 1989.

Martin, Irene and Kent Martin. *Development of an Alternative Gear for Harvesting Shad: Final Report, 1987-1988.* Prepared Under a Grant from the National Coastal Resources Research and Development Institute, Newport, Ore., 1988.

Mathews, Stephen and G. S. Brown. *Economic Evaluation of the 1967 Sport Salmon Fisheries of Washington.* Olympia: Washington Department of Fisheries, 1970. Technical Report No. 2.

Mathews, Stephen and H. O. Wendler. *Relative Efficiency and Economic Yield of the Columbia River Drift Gillnet and Indian Set Net Fisheries.* Olympia: Washington Department of Fisheries, 1970. Technical Report No. 3.

May, Earl Chapin. *The Canning Clan.* New York: Macmillan, 1937.

Meggs, Geoff. *Salmon: The Decline of the British Columbia Fishery.* Vancouver, B. C.: Douglas and McIntyre, 1991.

Meggs, Geoff and Duncan Stacey. *Cork Lines and Canning Lines; The Glory Years of Fishing on the West Coast.* Vancouver, B. C.: Douglas and McIntyre, 1992.

Legacy and Testament

Miller, Emma G. *Clatsop County Oregon: Its History, Legends, Industries.* Portland: Binfords and Mort, 1958.

Miller, Wallace J. *A Trip Along the Columbia River, from British Columbia to the Sea, with Numerous Illustrations by the Author and from Photographs.* N.P.: n.p., 1890.

Mundt, J. Carl, ed. *Limited Entry into the Commercial Fisheries.* Seattle: University of Washington, 1975.

Mundy, Phillip R., Terrance J. Quinn II, and Richard B. Deriso. *Fisheries Dynamics: Harvest Management and Sampling.* Seattle: University of Washington, March 1985. Technical Report WSG 85-1.

National Marine Fisheries Service. *Aquaculture and Capture Fisheries: Impacts in U.S. Seafood Markets.* Washington, D. C.: U. S. Department of Commerce, April 1988.

Native American Solidarity Committee. *To Fish in Common: Fishing Rights in the Northwest.* Native American Solidarity Committee, 1978.

Natural Resources Consultants. *Commercial Fishing and the State of Washington.* Seattle: Natural Resources Consultants, 1988.

Nehlsen, Willa, Jack E. Williams, and James Lichatowich. *Pacific Salmon at the Crossroads: Stocks at Risk from California, Oregon, Idaho and Washington.* American Fisheries Society, February 1991.

Netboy, Anthony. *The Atlantic Salmon, A Vanishing Species?* Boston: Houghton Mifflin, 1968.

_____. *The Columbia River Salmon and Steelhead Trout: Their Fight for Survival.* Seattle: University of Washington Press, 1980.

_____. *The Salmon: Their Fight for Survival.* Boston: Houghton Mifflin, 1973.

_____. *Salmon of the Pacific Northwest: Fish vs. Dams.* Portland: Binfords and Mort, 1958.

Newell, Dianne. *The Development of the Pacific Salmon-Canning Industry: A Grown Man's Game.* Montreal: McGill University Press, 1989.

Newell, Gordon, ed. *The H. W. McCurdy Marine History of the Pacific Northwest.* Seattle: Superior Publishing Co., 1966.

Nicandri, David. *Italians in Washington State: Emigration, 1853-1924.* Washington State American Revolution Bicentennial Commission, 1978.

North, George A. *A Ripple; A Wave; The Story of Union Organization in the B. C. Fishing Industry.* Vancouver, B. C.: Fisherman Publishing Co., 1974.

Northwestern School of Law of Lewis and Clark College. Symposium on Salmon Law. *Environmental Law,* 16:3 (Spring 1986). Entire issue.

_____. Symposium on the Public Trust and the Waters of the American West: Yesterday, Today and Tomorrow. *Environmental Law,* 19:3 (Spring 1989). Entire issue.

Olson, Mrs. Charles. *Cowlitz County, Washington, 1854-1948.* N. P.: n. p., 1947.

Oregon Department of Fish and Wildlife and Washington Department of Fisheries. *Columbia River Fish Runs and Fisheries 1957-1975; Status Report.* N. P.: n. p, June 1976.

_____. *Columbia River Fish Runs and Fisheries, 1960-1987.* N P.: n. p., October 1988.

_____. *Status Report: Columbia River Fish Runs and Fisheries, 1960-90.* N. P.: n. p., July 1991.

Oregon Historical Society. *Columbia's Gateway: A History of the Columbia River Estuary to 1920, Narrative and Maps.* Vancouver, Wash.: Pacific Northwest River Basins Commission, 1980.

Oregon State Planning Board. *A Study of Commercial Fishing Operations on the Columbia River.* Portland: n. p., Aug. 22, 1935.

Panayotou, Theodore. *Territorial Use Rights in Fisheries.* Rome: Food and Agricultural Organization of the United Nations, 1984. FAO Fish Report No. 289, Supplement.

Pearcy, William G., ed. *The Influence of Ocean Conditions on the Production of Salmonids in the North Pacific; A Workshop, Nov. 8-10, Newport, Oregon.* Corvallis: Oregon State University, 1984.

Pearse, Peter. *Turning the Tide: A New Policy for Canada's Pacific Fisheries.* Vancouver, B. C.: Commission on Pacific Fisheries Policy, 1982. Final Report.

Perry, Charlene. *Martinez; A California Town.* Martinez, Cal.: RSI Pubs., 1981.

Petrich, Mary Ann and Barbara Roje. *The Yugoslav in Washington State: Among the Early Settlers.* Tacoma: Washington State Historical Society, 1984.

Pinkerton, Evelyn, ed. *Co-operative Management of Local Fisheries: New Directions for Improved Management and Community Development.* Vancouver, B. C.: University of British Columbia Press, 1989.

Puustinen, Toivo. *Drifting Where the Dark Begins.* New York: Carlton Press, 1974.
_____. *Hello Kid.* N. P.: Hwong Publishing Co., 1979.

Radtke, Hans. *The Columbia River Non-Indian Gillnet Fishery Contribution to Personal Income.* Seattle: Resource Valuations, Inc., March 1987.

Radtke, Hans and William Jensen. *Fisheries Economic Assessment Model.* Portland: West Coast Fisheries Development Foundation, July 1985.

Rearden, Jim, ed. Alaska's Salmon Fisheries. *Alaska Geographic*, 10:3 (1983). Entire issue.

Reinikka, Merle. Ilwaco's Early Finns, Pacific County, Washington. Portland: *Finnish American Historical Society of the West*, 20:2 (1992). Entire issue.

Reiser, D. W. and T. C. Bjornn. *Influence of Forest and Rangeland Management on Anadromous Fish Habitat in Western North America: Habitat Requirements of Anadromous Salmonids.* Portland: Pacific Northwest Forest and Range Experiment Station, 1979.

Robbins, William G., Robert J. Frank, Richard E. Ross, eds. *Regionalism and the Pacific Northwest.* Corvallis: Oregon State University Press, 1983.

Scheiber, Harry N., comp. *Ocean Resources: Industries and Rivalries Since 1800.* Berkeley: Center for the Study of Law and Society, University of California, 1990. Working Papers on Ocean Resources History for the Tenth International Economic History Congress, Leuven.

Schoning, Robert, ed. *Science, Politics and Fishing: A Series of Lectures.* Corvallis: Oregon State University, 1981.

Schoning, Robert, T. R. Merrell Jr., and D. R. Johnson. *The Indian Dip Net Fishery at Celilo Falls on the Columbia River.* Portland: Oregon Fish Commission, 1951.

Scudder, Thayer and Thomas Conelly. *Management Systems for Riverine Fisheries.* Rome: Food and Agriculture Organization of the United Nations, 1985. FAO Fisheries Technical Paper 263.

Senn, Harry, John Mack, and Lloyd Rothus. *Compendium of Low-Cost Pacific Salmon and Steelhead Trout Production Facilities and Practices in the Pacific Northwest.* Portland: Bonneville Power Administration, September 1984.

Seufert, Francis. *Wheels of Fortune.* Portland: Oregon Historical Society, 1980.

Shaw, Susan A. and James F. Muir. *Salmon: Economics and Marketing.* Portland: Timber Press, 1987.

Shotwell, J. Arnold. *The Willapa Estuary; Background Studies for the Preparation of a Management Plan*. South Bend, Wash.: Planning Division, Department of Public Works, 1977.

Skogan, Joan. *Skeena: A River Remembered*. Vancouver: B. C. Packers Ltd., 1983.

Smith, Courtland L. *Fish or Cut Bait*. Corvallis: Oregon State University, n. d.

_____. *Oregon Fish Fights*. Corvallis: Oregon State University, 1974.

_____. *Salmon Fishers of the Columbia*. Corvallis: Oregon State University Press, 1979.

Snyder, John. *Salmon of the Klamath River, California*. Sacramento: Division of Fish and Game of California, 1931.

Sporleder, Lisa, comp. *Commercial Fishing Survey Results, 1989*. Fairbanks: University of Alaska, 1990.

Stacey, Duncan. *Blondies and Hairpins: The Salmon Net Fishery of British Columbia*. Vancouver, B. C.: Vancouver Maritime Museum, 1982.

_____. *Sockeye and Tinplate: Technological Change in the Fraser River Canning Industry, 1871-1912*. Victoria, B. C.: British Columbia Provincial Museum, 1982. Heritage Record No. 15.

Steinbeck, John. *Cannery Row*. New York: Viking Press, 1954.

Swanston, Douglas. *Influence of Forest and Rangeland Management on Anadromous Fish Habitat in Western North America: Impacts of Natural Events*. Portland: Pacific Northwest Forest and Range Experiment Station, 1980.

Tainter, Suzanne and Ray J. White. *Seines to Salmon Charters: 150 Years of Michigan Great Lakes Fisheries*. East Lansing: Michigan State University, May 1977. Extension Bulletin E-1000.

Tetlow, Roger and Graham Barbey. *Barbey: The Story of a Pioneer Columbia River Salmon Packer*. Portland: Binfords and Mort, 1990.

Thomas, J. Stephen, Lee Maril, and E. Paul Durrenberger. *Marine Resource Utilization: A Conference on Social Science Issues*. Mobile: University of South Alabama College of Arts and Sciences, 1988.

Van Syckle, Edwin. *The River Pioneers: Early Days on Grays Harbor*. Seattle: Pacific Search, 1982.

Washington Bureau of Statistics, Agriculture and Immigration. *State of Washington, 1907; Its Resources, Natural, Industrial and Commercial*. Olympia, Wash.: Bureau of Statistics, Agriculture and Immigration, 1907.

Washington Department of Community Development. *Economic Impacts and Net Economic Values Associated with Non-Indian Salmon and Sturgeon Fisheries*. Redmond, Wash.: ICF Technology, Inc., 1988.

Washington Department of Fisheries. *A Study of Washington's Commercial Salmon Fisheries*. Olympia: Washington Department of Fisheries, 1991.

Water Resources Research Institute. *Conflicts Over the Columbia River*. Corvallis: Oregon State University, 1980.

Wegars, Priscilla, comp. *Hidden Heritage: Historical Archaeology of the Overseas Chinese*. Amityville, N. Y.: Baywood Publishing Co., 1993.

Welcomme, R. L. *River Fisheries*. Rome: Food and Agriculture Organization of the United Nations, 1985. FAO Fisheries Technical Paper 262.

Wendler, Henry. *Regulation of Commercial Fishing Gear and Seasons on the Columbia River from 1859 to 1963*. Olympia: Washington Department of Fisheries, 1966. Fisheries Research Papers.

Wick, Carl I. *Ocean Harvest*. Seattle: Superior Publishing, 1946.

Wilkinson, Charles F. and Daniel Keith Conner, eds. The Law of the Pacific Salmon Fishery: Conservation and Allocation of a Transboundary Common Property Resource. *University of Kansas Law Review*, 32:1 (Fall 1983). Entire issue.

Williams, L. R. *Our Pacific County*. Raymond, Wash.: *Raymond Herald*, 1930.

Williamson, Henry. *Salar the Salmon*. London: Faber and Faber, 1935.

Willingham, William. *Army Engineers and the Development of Oregon*. Washington, D. C.: U. S. Government Printing Office, 1983.

Wright, E. W., ed. *Lewis and Dryden's Marine History of the Pacific Northwest*. Seattle: Superior Publishing Co., 1967.

Yee, Carlton S. and Terry D. Roclofs. *Influence of Forest and Rangeland Management on Anadromous Fish Habitat in Western North America: Planning Forest Roads to Protect Salmonid Habitat*. Portland: Pacific Northwest Forest and Range Experiment Station, 1980.

Articles

Adams, Emma. "Salmon Canning in Oregon." *Bulletin of the U.S. Fish Commission*, 1885, pp. 362-365.

Anon. "An Account of the Loffoden Islands of Norway." *Report of the Commissioner of Fish and Fisheries*, 1877, pp. 558-564.

Anon. "Astoria Originator of Modern Fishboat." *Astoria Evening Budget*, Feb. 28, 1927, pp. 11-13, 15.

Anon. "Diver Nets on the Columbia." *Pacific Fisherman*, 18:2 (Feb. 1920): 46.

Anon. "Early Chinese Fishermen." *National Fisherman*, October 1988, West Coast Focus, p. 4.

Anon. "Emden Joint-Stock Herring-Fishery Association." *Report of the Commissioner of Fish and Fisheries, 1876-77*, pp. 751-776.

Anon. "The First Salmon Cannery." *Pacific Fisherman*, 16:3 (March 1918): 53-54.

Anon. "Fish and Fishery Laws in Austria and of the World in General." *Report of the Commissioner for Fisheries, 1873-74*, pp. 570-679.

Anon. "Fishboats of Columbia River are Famous." *Astoria Evening Budget*, Feb. 25, 1929, p. 6.

Anon. "Newcomers to the Fishing Fleet." *Pacific Tidings*, 3:3 (Summer 1990): 7.

Anon. "One Hundred Years of Growth in Salmon Canning." *Pacific Fisherman*, 62:10 (Sept. 1964): 15-20.

Anon. "Power Applied to Lifting Gillnets." *Pacific Fisherman*, 29:5 (April 1931): 37-38.

Anon. "Salmon Fishing on the Columbia." *Pacific Fisherman*, 17:6 (June 1919): 26.

Anon. "William Hume." *Columbia County History*, 12 (1973): 50-53.

Apsler, Alfred. "Puget Island, Smorgasbord Paradise." *Seattle Times*, July 31, 1955, p. 5.

Arrestad, Sverre. "The Norwegians in the Pacific Coast Fisheries." *Pacific Northwest Quarterly*, (Jan. 1943): 3-17.

Barker, W. H. "Reminiscences of the Salmon Industry." *Pacific Fisherman Yearbook*, (Jan. 1920): 67-76.

Berwick, Arnold. "Norwegian Mountain Farms Then and Now." *The Sons of Norway Viking*, (July 1988): 252-255, 275.

Blumm, Michael C. "Native Fishing Rights and Environmental Protection in North America and New Zealand: A Comparative Analysis of Profits à Prendre and Habitat Servitudes." *Wisconsin International Law Journal*, 8:1 (Fall 1989): 1-50.

Chandler, Alfred D. "The National Marine Fisheries Service." In William Chandler, ed., *Audubon Wildlife Report, 1988/89*. New York: Academic Press, Inc., 1988, pp. 3-98.

Cleveland, Alfred A. "Social and Economic History of Astoria." *The Quarterly of the Oregon Historical Society*, 4:2 (June 1903): 130-149.

Cobb, John. "Pacific Coast Fishing Methods." *Pacific Fisherman Year Book*, (January 1916): 19-33.

Collins, J. W. The Fishing Vessels and Boats of the Pacific Coast. *Bulletin of the U.S. Fish Commission, 1890*, pp. 13-48.

———. "Gill-nets in the Cod Fisheries: A Description of Norwegian Cod-nets, etc., and a History of Their Use in the United States." *Report of the Commissioner of Fish and Fisheries, 1884*, pp. 265-286.

Cook Truman B. "Fish Boats and Engines, Coastal Freighters." *Oregon Historical Quarterly*, 83:1 (Spring 1982): 53-65.

Costa, Achille. "On the Fisheries of the Gulf of Naples." *Report of the Commissioner of Fish and Fisheries, 1876-77*, p. 139.

Crawford, Peter. "Cowlitz Journal." *Daily News* (Longview, Wa.), Oct. 13, 1852, p. 2.

Creed, Carolyn. "It's Not a Job, It's a Lifestyle." *Crosscurrents*, 2 (Autumn 1988): 85-29.

Dambeck, Karl. "Geographical Distribution of the *Gadidae* or the Cod Family, in its Relation to Fisheries and Commerce." *Report of the Commissioner of Fish and Fisheries, 1879*, pp. 531-557.

DeLaney, Paul. "Toilers of the Columbia." *Skamokawa Eagle*, Oct. 6, 1904 to Jan. 5, 1905. Serialized novel.

Fiske, Shirley. "Resource Management as People Management: Anthropology and Renewable Resources." *Renewable Resources Journal*, 8:4 (Winter 1990): 16-20.

Friehle, M. "An Account of the Fisheries of Norway in 1877." *Report of the Commissioner of Fish and Fisheries, 1876-1877*, pp. 712-733.

Gile, Albion. "Notes on Columbia River Salmon." *Oregon Historical Quarterly*, 56 (1956): 140-153.

Hanna, Susan. "The Eighteenth Century English Commons: A Model for Ocean Management." *Ocean and Shoreline Management*, 14 (1990): 155-172.

Howay, F. W. "Brig *Owhyee* in the Columbia, 1827." *Oregon Historical Quarterly*, 34:4 (Dec. 1933): 324-329.

Howell, Benita and Eugene Hunn. "Environmental Protection." *Folklife Center News*, 12:3,4 (Summer-Fall, 1990): 14-15.

Hume, Robert. "Beginnings of Salmon Canning on the Pacific Coast." *Pacific Fisherman*, 2:1 (Jan. 1904): 19-21.

———. "The Salmon Popagation [sic] Problem." *Pacific Fisherman*, 6:1 (Jan. 1908): 25-27.

Johnson, Dale. "Alexander Abernethy: His Political Life and Times." *Cowlitz County Historical Quarterly*, 17:4 (Feb. 1976): 2-11.

Johnson, D. R., et al. "The Effects on Salmon Population of the Partial Elimination of Fixed Fishing Gear on the Columbia River in 1935." Portland: Oregon Fish Commission, Contribution no. 11, 1948, pp. 10, 28-32.

Johnson, Ralph W. "Regulation of Commercial Salmon Fishermen, a Case of Confused Objectives." *Pacific Northwest Quarterly*, 55:4 (Oct. 1964): 141-145.

Kaste, Ruth. "Gillnetters Complain About Sand Bars, Sunken Logs." *Daily News* (Longview, Wa.), Aug. 22, 1987, p. A3.

Kaups, Matti. "Norwegian Immigrants and the Development of Commercial Fisheries Along the North Shore of Lake Superior: 1870-1895." In Harald S. Naess, ed., *Norwegian Influence on the Upper Midwest: Proceedings of an International Conference, May 22-24, 1975*. Duluth: Continuing Education and Extension, University of Minnesota, 1976, pp. 21-34.

Keegan, T. E. P. "The Old and The Modern Ways of Canning Salmon." *Pacific Fisherman*, Yearbook 1953, pp. 91, 93, 95.

Kirkpatrick, C. A. "Salmon Fishery on the Sacramento River." *Hutchings' California Magazine*, 4:12 (June 1860): 529-534.

Lomax, Alfred. "Hawaii-Columbia River Trade in Early Days." *Oregon Historical Quarterly*, 43 (1942): 328-38.

McCay, Bonnie. "Systems Ecology, People Ecology, and the Anthropology of Fishing Communities." *Human Ecology*, 6:4 (1978): 397-422.

Madsen, Lillie. "Astoria Fishermen Find Winter Tasks." *Sunday Oregonian*, Feb. 2, 1930, Sect. 6, p. 2.

Mahar, Dulcy. "Point of View: Kai Lee." *Northwest Energy News*, 9:5 (Sept.-Oct., 1990): 16-24.

Marchak, Patricia. "What Happens When Common Property Becomes Uncommon?" *B. C. Studies*, 80 (Winter 1988-1989): 3-23.

Martin, Irene. "Drift Rights on the Columbia River." *Pacific Fisheries Review (The Fishermen's News)*, 40:5 (Feb. 1984): 87-91, 101-102.

_____. "Early Days of Fishery on Lower Columbia River." *Columbia River Gillnetter*, (Feb. 1975): 3, 7-9.

_____. "Ethnohistorical Notes on the Wahkiakum Indians." In Rick Minor, *Further Archaeological Testing at the Skamokawa Site (45-WK-5), Wahkiakum County, Washington*. Seattle: Office of Public Archaeology, University of Washington, 1980, pp. 40-52.

Martin, Kent. "Play by the Rules or Don't Play at All: Space Division and Resource Allocation in a Rural Newfoundland Fishing Community." In Raoul Andersen, ed. *North Atlantic Maritime Cultures*. The Hague: Mouton, 1979, pp. 277-298.

Milner, James W. "Report on the Fisheries of the Great Lakes; The Result of Inquiries Prosecuted in 1871 and 1872." *Report of the Commissioner of Fish and Fisheries, 1872 and 1873*, pp. 1-75.

Morison, Samuel E. "New England and the Opening of the Columbia River Salmon Trade, 1830." *Oregon Historical Quarterly*, 28 (1927): 111-132.

Mortimore, G. E. "*Samson V* is Chugging Toward Oblivion." *Vancouver Sun*, Oct. 2, 1980, p. A5.

Orbach, Michael K. " 'Rights' to Fisheries Resources." *Report of the Workshop on Extended Jurisdiction, May 10-11, 1976*. Woods Hole, Mass.: Woods Hole Oceanographic Institution, 1976, pp. 22-23.

Ostrom, Elinor. "Institutional Arrangements and the Commons Dilemma." In Vincent Ostrom, David Feeny, and Hartmut Picht, eds., *Rethinking Institutional Analysis and Development: Issues, Alternatives and Choices*. San Francisco, ICS Press, 1988, pp. 103-139.

Passi, Michael. "Fishermen on Strike: Finnish Workers and Community Power in Astoria, Oregon, 1880-1900." In Michael Karni, Matti Kaups, and Douglas Ollila, eds., *The Finnish Experience in the Western Great Lakes Region: New Perspectives.* Vamilla, Finland: Institute for Migration, 1975, pp. 89-103.

Pollard, Lancaster. "The Salmon Fishery of Oregon, Washington and Alaska." *Americana*, 30:4 (1942): 638-667.

Popper, Frank and Deborah Popper. "The Reinvention of the American Frontier." *The Amicus Journal*, (Summer 1991): 4-7.

Rockwell, Cleveland. "The Columbia River." *Harper's New Monthly Magazine*, 66:391 (December 1882): 3-14.

_____. "The Great Columbia River Basin." *Pacific Monthly*, 7:3 (March 1902): 97-111.

Schulz, Alexander. "Account of the Fisheries and Seal-hunting in the White Sea, the Arctic Ocean and the Caspian Sea." *Report of the Commissioner of Fish and Fisheries, 1873-74, 1875-76*, pp. 35-96.

Sehmsdorf, Henning K. "'I Went Through a Lot of Misery': The Stories of Fred Simonsen, Norwegian American Fisherman." *Northwest Folklore*, 10:1 (Fall 1991): 5-42.

Smith, Courtland. "Fisheries as Subsistence Resources: Growth and Decline of the Columbia River Salmon Fishery." In M. Estellie Smith, ed., *Those Who Live from the Sea*. New York: West Publishing Co., 1977, pp. 215-234.

_____. "The Life Cycle of Fisheries." *Fisheries*, 11:4 (July-August, 1986): 20-25.

_____. "Resource Scarcity and Inequality in the Distribution of Catch." *North American Journal of Fisheries Management*, 10 (1990): 269-278.

Smith, Hugh. "Notes on a Reconnaissance of the Fisheries of the Pacific Coast of the U. S. in 1894." *Bulletin of the U. S. Fish Commission, 1894*, p. 2.

Smith, J. and A. Kornberg. "Some Considerations Bearing Upon Research in Canada and the United States." *Sociology*, 3 (1969): 342; as cited by Joan Vincent. "The Structuring of Ethnicity." *Human Organization*, 33:4 (1974): 376.

Spier, Robert. "Food Habits of the 19th Century California Chinese." *California Historical Society Quarterly*, 37 (March 1958): 79-85; (June 1958): 129-136.

Sylvester, Avery. "Brigs *Pallas* and *Chenamus*." *Oregon Historical Quarterly*, 34:3 (Sept. 1933): 259-272.

_____. "Voyages of the *Pallas* and *Chenamus*, 1843-45." *Oregon Historical Quarterly*, 34:4 (December 1933): 359-371.

Tettey, Ernest O., et al. "Implications of Tax Policy on Investment in a Common-Property Resource." *North American Journal of Fisheries Management*, 6 (1986): 100-104.

Townsend, Ralph E. "Entry Restrictions in the Fishery: A Survey of the Evidence." *Land Economics*, 66:4 (Nov. 1990): 359-378.

_____. "On 'Capital-Stuffing' in Regulated Fisheries." *Land Economics*, 61:2 (May 1985): 195-197.

Turque, Bill. "The War for the West." *Newsweek*, (Sept. 30, 1991): 18-32.

Wade, Murray. "Right Angles." *Oregon Magazine*, 26:1 (January 1931): 32.

Weaver, James. "The Sea Fisheries of Austro-Hungary from 1877 to 1883." *Report of the Commissioner of Fish and Fisheries, 1883*, pp. 1197-1199.

Weilepp, Bruce. "Sailing Gillnet Boats of the Columbia." *National Fisherman*, 71:12 (April 1991): 44-47; 72:1 (May 1991): 44-47.

Wicks, Walter. "The Early Gillnet Fishermen." In Art Downs, ed., *Pioneer Days in British Columbia*. Surrey, B. C.: Heritage House, 1975-1979, pp. 76-79.

Wood, William. "H and B Seining Grounds." *Columbia County History*, 5 (1966): 39-40.

Media

From Potlatch to Potluck: A Four-Part Series on the History of Wahkiakum County, Washington. Slide/Tape Program. Written by Irene Martin. Produced by David Myers. Olympia: Washington Commission for the Humanities, 1985.

Logging the Way I Seen It. Video. Produced by Ken Eurick, 1991.

Remembering Uniontown. Video. Written by Paul George Hummasti. Produced by Lawrence Johnson. Clatsop County Historical Society, 1985.

Work is Our Joy: The Story of the Columbia River Gillnetter. Video. Written by Irene Martin. Produced by Lawrence Johnson. Oregon State University Extension Sea Grant and the Columbia River Maritime Museum, 1989.

Index